IF THESE HALLS COULD TALK

A Historical Tour through San Francisco Recording Studios

by Heather Johnson

THOMSON
COURSE TECHNOLOGY
Professional ■ Technical ■ Reference

If These Halls Could Talk: A Historical Tour through San Francisco Recording Studios

Publisher and General Manager, Thomson Course Technology PTR: Stacy L. Hiquet
Associate Director of Marketing: Sarah O'Donnell
Manager of Editorial Services: Heather Talbot
Marketing Manager: Mark Hughes
Executive Editor: Mike Lawson
Project Editor: Mary Cosola
Technical Reviewer: Blair Jackson
Thomson Course Technology PTR Editorial Services Coordinator: Elizabeth Furbish
Copy Editor: Steve Honeywell
Cover Designer & Interior Layout Tech: Stephen Ramirez
Indexer: Sharon Hilgenberg
Proofreader: Kate Welsh

Bay Bridge photo © Nathan Jaskowiak; Plant Studio B photo courtesy of Tom Rider; SQB70 Console Ellen Burke photo courtesy of Stephen Barncard; Coast A Mission photo courtesy of John Cuniberti; HMW CR photo courtesy of Elliot Mazer; Talking House Image photo courtesy of John Storyk, Walters Storyk Design Group; Hyde St. Helios Desk photo courtesy of John Cuniberti; The Plant 2000 The Garden photo courtesy of Tom Rider; Perro Setup B photo courtesy of Stephen Barncard; Coast B Mission photo courtesy of John Cuniberti; Automatt B, CR photo courtesy of Kaz Tsuruta Photography; Coast Harrison photo courtesy of John Cuniberti.

ISBN: 1-59863-141-1
Library of Congress Catalog Card Number: 2006923262

Printed in the United States
06 07 08 09 10 PH 10 9 8 7 6 5 4 3 2 1

THOMSON
COURSE TECHNOLOGY
Professional ■ Technical ■ Reference

Thomson Course Technology PTR, a division of Thomson Learning Inc.
25 Thomson Place
Boston, MA 02210
www.courseptr.com

For John VanEtten

Foreword

The San Francisco recording community adopted me in 1978. But the big difference was I got to choose San Francisco! I think that is really the underlying connection we—the studios, the musicians, and the culture—all have with this area. Even those born here choose to stay because there is something absolutely magical about this place. Others, like me, chose to come here because we sensed there was something new and different and the possibilities were endless.

From the very beginning of our recording history, an independent and optimistic streak seemed to infect everyone involved with audio. Whether it was advertising, radio, or even something as basic as Ampex tape and tape machines, people felt then as they do now that they were on the cutting edge of recording and later, technology. I can't think of any other area that garnered so much attention from outside companies as San Francisco and the Bay Area. Of course Columbia Records would have studios in Hollywood and New York, but like so many others they saw great opportunities here to capture and promote whatever new was coming down the pike, as did Wally Heider and Chris Stone and Gary Kellgren.

I came to San Francisco to work with people I admired: Fred Catero and David Rubinson. But the city and its reputation had just as strong a pull. Whether it was Haight-Ashbury, the demonstrations at San Francisco State, the love-ins, Bill Graham and the Fillmore, everything seemed to be happening here, including some of the most adventuresome music anywhere. Roy Halee and I worked together in Los Angeles for many years, and he would rave about the sound of the rooms at what was then known as CBS San Francisco. "You think this is a patch bay?!?!?!", he said, pointing to the one we had at ABC Studios in Los Angeles. "Why, the patch bay we have in Studio B at CBS covered the whole wall!" Imagine how I felt when I got hired at what became The Automatt and walked into Studio B and saw "Roy's patch bay." San Francisco studios saw everything from seminal recordings by Big Brother & the Holding Company, Sly Stone, Herbie Hancock and the Sons of Champlin to the first digital multitrack recording with Carlos Santana.

From the soundtrack for *Apocalypse Now*, handmade consoles, and recording rooms that were sonic gems to companies such as Digidesign, Sonic Solutions, Lucasfilm, and Apple, that independence and optimism continues to this day. Heather Johnson's book has captured the essence of the San Francisco studio and recording community for the first time in a narrative that contains all its glorious history. But be forewarned...after reading it you too will want to choose San Francisco.

Leslie Ann Jones
Director of Music Recording and Scoring, Skywalker Sound, Marin County, California

Acknowledgments

This is the last page I wrote for this book, but it is the most important one to me. Faced with an unbelievably short time frame to write this book, I dove in headfirst, not completely knowing how I would arrive at a completed manuscript or what the final form would look like. The last six months have been a haze, my mind simultaneously occupied by studios and sessions of the past and life in the present. My computer and cat saw more of me than anyone else did during this book's gestation, but it never would have happened without the numerous producers, engineers, studio owners, and others who generously gave their time for interviews, answered my fact-checking e-mails, and dug through their personal archives and sometimes-hazy memories of San Francisco studio history. Many of the people I spoke with said that the years they spent as part of San Francisco's recording community were some of the most important and special times in their lives. I feel very honored to share those experiences with you. I especially want to thank George Horn for his guidance during this book's infancy; Dan Alexander, Stephen Barncard, John Cuniberti, and Chris Stone, who went out of their way to help; and to David Rubinson, my *éminence grise*, for invaluable feedback, for setting me straight on union rules and evil tax laws, and for sharing parts of his life that he packed away years ago.

I also want to thank the entire staff of *Mix* magazine for their support and for letting me dig through the archives: George Petersen, Sarah Benzuly, Barbra Schultz, Sarah Jones (for understanding), Blair Jackson (for his expert editorial guidance, and for assuring me my panic attacks were normal and would not stop), and especially to editor Tom Kenny, for his flexibility, advice, and encouragement every step of the way.

A special thanks also goes to project editor Mary Cosola—her suggestions and corrections hugely improved my rough drafts—and to Mike Lawson and Thomson for giving me the means to bring this vision to life.

On a personal note, I thank my mother, Margaret Johnson, for not getting mad when I worked at her kitchen table on Christmas Day; my running club, the KStars, and our coach Andy Chan for their friendship and positive energy; and my petite Soleil, my feline muse.

About the Author

Heather Johnson is a San Francisco–based music, entertainment, and professional audio journalist, author, and contributing editor to *Mix* magazine, the industry's leading professional audio publication. Her work has appeared in *Mix, Electronic Musician, Performing Songwriter, Audio Media, No Depression,* and *Country Music* magazine, among many others. Formerly based in Nashville, Johnson served on the Board of Directors for the Nashville Association of Professional Recording Services (NAPRS) for seven years. Johnson currently serves on the Board of Governors for the San Francisco Chapter of the Recording Academy. This is her first book.

Contents

Introduction

The San Francisco Bay Area's spirit of adventure, of charging ahead to untended ground no matter what the rest of the world thinks, goes as far back as the 1848 Gold Rush and the Comstock Lode and silver mines of 1859, when people arrived in droves in search of a better life. Those sorts of roots are hard to shake. A century and a half later, people still pack up their belongings and traverse across the U.S. to the City by the Bay in hopes of finding prosperity or maybe just the freedom to be themselves without persecution. Naturally, a city founded largely by independent thinkers and free spirits would evolve into one of the most progressive and aggressive regions in terms of social and technological development and a natural nesting place for creative individuals of all professions, arts and entertainment included.

Considering the area's high concentration of creative individuals, it's no surprise that the Bay Area's earliest radio station, reportedly the first to broadcast human voices, was the result of an experiment—by Stanford graduate Charles Herrold, founder of Herrold College of Engineering and Wireless in San Jose, who began regular broadcasts in 1910.

As the radio industry evolved, San Francisco remained a market leader and trendsetter. In the 1920s, stations such as KPO, purchased by NBC in 1933, and KTAB, later to become KSFO, dominated the market. KPO committed to an "all live" format and set up remote stations throughout the city to broadcast concerts from halls such as The Warfield, as well as from their own impressive studios. In the early 1930s, people huddled around their radios to listen to soap operas, quiz shows, dramas, comedies, anything to take their minds off of the Great Depression. Around 1934, stations began recording these performances on lacquer discs, which allowed them to record an orchestral or big band performance, for example, and play it at a later date. Hence, the city's first real recording studios. Most of the recording in San Francisco took place live in the radio studios—grand, acoustically treated spaces with room to fit musicians and an audience—or live in the clubs, until some small studios began cropping up in the mid '50s.

Beginning in the mid '50s, too, San Francisco was home to a very different kind of cultural Renaissance that brewed underneath the mainstream culture. With North Beach as a nerve center, a young group of writers and poets—dubbed "beatniks" by *San Francisco Chronicle* journalist Herb Caen—including New York transplants Allen Ginsberg, Gregory Corso, and Jack Kerouac and locals such as Phil Whalen, Phil Lamantia, Kenneth Rexroth, Gary Snyder, and Michael McClure, provided an alternative view of American society to free-thinkers who refused to buy into the conservative paradigm of Eisenhower America. Ginsberg's "Howl" alone, performed live for the first time at the Six Gallery in San Francisco in 1955, would be credited for sparking a resurgence both in American poetry and liberal thought.

When the Beats weren't hanging out in North Beach cafés such as Vesuvio, Caffè Trieste, Caffè Tosca, and Enrico's Sidewalk Café, they often ventured into one of the city's jazz clubs (the preferred genre among the hip literati), where the music stayed smokin' hot into the next morning. In the late '50s, as well, a significant folk scene sprang up in Berkeley, the Peninsula area south of San Francisco, and in the city itself.

The jazz and blues that permeated San Francisco at this time began its surge around World War II. This took place primarily in the Fillmore district, where many African-American industrial workers, artists and musicians settled after President Roosevelt signed an order to relocate the Japanese, some of whom lived in the Fillmore, to internment camps. Over the next several years many nightclubs opened in the area. Trumpeter Chet Baker, stationed in San Francisco during the Korean War, would sometimes sneak out of the barracks at Fort Mason to sit in on a jam session at Jimbo's Bop City (located in what is now the heart of Japantown), famous for its post-midnight jam sessions.

By 1955, the Fillmore bustled with activity nearly comparable to the Harlem Renaissance. Jazz giants such as Ella Fitzgerald, Billie Holiday, Ray Charles, Louis Armstrong, Duke Ellington, Charlie Parker, Charles Mingus, and Gerry Mulligan all passed through town to play in the homey, dimly lit watering holes of the Fillmore district. A young John Handy played Bop City with the great John Coltrane. Venues such as Jack's, Café Society, the Blue Mirror, and Club Alabam attracted bands led by Wes Peoples and Saunders King, among others. Other popular venues around town included El Matador, Jazz Workshop, Facks (its building on Bush Street would later house Coast Recorders), and the Blackhawk, which stood as one of the premier jazz venues from 1949 to 1963 and was the site of many classic live recordings.

The few resourceful technical innovators who had the foresight to record some of the jazz club happenings of the '50s and '60s usually had to lug around heavy equipment stuffed into station wagons or even strapped to the hoods of cars. Wally Heider, Orrin Keepnews (a New Yorker at the time), Sol and Max Weiss, and George Horn, all of whom make appearances in this book, could be found in San Francisco nightclubs capturing the music of the era.

Owned by Guido Caccienti and pal Johnny Noga, the Blackhawk hosted some of the biggest names of the 1950s at its 200 Hyde Street location. Already a Saturday night regular, Miles Davis debuted his "working band," featuring his powerful *Kind of Blue* band—pianist Wynton Kelly, bassist Paul Chambers, and drummer Jimmy Cobb, along with Hank Mobley on tenor sax—at the venue in 1961. Thelonious Monk, Shelley Manne, Cal Tjader, and Dave Brubeck also recorded albums at the club.

Vince Guraldi's first official booking came from the Blackhawk, as a fill-in for the legendary Art Tatum. Engineer Reice Hamil recorded many Blackhawk albums, including Monk's *At the Blackhawk,* recorded on April 29, 1960, for Riverside Records, co-owned by Keepnews and based in New York. Hamil owned a portable Ampex 600 machine packed in a sturdy Samsonite case, which he used to tie onto the back of his tiny Porsche.

Noga later sold his interest in the club to the Weiss brothers, who owned a small pressing plant called Circle Records, the launching pad for their soon-to-be label, Fantasy Records. These, along with clubs such as the Trident in Sausalito, Hungry i in North Beach, and later, venues such as the Fillmore Auditorium and Winterland Arena, would become sites for numerous live recordings.

When the city's first commercial studios appeared on the scene, the same acts that recorded their live albums in San Francisco finally had the option of making a studio album in their native city, too. The abundance of local talent that made the city's radio broadcasts come alive and filled coffeehouses, nightclubs, and concert halls would bring these early recording rooms to life.

From its early roots as a haven for various ethnic music forms, jazz, blues, and R&B, the city evolved to become a center for folk, pop, country, reggae, avant-garde, electronic, new age, rap, hip-hop, and of course rock in all its various forms. The list of nationally known bands to come out of the area is astounding. The '60s gave us Jefferson Airplane, the Grateful Dead, Santana, Janis Joplin, Sly and the Family Stone, Creedence Clearwater Revival, and Steve Miller. In the '70s, local acts such as Boz Scaggs, the Doobie Brothers, Journey, Tower of Power, Eddie Money, Sammy Hagar, the Pointer Sisters, Herbie Hancock, Sylvester, Dead Kennedys, and The Tubes entered the scene. The '80s gave us everyone from Huey Lewis, Tommy Tutone, MC Hammer, and Robert Cray to Faith No More, Primus, Digital Underground, Joe Satriani, Chris Isaak, and Metallica. The '90s saw many more local acts hit it big, including Smashmouth, Third Eye Blind, 4 Non Blondes, Train, En Vogue, Counting Crows, NOFX, and Green Day. In recent years we can add The Donnas, Dan the Automator, and DJ Shadow, among others. That only scratches the surface of the talent residing in this area.

About *These Halls*

Studios specializing in audio for film, TV and radio commercials, video games, and music exist throughout the entire Bay Area, from as far south as Monterey all the way up to Marin and Sonoma counties to the north and to Sacramento in the east. To cover them all in one book would probably require an encyclopedia-sized tome. With that in mind, I had to set some boundaries. First, I decided to focus mainly on *music* recording studios, allowing the musical history made within those walls to naturally come forth through the words of the many artists, producers, and engineers who contributed to this book. After all, these soundproofed buildings and their fancy equipment don't amount to much more than scrap metal and wood without them, so they're as much, if not more, a part of the Bay Area's recording history than the studios themselves.

With some notable exceptions, I narrowed my geographical range to the city of San Francisco, venturing outside of the metropolitan area only when historically necessary. For example, to write this book without including legendary facilities such as The Plant in Sausalito or Fantasy Studios in Berkeley wouldn't be much of a book. I also decided not to cover home studios and artists' private studios here, although hundreds are scattered all over the Bay Area, many of them on par with the commercial studios.

I do, however, intend to take you through a range of historic spaces and little-known places, giving you an inside look at where bands of all levels, budgets, and genres would record, as well as a behind-the-scenes look at how some of the music's most famous records got made and the often odd dramas that occurred in the process. Think of this as a guided tour when you're on vacation: You get to see most of the high points, and if you look closely, you'll catch a few things on the perimeter that only the locals know about.

Enjoy the ride!
Heather Johnson
San Francisco, 2006

SECTION ONE

The Fifties Through the Mid-Sixties: The Pioneers

If you could take an audio snapshot of the music coming out of San Francisco's few recording studios during the 1950s, most of what you'd hear would be the saccharine harmonies of advertising jingles used on local radio and television commercials. In post–World War II America, television use was skyrocketing; however, radio still had its fair share of listeners, drawn by popular DJs spinning new pop and rock singles and local personalities hosting live performance broadcasts. Both of these media, of course, relied on the support of their advertisers, and many of the agencies representing these companies were based in San Francisco. Naturally, when it came time to record the jingle for that new washing machine, they brought their business to one of the area's few studios.

But as far as recording artists go, most of the "name" acts based in the area recorded in Los Angeles, a city already established as a major recording center. Capitol Records set up shop there in 1942, with its first studio opening in 1949. As the only L.A.–based label that was part of the "Big Six" (Columbia, RCA, Decca, Capitol, MGM, and Mercury), Capitol held court as the primary player in L.A. until Warner Bros. came along in 1958. Independent labels such as Challenge, Del-Fi, Keen, Specialty, and Titan, among others, further established the city as an "A" market in the music business.

At the same time, San Francisco's musical talent pool was growing and would continue to do so at a steady pace up to 1965, when the activity would increase to levels more like white water rapids, and then to an ocean of excess as the decade closed. An abundance of new folk, rock, jazz, R&B, and other genres of acts started taking shape. In turn, a number of small and independent labels set up shop to support them. These artists needed spots to record, too, and many of the same studios that buttered their bread with advertising work began to take in the varied acts that either predated or served as a catalyst to the San Francisco rock explosion that would follow.

Until the late '60s, only a few major studios existed in San Francisco: Coast Recorders, Commercial Recorders (both primarily jingle houses that took on music recording), Golden State Recorders, and Columbus Recorders. All were dedicated music-recording facilities owned by passionate lovers of music and/or audio—a quality that's almost essential in a business that often brings greater creative than financial rewards. In the section to follow, we'll walk you through these four studios, as well as a handful of smaller facilities that emerged around the same time and produced an equally interesting body of work.

CHAPTER 1

The Original Coast Recorders

Sound Recorders, one of the earliest known commercial studios in San Francisco, opened in 1946. Jingles for radio, mostly, poured out of this second-floor space at the corner of Post and Powell Streets, while the United Airlines ticket office booked flights downstairs and trolleys outside carried businessmen and shoppers through bustling Union Square. Toward the end of the 1950s, advertisers could finally purchase 30- or 60-second spots rather than sponsor an entire radio program, so naturally, the city's top ad agencies needed a place to produce these bright, brief bursts of words and music. The demand for these short spots increased as Top 40 AM radio began to dominate in the early 1960s.

Sensing a prime business opportunity in the Bay Area's commercial industry, audio legend Bill Putnam purchased Sound Recorders in 1962. Putnam had founded Universal Recording Corporation, a successful recording studio and audio equipment manufacturing business (the precursor to Universal Audio) in the Chicago area in 1947, and United Recording Corporation in Hollywood in 1957. Rooms stamped with the Putnam name were considered prime acoustic real estate, and some of his recording techniques—he is acknowledged to be the first to use artificial reverberation for commercial recordings, developed the first multi-band equalizers, and was one of the first to record in stereo, among other achievements—advanced the field in innumerable ways.

When Putnam picked up Sound Recorders, the expanding United umbrella already included both United and Western Studios in Los Angeles, Universal Audio (manufacturers of prized UREI compressors and amplifiers), and the URCON studio in Las Vegas.

Putnam promptly christened his new purchase Coast Recorders and moved the operation and its clientele to 960 Bush Street, a large building in the tony Nob Hill area, not far from the activity of Union Square. The building wasn't ideal for recording, which is probably one reason why Putnam almost immediately began looking for another space, but he inherited a veritable landmark with a fascinating musical history.

Long before Putnam moved in his custom recording equipment, music ranging from the highly spiritual to the deliciously sinful reverberated through 960 Bush. Hymns and sacred music filled the sanctuary during its original incarnation as a church. During the first half of the 20th century, the house of worship either closed or moved (few records were kept, so the exact date and reason for its move are uncertain), and in the early 1930s, a theater called Hawaiian Gardens moved in.

Longtime San Franciscans remember 960 Bush as a home for the San Francisco Repertory Theater, the Bush Street Theater, Barney Gould's Emperor Norton Theater, the Balalaika, and the Club Kamokila. In 1956, The Andros Brothers assumed the space to open the nightclub Fack's. Mel Torme, June Christy, Earl "Fatha" Hines, Buddy Greco, and the Hi-Lo's, among others, played there. Duke Ellington was *supposed* to perform one night, but was greeted by a padlocked door; apparently, the I.R.S. shut the place down because the Andros Brothers owed them $36,000 in back taxes. Ellington returned when the club reopened for a short time as The Neve. For a brief period in the 1960s, the Quake, later named the Million Cellar, presented topless dancing in a Gold Rush–type atmosphere on the bottom floor. The red velvet curtains, stage, and large crystal chandelier from The Neve/Fack's era were still there when Coast Recorders moved in, serving as reminders of the numerous gala events, dramatic performances, and swanky soirées that happened through the years.

Coast Recorders in 1964, with the Million Cellar club conveniently next door.

© 1964, Alan Canterbury. Photo courtesy of San Francisco History Center, San Francisco Public Library.

After extensive renovations, Coast Recorders, a United Affiliate, officially opened its doors in October, 1963, equipped with some of Putnam's custom equipment, a 3-track tape machine, and remote recording services. They aimed to satisfy the needs of the Bay Area, which, at the time, meant accommodating a mix of advertising agencies and musicians. Putnam sent up Don Geis from L.A. to serve as chief engineer, and Geis busily recorded jingles for commercial clients and random singles, demos, and other projects for a smattering of Bay Area bands.

Coast Recorders claimed to offer "state-of-the-art" equipment in its promotional materials, and it did. In 1963, "world class" generally meant 3-track recording, but it wasn't long before 4-track came along. Coast made the necessary modifications to become a 4-track studio, but that's right where it stayed until 1969, when competitors in town offered 8- and 16-track options. But Putnam had bigger plans for Coast Recorders, so instead of purchasing a new machine for 960 Bush, he allowed Coast to rent Columbus Recorders' 3M 8-track machine, which was *the* most advanced machine in San

Francisco when owner Frank Werber purchased the heavy beast in the mid-1960s.

Coast Recorders' original space also offered a large live room, which worked well for orchestral dates and certain jazz recordings but wasn't as good for the burgeoning rock bands who were unaccustomed to such expansive surroundings. These bands felt uncomfortable in the room, which was roughly the size of a 300-seat club, shaped like a big empty box with a small stage at one end and a chandelier up above.

In the mid-1960s, engineer Bob Shumaker played drums in a band called The Answer (a great name for a sixties band, he says, because "everyone was looking for it!"), who recorded at Coast on Bush. "There were three monitors; we were recording mono in 1965, not stereo." The studio had no iso booths, he recalls, because "no one really knew about them in those days. I don't remember seeing gobos either, but maybe there were some. We set up the drums on the stage, and the rest of the band was beneath me. We recorded 20 songs that day."

Universal Audio Archives/David Kulka

Jan Ashton of local rock band the Mojo Men in session at Coast Recorders in 1967.

Shumaker also sat in on a pre-1966 session with Denise Kaufman, who later joined the psychedelic girl group Ace of Cups, a popular fixture in the late-1960s San Francisco ballrooms, despite not releasing any records. Before joining the Cups, Kaufman recorded the single "Boy What'll You Do Then" under the name Denise & Co. at Coast. It later became "the most sought-after garage band record of all time," says Shumaker, "because all of the copies, save for one or two, were stolen from her producer's car trunk."

Coast's more mainstream clients included crooners such as Jack Jones, who flew in from Lake Tahoe in 1965 to re-record and edit his new album, *Dear Heart*. In an early United and Affiliates newsletter, Geis said that artists working the resort hotels and music halls of touristy Reno and Tahoe seemed to gravitate to Coast due to its close proximity to their nightly gigs. The Charlatans also recorded at Coast while working in Nevada, but lived in a world far removed from the squeaky-clean pop singers. Straight out of the Red Dog Saloon in Virginia City, The Charlatans were part of the vanguard of the area's psychedelic movement. Ringleader George Hunter, guitarist Mike Wilhelm, piano player Mike Ferguson, bassist Richard Olsen, and drummer Dan Hicks blew into town like a stray tumbleweed, taking a break from their three-and-a-half-month stint at the Red Dog. The Western-themed bar/restaurant/nightclub had become quite the happening scene for the burgeoning drug counterculture; its Victoriana setting was made all the more surreal with generous amounts of LSD, visits from Ken Kesey's Merry Pranksters, and live music from the nattily dressed Charlatans. Though Wilhelm and Hicks were proficient players, the band itself didn't always have their set down, but darn it, they sure looked good, and could pull off shows that lasted until the sun came up. "Since there's no closing time in Nevada, we'd play as long as there were people there," says Wilhelm. "One time we played until 7 a.m.!"

After one of their nightly gigs wound down at the reasonable hour of 1 or 2 a.m., the group boarded the night train from Reno to San Francisco. They were headed for Coast to record a demo for Autumn Records, which had already amassed an extensive local roster thanks to co-owners Tom Donahue and Bobby Mitchell, both popular DJs on radio station KYA, and their multi-talented in-house producer, Sylvester Stewart, who would become better known later as Sly Stone.

An exceedingly chipper Stewart greeted the group, who showed up at Coast with suits rumpled and on no sleep, having knocked back a few drinks in the bar car chased by hits of LSD to stay awake. They knew young Sly; they had seen him not long before playing bass and leading the house band at the Cow Palace. "We showed up and he was just wired," Wilhelm recalls. "He said, 'I'm Sly Stewart and I'm here to help you guys, so if you need any musicians, like, I play bass, I play guitar, I sing, whatever you need!'"

Donahue then presented the group with sheet music for a couple of songs, one of which Wilhelm recalls as a protest song, which "wasn't really our bag." Another had references to modern society, which didn't fit with the group's well-crafted Victorian image. Wilhelm recalls telling Donahue, "Hey man, The Charlatans don't hang out at airports." He continues, "We studiously avoided any song that might pin us to a certain point in time. So we didn't really want to cut these tunes, plus we didn't know 'em, and here's Sly Stone bouncing around going 'I play everything.' We're thinking, 'Well what do you need us for!' Basically we just insulted him and kicked him out of his own session. We cut four tunes, a couple of which are okay, but we were so fried from the night before, we just weren't in the mood." The group recorded live, no overdubs, in less than an afternoon, then promptly took their burnt-out selves back to Virginia City, leaving any future with Autumn Records in the dust.

The following year, with their Red Dog tenure behind them, the group agreed to record an album for the Kama Sutra label with producer Eric Jacobsen (who also produced work for the Lovin' Spoonful, Tim Hardin, and, much later, Chris Isaak), who had signed the group based on the strength of a demo they had sent him. Once he had them in the studio, however, Jacobsen apparently had second thoughts.

"He thought we really had something, but then we got in the studio and he didn't think we had it!" says Wilhelm. "We recorded take after take, trying to get this elusive something that he wanted, but I guess he just decided, 'These guys can't sing, they can't play' and kind of lost interest."

As producer of the more good-time hook-heavy music popular at the time, Jacobsen may have wanted something more radio friendly than The Charlatans' ecelectic, folk- and blues-based guitar rock. Despite the differences, the Kama Sutra demos were later considered some of the greatest "lost" recordings of the sixties, but they didn't come without struggle.

"Erik would drag us through take after take, and we were trying to figure out what the heck he was looking for," says Wilhelm. "I remember one time we were 50 takes in on something and instead of just stopping us when he didn't like it, he'd let us go through the whole take and have us do the whole thing again. After you sing something so many times, how do you retain any kind of freshness?"

Jacobsen gave up on the band, but the label saw potential in those 3-track recordings, and decided to release "Codeine Blues" as a single. The group finished the single, and Hunter and Ferguson promptly designed an ad for the music trades. The ad included the group's logo, a photo of the band, and, in their trademark old-timey lettering, the words: "Codeine Blues: Remedy for a Drug Market."

"Oops! Drug song! Never mind that it was an anti-drug song," Wilhelm says, "but the label balked and never did put it out." They did concede to release another single, on the Kapp/Kama Sutra label, of the Leiber Stoller tune "The Shadow Knows," with "32-20 Blues" on the flipside. The single, says Wilhelm, "went absolutely nowhere, and it wasn't until years later that I actually saw a copy of it. I never really believed they actually put it out!"

The Charlatans didn't put out a full-length album until 1969, after most of the original lineup had moved on, but they carved out a path for the mass of psychedelic rock bands to follow. They had the look, the logo, and the posters done before they had ever played a note, and the vision to do something different.

Despite the occasional session, Coast never earned a reputation as a rock room; instead, it held on to its original notoriety as a jingle studio, and became a popular spot for jazz artists, some of whom knew Putnam from his tenure in Chicago, when he recorded projects for top-drawer acts such as Stan Kenton, Tommy Dorsey, Count Basie, Dizzy Gillespie, Ella Fitzgerald, Sarah Vaughn, Nat "King" Cole, and Duke Ellington, who later became a frequent visitor at Coast.

Universal Audio Archives/David Kulka

Vince Guaraldi, director of the San Francisco Boys Choir, helmed a session with the 50-voice group at Coast in 1967.

Advertising clients, some left over from the Sound Recorders days, filled up the rest of the calendar, eager to work in Coast's clean-sounding studio. Radio spots were created for many companies, including Comet, Mother's Cookies, Pacific Telephone, and Pacific Gas & Electric. (At least one spot featured location recording, with Geis recording dishwasher sounds in his own kitchen). Upstairs neighbors Diana Production Company, then owned by Cournoyer, brought in spots from Mercury, Donald Duck Orange Juice, and Lejon Wine, among others. West Coast Productions, also located in the Coast building, produced spots for a wide range of clients, including Sapporo beer, Datsun, and Bank of Hawaii.

Toward the end of the Coast-on-Bush era, Dan Healy occupied the room for a stretch to produce and engineer a slew of bands for Mercury Records. Though he's best known for his longtime studio and live sound work for the Grateful Dead, Healy's credits extend to albums with Quicksilver Messenger Service, Sir Douglas Quintet, and Michael Bloomfield, among others. So swamped was he with work, Healy would finish a session at one studio during the day, then jet over to Coast the same day to record another act. The

Steve Miller Blues Band, another ballroom regular before polishing their sound and dropping "Blues" from their name, was one group caught in Healy's double-shift. Like The Charlatans, their first studio experience took place on Bush Street. It was, in all due respects, a nightmare.

"We got thrown out of the studio lock, stock, and body!" recalls Healy. "I don't remember who did it...maybe it was Boz Scaggs[then a member of Miller's band]...but somebody put an American flag over the B3 console. Mel Tanner, who was the manager at the time, basically came in and said, 'Get your shit and get the heck out of here.' They just went nuclear! These guys were all World War II vets and didn't understand that we didn't mean any disrespect. None of us were really that political. Our message was more about how to live your life and be a decent person."

Coast Recorders would soon move to new digs on Folsom Street (see Chapter 6), and would occupy two more locations after that during its long tenure in the city. Throughout their roving ways, Coast would continue to specialize in jingles and jazz, with a few rock acts peppered in between, and endure as the only Bill Putnam room in San Francisco.

CHAPTER 2

Commercial Recorders

In 1962, bassist Lloyd Pratt and piano player Steve Atkins started Commercial Recorders in a building that used to house one of the original turn-of-the-century San Francisco firehouses. A photography studio operated on the first floor of 149 Natoma between 2nd and 3rd and Mission and Howard Streets in the heart of downtown. With the arrival of Pratt and Atkins, one of the city's most successful jingle studios kept the second floor abuzz with activity.

A San Francisco native raised near Dolores Park in the Mission District, co-founder Pratt arrived on the studio scene after a long career as a singer and bass player. The Sequoia High School graduate joined the Page Cavanaugh Trio while serving in the Army during World War II. After their discharge, the trio—pianist/vocalist Cavanaugh, guitarist Al Viola, and bassist Pratt—with their Nat "King" Cole–inspired playing, generated such mid- to late-'40s hits as "The Three Bears," "Walkin' My Baby Back Home," and "All of Me." A three-year touring stint with Frank Sinatra bolstered their success. While Cavanaugh and Viola continued to work steadily in the L.A. area, Pratt returned to San Francisco and studied to become a music teacher. Though rewarding, the teaching career didn't offer the excitement of performing, so Pratt left the world of academia and returned to show business; he's rumored to be the only white man to have played with the Count Basie band.

For his day job, Steve Atkins played vibes and trombone in the staff band for Channel 7, the local ABC affiliate. He later joined Channel 5, where he led a trio for an afternoon show hosted by John Bartholomew Tucker. At night, Atkins navigated the club scene as an in-demand piano player (he even worked at Fack's No. 2 for two years) and actually met Pratt when the two played at a club at the corner of Powell and Bay Streets. In addition to working as a musician for hire, Atkins got occasional work as an arranger for a local ad agency, with Pratt often playing bass on the sessions. Disgruntled by the lack of studios in the area, Atkins and Pratt decided to build their own.

Pratt was eager to revisit his passion for engineering and production; Atkins had the writing, arranging, and conducting skills; both were monster musicians. Together they formed Comm-Spot Productions, a commercial production company; and Commercial Recorders, a space that gave them the sonic results they had been looking for.

During its seven-year run, Pratt and Atkins hosted, on average, 90 percent of the commercials running on San Francisco radio, assembled in both large and small scale in the studio's 40×40×20 (width × depth × height) recording room. A pole, left over from the building's fire station days, ran through the middle. Partly because of the studio's high ceilings, Pratt and Atkins elevated the control room to about shoulder height. That control room housed an old 2-bus RCA tube console, praised by those who used it for its warm, musical sound. Recording options included an Ampex ½-inch 3-track (later converted to 4-track), as well as two Ampex 350 2-track stereo machines and about 15 microphones. Live echo chambers resided in the basement.

Much like today's commercials, some of Commercial's radio ads combined voiceovers with music libraries, although the clients with deeper pockets brought in some of the best musicians in town. "The top musicians always get the calls for recording, because they're the top musicians," says Atkins. "That holds true to this day. When you've only got one hour to do a lot of work, you want the best possible people in there."

Jazz luminaries such as Vince Guaraldi and Cal Tjader could be found playing as part of a trio or quartet, usually conducted by Atkins if he wasn't sitting in on the sessions himself. "We could have anything from a trio to a 30-piece orchestra in there, depending on what was going on that day," he says.

Celebrity vocalists could sing through an old RCA ribbon mic or Telefunken tube in the spacious room, which Dan Healy says had a sound that would knock your socks off. "Every day we'd have somebody famous reading a spot," he says. Healy got his start at Commercial Recorders in 1964—mopping floors. For free. "This was in the heyday of Willie Mays when the Giants ruled the baseball world, and we did all of the Giants commercials with Russ Hodges and Lon Simmons, two legendary baseball announcers. They'd come in two to three times a week." Healy came in right around the time Atkins left the company to pursue more work writing and producing jingles from an office in Columbus Tower, which housed Columbus Recording (covered in Chapter 3).

Healy was just a teenager when he volunteered his services to Pratt and Atkins, but he came from a strong musical background and, like a lot of budding engineers, had liked to fiddle with radios as a kid. He learned the art of engineering and producing at first via osmosis, taking care of his janitorial and maintenance duties at night so he could "hang out" during the day.

"I got to watch, and I got to learn," Healy says. "The ad agencies bought the time, and each agency had these famous crack commercial producers. So I got to not only watch the engineering, I got to witness and watch the producers direct the announcers in how to speak, talk, and direct the commercials. I got a fantastic education that in later years really paid off for me."

Healy produced a number of commercials and radio broadcasts in later years, but during his time at Commercial, his interests leaned more toward his friends' rock bands. He lived on a houseboat in Larkspur, a short walk down Boardwalk 3 from concert promoter Bobby Collins, who often let the guys from Quicksilver Messenger Service crash on his floor. Nobody really had much money in this small bohemian community; a broken guitar amp often meant a missed gig. "We were the rebels-without-a-cause group, so we didn't have the normal connections, either. We were outcasts and we wanted it that way," says Healy.

It didn't take long for the neighbors to figure out that Healy had a day gig at a studio and that he knew important things, such as how to fix a guitar amp so they wouldn't miss the next gig. A friendship with Quicksilver Messenger Service, especially lead guitarist John Cipollina, developed, and eventually Healy made it to one of their gigs. Opening act: The Grateful Dead. As the story goes, Healy was called on stage to figure out why the music suddenly stopped (probably a broken amp). He ended up fixing the problem, and then hung around backstage shooting the breeze with Jerry Garcia. Healy never did catch Quicksilver's set like he promised, but he did catch a clear vision of his future as a studio and live engineer. Still on the clock at Commercial, Healy switched his cleaning shift to days and snuck in his friends' bands at night. "Of course Lloyd Pratt and the guys would come in the next morning, and everybody would just be out of there by the time they came in," Healy recalls. "The place would be thick with cigarette smoke, and there I'd be, sweeping the floors! Lloyd never said anything about it."

A couple of years later, when the record labels began scoping out the happening San Francisco rock scene, Commercial Recorders made a deal with Mercury Records. One of the first majors to set up offices and studios in the city, Mercury pursued a handful of what they felt were the most promising bands for demo deals. Commercial, knowing they would need a cheap place to record their demos, offered the label a budget weekend rate. Neither Pratt nor Atkins really wanted to work on their days off and they weren't too familiar with the new rock music anyway, so they turned to their resident maintenance guy/janitor/engineer-in-training Healy, who happened to be *way* into the rock scene. An insider, the musicians knew him, liked him, and partied with him outside of the studio.

"The music community wasn't that big then," Healy recalls. "All the bands knew each other and hung out together. I guess because the whole scene was a bunch of people who had gotten out of high school and had some sort of wanderlust and left home. We all somehow gravitated to San Francisco and stumbled into each other and the whole music scene was born."

Because of his close relationship with many musicians, Mercury saw Healy as a missing link between their structured corporate world and the independent, go-with-the-flow hippie bands. "There was a lot of friction between the straight engineers and studio scenes," says Healy. "So they were immediately looking for a new generation of engineers that could interface with the new generation of musicians." Healy's insider status and musical knowledge led to a one-year producer contract with Mercury, and he moved up from demo recordings to full-blown album projects. He was 20 years old. During that year he produced Tex-Mex group Sir Douglas Quintet's career-boosting album, *Mendocino,* the band Fifty Foot Hose's sole album, *Cauldron* (for the Mercury imprint Limelight), and a few others. By that time, the four tracks at Commercial Recorders weren't enough for what Healy wanted to accomplish, so he sought out another studio and found one in the basement of one of the most recognizable buildings in North Beach—Columbus Tower—the same address that Steve Atkins had moved to just a few years before.

After Atkins and Healy moved on, Pratt continued to run a busy jingle production business. In 1969, Pratt merged his business with Coast Recorders, giving Coast even more muscle in the advertising world. Not long after, Bill Putnam named Pratt director of agency recording. Sadly, Pratt didn't have much time to settle into his new position. He died of a heart attack in 1970.

CHAPTER 3

Columbus Recorders

A few years after the Kingston Trio hit it big in 1958 with their self-titled Columbia debut and singles such as "Tom Dooley," manager Frank Werber re-invested the group's earnings to form Trident Productions, a multi-faceted enterprise located in the historic Sentinel Building at the corner of Columbus and Kearney, at the financial district, Chinatown, and North Beach border.

The triangle-shaped, copper-clad structure, also known as Columbus Tower, housed Trident's management, production, publishing, and promotion divisions. The real action, though, happened in the basement—ground zero for Columbus Recorders. The studio had a smallish tracking room—not much bigger than most control rooms these days—but it was adorned with redwood walls that gave the studio a stylish feel reflective of the owner's good taste. It would serve as a model for studios to come. There was another perk. "You could walk up the back stairs and be right at the back door of Zim's Hamburgers," says multi-instrumentalist/songwriter Bill Champlin, who recorded there with his band Sons of Champlin. "How much more could you ask for?"

To complement the comfortable recording environment, Werber's studio offered a solid array of equipment. In addition to multiple echo chambers, the studio contained a custom-built

10-input Langevin console, which was an impressive deck for the time. A mastering room with a Scully mono lathe was installed upstairs. Hank McGill served as the studio's first house engineer and operations director.

Columbus Tower, at 916 Kearny, home to Columbus Recorders and Frank Werber's Trident Productions enterprises.

© 1964, Alan Canterbury. Photo courtesy of San Francisco History Center, San Francisco Public Library.

The opening of Columbus Recorders gave the Kingston Trio a regular place to record until their "official" retirement in 1967. As the trio's career slowed, Werber found other acts to manage and produce under the Trident Productions, Inc., banner, including the Limeliters, Mystery Trend, and Blackburn & Snow, among others. "In terms of what they were trying to do, they were sort of San Francisco's answer to Stax/Volt," Champlin says of Werber's enterprise.

Werber discovered the We Five in 1965, a folk-rock quintet led by singer/guitarist/banjoist Mike Stewart, who also arranged most of the group's music and, not so coincidentally, was the brother of Kingston Trio member John Stewart. Bassist/vocalist Pete Fullerton, lead vocalist Beverly Bivens, electric guitarist/vocalist

Bob Jones, and acoustic guitarist Jerry Burgan rounded out the five-piece group. The We Five did well with reworkings of everything from "My Favorite Things" from *The Sound of Music* to Stewart-penned originals, but they scored their first big hit in 1965 with "You Were On My Mind," a song written by Sylvia Fricker of the Canadian folk duo Ian & Sylvia. They hit the Top 40 again in 1966 with "Let's Get Together," but with not nearly the same luster. They recorded a second album with Werber, *Make Someone Happy* (which has been compared to the sound of Jefferson Airplane's first album), before they split up. This ended their career, despite Stewart's attempts to reconfigure the group later.

In addition to working with We Five, Stewart lent his vocal talents to another up-and-coming Trident Productions band, Sons of Champlin, a highly skilled ensemble that evolved out of a Marin County R&B outfit called the Opposite Six in late 1965. "When we signed with Werber, we had to go to court to get the signatures okayed by the judge because we were all [underage]," says frontman Bill Champlin. "I was maybe 17 at the time."

Before signing with Capitol and becoming an important but overlooked part of the S.F. rock scene as The Sons, the quintet embodied a more straightforward garage-rock sound that Werber once described as the "Beach Boys with balls." In the mid 1960s, the group recorded an album's worth of material for MGM-Verve at Columbus Recorders with producer Randy Steirling, whom Werber brought up from L.A. Hank McGill engineered. "We recorded the whole album there, 4-track to 4-track," says Champlin. "We'd make a submix of the first four tracks and fly it to one track of the second 4-track, then you'd have three more tracks to record on. Engineers in those days had to always be mixing, which was a cool thing, because we were always paying attention to the mix instead of thinking, 'I'll fix it later.' You had to hear it right all the time."

Verve only released one single from those sessions, "Sing Me a Rainbow" backed with "Fat City," although the remaining tracks can be found on *Fat City*, a collection of previously unreleased Sons of Champlin material issued in 1999 through Big Beat Records. Not long after the Verve sessions, in 1967, Werber and The Sons parted ways.

"We weren't getting along," says Champlin. "Werber wanted us to do a demo of this Barry Mann song, 'Shades of Grey,' and we just overproduced the shit out of it. He wanted us to redo it [one way] but we wanted to take it somewhere else. We wanted to turn it into this big production, showing, 'Yeah, look what we can do.' My band and the producer got in trouble for it, and I thought, 'If you're going to put a ceiling on us in this stage in our careers…I don't want to go there. Me, Tim, and Terry were really opening up and becoming aware of so many other kinds of music."

They held on to their artistic freedom, but Champlin wonders if they passed up an important opportunity. "We didn't realize at the time that Werber was trying to groom us for something. He thought that we had a real good shot to make a big splash if we played the game right, but we didn't. We never really played much of the industry game. That's probably why not very many people know who we are!"

However, passing on that shot at mainstream success gave them the freedom to expand their sound, adding a horn section and incorporating elements of jazz and R&B and becoming a bright spot in the San Francisco music scene. It also allowed them to sign with Capitol Records later.

Despite The Sons' departure, business was especially fertile at Columbus Recording in 1967. Among other projects, the Grateful Dead came in to record one song with arranger/producer Jon Hendricks. The studio tallied up enough profits that year to upgrade their tape machine and purchased a 3M 8-track—the first in the city—for $15,000. Naturally, it became an in-demand item for tracking and mixing clients both in-house and at other studios.

"We used to rent that machine to Coast Recorders for $200 a day," recalls George Horn, who assumed McGill's role in 1968. "Creedence Clearwater Revival did their first album on that machine while they were at Coast." The combination of the newly modified Langevin and the 3M 8-track attracted many producers and engineers, including Dan Healy, who recorded many of his Mercury Records projects at Columbus following his tenure at Commercial Recorders.

One of the most interesting projects Healy worked on at Columbus wasn't for Mercury, though, and it didn't involve cutting tracks in their studio. The Grateful Dead's second LP, *Anthem of the Sun*, shattered the mold of conventional recording. The Dead thrived on the spontaneity of the live setting and resisted most forms of organization. The studio environment limited their potential and often felt like it was too...controlled. Getting a decent take from the band, Healy says, was "like pulling teeth. It had to do with the way the whole scene was structured, which was raw unadulterated anarchy. Plus, personally and collectively they always thought that they sucked, and that carried into the studio. Nobody was ever satisfied with their tracks or overdubs, so we'd do them over and over and over for weeks, even months. As a result, their records ended up being really over-recorded and overproduced and overplayed. They lacked spontaneity." The group started their second album at RCA's Studio A in Hollywood in the summer of 1967 with their label-approved producer, Dave Hassinger, who had also produced their self-titled debut album in just four days of "live" recording in the same studio. Actually, the lead-off track from that album, "The Golden Road (To Unlimited Devotion)" was tracked after the RCA sessions, at Coast Recorders and required many more takes than the Hollywood material. They challenged Hassinger every step of the way. The project moved to American Studios in North Hollywood, where they continued to test their producer. They allegedly contemplated recording in a desert to record in a more "purified" atmosphere. As the now-frazzled Hassinger had discovered, working with the Grateful Dead was like "trying to organize a school of fish," says Healy. "Just when you think you've got something together, it blows up and goes in the opposite direction."

That's exactly what happened when the project moved a third time to a pair of 8-track studios in Manhattan: Olmstead Studios and Century Sound. Recording lurched along, with Hassinger trying to set boundaries on a band that wanted none. He disapproved of the constant experimentation on the album—for instance, one of Dead bassist Phil Lesh's friends, avant-garde composer and keyboardist Tom Constanten, contributed a section of music for one song played on a "prepared piano," a technique originated by John Cage in which different objects, ranging from coins to spoons, were placed in a piano's strings, altering the sound of each note in bizarre ways. The final straw may have been when rhythm guitarist Bob Weir asked Hassinger if he could create the sound of "heavy air." According to Weir, Hassinger stared back blankly before leaving the room—and the project—for good.

With one of their favorite producers gone and nothing more than a couple of instrumental tracks to show for more than three months of studio time and mountains of equipment rental bills, Warner Bros. vice president Joe Smith sent a letter to then–Dead manager Danny Rifkin, stating, "You are now branded as an undesirable group in almost every recording studio in Los Angeles. I haven't gotten all the New York reports in as yet, but the guys ran through engineers like a steamroller."

The band turned to their friend Healy, who had revamped the Dead's sound system and mixed their live shows, to help them get something on tape. They had a few concerts coming up in the Pacific Northwest, so Healy and the band agreed to record them in lieu of more studio sessions. He found a Viking ¼-inch 4-track, which Healy describes as "a funky machine for its time, but it ran at 15 ips." He hot-rodded it by adding another ¼-inch 4-track head and at least six Altec 1567 4-channel mixers to create a portable recording device that he could take on the road. He recorded five shows, and when he and the band got home, retreated to Columbus Recorders to cobble together an album. Shows were recorded at different speeds, some on ½-inch, some on ¼-inch. They listened to every song on every tape, picked either the best performances or parts of the best performances for each song, and put them together in a collage that became the album.

"A lot of it was done by hand because there was no synching equipment in those days," he explains. "Also, there might be a song where the first half from one night would be better and the second half from another night would be better, but because we were so radical in those days, you couldn't just cut the songs together because, shit, it might be in a different key. Or it might be in a totally different time signature! So, I would take one performance from the 4-track recordings and lay it on the 3M 8-track [at Columbus] on to four tracks. Then I'd take the other one, and I'd play that back, and I'd get the 4-track machine and start them together so that the same song would be played simultaneously, and then I'd crawl underneath the 3M 8-track and rub my hands on the fly wheel—they didn't have variable speed; anything you did, you did out of your own creativity and it was really, going to the junk-yard and hammering something together—and listening with a pair of headphones, I'd put one performance in one ear, the other in the other ear, and then I'd listen and rub my fingers on the flywheel of the machine to keep them in sync for the transition point. Then I'd have them synched up perfectly when it went from one part of one song to the second part of same song from another night. Then when we'd mix it down, we'd mix it that way so it would all come out sounding like one song." The final version contained thousands of edits, spliced by hand.

Healy probably had no idea at the time that his experiments with a 3M 8-track would lead to an album that pushed the boundaries of the 12-inch LP medium, completely redefined the concept of a recorded live performance, and led to an album as unconventional and revolutionary as the band itself. "It was a psychedelic collage literally put together outside of any record company direction. The inmates were running the asylum," Healy says. "It created a huge wave in the industry. As soon as other bands heard about [the album], the idea of straight recording went out the window." For the Dead, the experience also inspired them to produce more live albums (although more studio albums would follow) and construct their own recording facilities at spots throughout Marin County.

Not long after Healy crawled out from under the 3M machine, George Horn hired a young and very green engineer named Phil Edwards. Edwards majored in music at San Francisco State and took a few classes in broadcast electronics on the side. He also played saxophone with his brother in a band called the Edwards Brothers and worked occasionally as a sideman. He had a lot of moxie for a kid in his early 20s. Edwards first visited Columbus Recorders with his band's drummer (who coincidentally later joined The Sons). They met with Horn, who informed the drummer he had no need for his services as a studio musician, but he did need a mixer. Though he had no technical experience, Edwards piped up anyway. "Oh I can do that!" he said. Horn took his name and number and the two left to resume lives as student/musicians.

Months later, however, during an Ornette Coleman show at the Greek Theatre in Berkeley for which Edwards was hired to play flute, he bumped into Horn again, who rolled in with engineer Healy and that heavy 3M 8-track to record the performance. They spoke only briefly before the show, but the conversation must have left an impression on Horn, because "about a month later at 7 a.m., I got a call, saying, 'Can you come in and mix a 4-track date?'" recalls Edwards. "I said, 'Well sure!' I had just enough knowledge to fake my way through it. Later George took me out to lunch and said, 'How would you like a part-time job?'" Edwards accepted.

Edwards remained at the facility until it closed in 1970, engineering whatever unmanned projects came through the door, including folk singer Tim Hardin and various Dan Healy sessions for Mercury Records. "They'd record at Coast on Bush Street and mix at Columbus," says Horn. Columbus also did its fair share of commercial work, some of which migrated from its competitor. "We got a client from Honig-Cooper & Harrington who wanted to do some voiceovers," recalls Edwards. "All of a sudden we had all of Honig's accounts. Unbeknownst to me, there were a couple of clients who were unhappy with Coast. Coast had a huge problem with a spot welding machine in the next building that was creating all sorts of havoc on the console, spikes and stuff, so they were having difficulty doing sessions. So we started [working with Honig] and they were happy."

Columbus Recorders began its slow burn to cessation when Werber became part of a major drug bust. According to an article in the October 16, 1968 *San Francisco Chronicle*, two owners of the Sausalito bar Latitude acquired 258 *pounds* of marijuana. (A friend of Werber's said the two men had made advance arrangements with about half-a-dozen people to purchase the marijuana, Werber being one of them.) However, upon landing their plane in Laredo, Texas (where they were to pick up the weed), the two men were caught by federal authorities. They then flew back to California with the pot, but accompanied by two federal agents. When they delivered the marijuana to Werber's DeSilva Island home, a stakeout ensued. The authorities charged Werber with transporting and concealing marijuana—a Federal offense. In his home city, he was charged with importing marijuana into the state for possession and sale.

Defending himself in court, Werber cleared himself of the federal charges but served a one-year sentence in San Quentin for the state charges. "He was never the drug dealer that they tried to make him out to be," says Horn. "He was just the type of guy who you could never go to his house and not leave with a bag of marijuana. It was just his thing. Like some people give out cigars, he gave out little baggies of marijuana."

The legal ordeal consequently drained a large portion of Werber's monetary assets. The $412,850 in taxes that the Federal government ordered Werber to pay on the marijuana, which agents say they seized in his possession, drained even more. At the same time, competition in San Francisco's studio scene had become exceedingly tough, especially for smaller rooms such as Columbus. Werber and Horn had initially discussed expanding the studio, but after the court battles, he closed the studio in 1970, handing the now-famous Columbus Tower space to San Francisco native Richard Beggs, an engineer and soon-to-be sound designer who rented out the space to work on commercials and demo recordings.

As fate would have it, Francis Ford Coppola purchased the building and moved his American Zoetrope offices there in 1972, after a pretty good run on the second floor of Coast Recorders on Folsom Street. Though separate entities initially, Coppola began using Beggs' studio as a screening room on *Godfather II*. "They would screen dailies there," Beggs said in an interview with *Mix* magazine. "The screen came down on the wall where my glass was, so I'd be working in there on some commercial for PSA or Pacific Telephone or Foster Farms chicken, and I had this huge image four feet in front of me—I could see this movie playing out in reverse. It was pretty claustrophobic. Anyway, Francis was very courteous. Even though he owned the building, I had my lease and he was respectful of that. But slowly I became integrated into that organization. There were odd jobs that needed to be done from an audio point of view. I had a good live space for voice-overs. Someone would come in to do some sound effects. I did a lot of dribs and drabs—nothing that would ever deserve a screen credit. But by the next one, *Apocalypse Now,* I'd been sucked in." Beggs has worked on Zoetrope projects (and many others) ever since.

Frank Werber

Frank Werber's story is classically San Franciscan: He arrived with nothing but carved out a rich legacy as one of the most influential music-business figures of the 1960s. Armed with the power to grant a band a fortune with a flash of a signature, Werber built an empire around the Kingston Trio's success, helping them earn unheard-of sales numbers for a folk group in the early 1960s.

His multifaceted career began as an aviation photographer and midshipman in the Navy, followed by odd jobs as commercial artist, gold miner, cab driver, horse rancher, ski-lift operator, construction worker, and press photographer. The restless soul reportedly landed in San Francisco with only 15 cents in his pocket, but a few months later, a chance meeting with restaurateur and scene-maker Enrico Banducci led to his involvement in the night-club business, managing the famous Hungry i nightspot and bringing the club national recognition through his networking and PR skills. Four years later, he opened his own public-relations office. During this time, Werber stumbled upon a group of young Stanford University students singing for pretzels and beer in a college pub called the Cracked Pot. He was so impressed that he signed on to be their manager and promptly began grooming the young men, taking them to vocal coach Judy Davis and putting them through rigorous rehearsals at a North Beach loft. Emerging as the Kingston Trio, the group began a one-week residency at the Purple Onion in 1957. One week evolved into seven months, followed by a short tour and a deal with Capitol Records in 1958. Of the 13 albums the Trio recorded for Capitol, five became certified million sellers. "Tom Dooley" was their first million-selling single, with hits such as "Tijuana Jail," "M.T.A.," "Worried Man," "Everglades," and "Where Have All The Flowers Gone" soon to follow.

An astute businessman and entrepreneur, Werber launched Trident Productions, a conglomerate that included music production and business, real estate, land development, restaurant and night-club supervision, and nearly every facet of the Kingston Trio's affairs, from publishing to song-book and sheet-music sales, television and personal appearances, to development of new shows.

Werber joined forces with Decca Records and Universal Pictures to form his independent production company, recording the Kingston Trio as well as numerous other successful acts. He also negotiated the sale of Kingston Trio albums with Decca Records as sole exclusive distributor, and subsequently, from Universal, obtained many motion-picture and television guarantees for the trio. On the live scene, Werber launched the Trident Club in Sausalito in 1961, one of the swankier jazz clubs in the area, which he kept until 1980. In 1969, he was involved in the early planning stages of the ill-fated Wild West Festival, a multi-media arts and music event, billed as a sort of West Coast Woodstock that was supposed to sprawl through Golden Gate Park but eventually collapsed due to political infighting and a lack of civic support.

In his rare free time, Werber played as hard as he worked. He had a passion for photography, skiing, diving, and sailing, and spent many a weekend steering the Shearwater, his 60-foot Alden Ketch, on San Francisco Bay. On land, he often sped around Marin County on his Honda motorcycle or, later, in his Ferrari 300 SL. He sought refuge at his secluded home on DeSilva Island, a private community in southern Marin County. He currently lives in New Mexico, although he still maintains a membership to the San Francisco Chapter of the Recording Academy after more than 45 years with the organization.

CHAPTER 4

Golden State Recorders

Maybe he sought a better quality of life, maybe he wanted to be closer to his brother and other family in San Francisco, or maybe he saw an opportunity to accommodate a new kind of music emerging in a market far less competitive than Los Angeles. For one, or maybe all, of the above reasons, Leo De Gar Kulka (a.k.a. "The Baron") migrated from L.A. to San Francisco in 1964 to open Golden State Recorders at 665 Harrison Street between 2nd and 3rd Streets, a gritty area at the time, now a mix of modern lofts, fancy restaurants, and the Giants' home, AT&T Park. A classic example of the "mom and pop" studio, Leo Kulka ran the studio and engineered most of the sessions. He employed a small staff, including an office manager/bookkeeper, one staff engineer, and an assistant engineer. On busier days, his wife came in to help out.

For the first few years, that small group ran one of the few music recording studios in town with a recording room comparable in size to established L.A. and New York facilities. The studio area was at least 50×50 feet, with high ceilings, a vocal booth, and the requisite gobos to break up the square footage during a session. "At the time it was a good room; a big box, really," George Horn describes it bluntly.

"One of the advantages of [the room's size] was you could record a broad variety of music," adds Vance Frost, who worked as an assistant engineer at Golden State in 1968. He returned in 1971 to serve as its lead engineer and manager until 1976. "We'd do large-scale recordings, like big bands, a few orchestral dates, and 30- to 60-voice gospel choirs."

Golden State had the size.but it lacked the pristine quality of certain major market studios—which is just why a lot of clients liked it. Reflecting the no-nonsense attitude of its owner, Golden State felt lived in and unpretentious. It didn't have much in the way of décor—no colored lights, no dimmer switches. You had two options: lights on, lights off—all or nothing. Kulka did add a few switches later so clients could at least control *which* lights turned on and off.

After spending several years in L.A., Kulka probably had had enough of "slick" anyway. In 1957, following a staff-engineering gig at Radio Recorders on Santa Monica Boulevard, Kulka founded International Sound at Sunset and Western in Hollywood. His mastering room there featured a Neumann cutting lathe with a stereo head. He had a Neumann mastering room at Golden State as well, along with a custom 4-bus console built by staff engineer Mike Larner. This was later expanded to 8-bus.

"In those days, most recording consoles were custom because there weren't really any manufacturers who made them," says nephew David Kulka, president of Studio Electronics, a Burbank-based pro audio support firm. Kulka made much of his other equipment himself. "Who knows how it was made or what it was made of," says producer/engineer Elliot Mazer. In addition to working in the studio, Mazer and engineer David Diller used Kulka's remote truck (an odd thing that looked like an old bread van) to record a series of shows at The Fillmore. "It didn't matter when you put up a mic and heard the guitar or drums. It sounded good and off you went." A live echo chamber, accessed by walking through the electrical shop behind the control room and climbing up a ladder and through a porthole, added character—and still more reverb—to an already live room.

In addition to the handmade gear, Golden State offered an Ampex Model 200 (the first model issued by the Bay Area–based company), brought by Kulka from L.A., as well as a couple of AG440 mono 2- and 4-track machines and at least one Ampex 350 reel-to-reel recorder. All great machines, but Kulka was slow to upgrade: When 16-track became available in the late 1960s, Golden State hung back at four.

In its early years, Golden State, and Kulka's engineering skills, appealed mostly to a niche of respected soul and blues artists, including Rene Hall and Wally Cox. Both of these artists already had a few decades of experience under their belts when they recorded with Kulka at Golden State. Kulka also signed some of these acts himself, either leasing sides to outside labels such as MTA and Acta or issuing singles through his Golden Soul imprint. Much of this material remained unreleased until decades later, when the public discovered his recordings from San Francisco TKOs, The Savonics, The Spyders, Jeanette Jones, and The Generation (featuring Lydia Pense, later of Cold Blood).

The studio also attracted a few L.A.–based artists and producers and a solid cast of local musicians, such as the Beau Brummels, Sons of Champlin, Big Brother & the Holding Company, The Charlatans, and a slew of obscure acts. Some achieved later success, while others—such as the C.A. Quintet (oddly, from Minneapolis, but they recorded their first and only album at Golden State)—remained relatively unknown.

The same year Golden State opened its doors, the Beau Brummels recorded *Introducing the Beau Brummels* for Autumn Records with producers Bobby Mitchell and Sylvester Stewart (a.k.a. the infamous Sly Stone), which included their first hit, "Laugh Laugh." Their importance has perhaps been underrated in the Bay Area: Led by guitarist-songwriter Ron Elliott and vocalist San Valentino, the group was one of the first in the U.S. to respond to the British Invasion and also among the first U.S. folk-rock groups. "Laugh Laugh" reached the Top 20 and its follow-up "Just a Little" made the Top 10. However, Autumn Records, despite its good intentions, didn't have the promotional muscle to propel the group to long-term national success. They produced several more strong albums with Autumn and stayed until 1966, when Warner Bros. purchased the company.

In 1965, label co-owners Tom Donahue and Mitchell brought in another one of their acts: an odd blues- and R&B-influenced rock band called The Warlocks. Half a year earlier, they had been an anarchic acoustic group called Mother McCree's Uptown Jug Champions. In one day at Golden State, they recorded six songs—four originals, one traditional, and a cover of Gordon Lightfoot's "Early Morning Rain"—none of which were ever released until a box set 30 years later. With Kulka at the board, they recorded under the name The Emergency Crew, reportedly because bassist Phil Lesh had spotted an album in a record store by another group called The Warlocks. Soon after, they permanently changed their name to the Grateful Dead, putting an end to any risk of band name infringement.

During their time at Autumn Records, Donahue and Mitchell had become popular voices around town as KYA DJs, producing shows at the Cow Palace, and running a management company and radio-tip sheet. They brought many other groups to Golden State to record under the Autumn Records banner, often with the help of Stewart, their secret weapon. In addition to the Beau Brummels, Stewart produced Bobby Freeman's hit "C'mon and Swim" and other cuts for the Mojo Men, The Vejtables, and the Great Society. This last group was the launching pad for future Jefferson Airplane siren Grace Slick

Under Autumn Records' wing, the Great Society often rehearsed in Donahue's office, and it wasn't long before Donahue asked Stewart to produce them. According to band member Darby Slick (Grace's brother–in-law; her husband Jerry Slick was also in the band), the hot-shot multi-instrumentalist started making arrangement suggestions, and one by one, the band rejected them. In his book, *Don't You Want Somebody to Love*, Darby Slick says that Stewart asked, "What the fuck do you need with a producer if you're going to axe all my ideas?" "Did we ask for a producer?" Darby said. "Maybe not," answered Stewart, "and you can bet your asses I didn't ask for you either."

Stewart later cooled down and came with them to Golden State to help them record "Free Advice" and "Somebody to Love." Darby Slick had written this song days before while coming down off of LSD after his girlfriend failed to come home one night. They recorded "Somebody to Love" first. As Darby Slick recalls, the Great Society "played their hearts out" during that first take, feeling "drained, but triumphant," at the end. And then, the dreaded words: "Sorry, I messed up," said the engineer. "Can you give it to me again?"

It took them more than 50 takes to get another version that came close to a keeper, and even then, it didn't match the luster of the missed Take One. After a couple dozen tries, Stewart walked out, disgusted. "Free Advice" came more quickly. Because the song was pitch lower than guitarist/vocalist David Miner's range, he stretched out on a sofa in the studio, mic lowered to just above his face, and with his hands stretched behind his head in perfect lounging position, nailed the song on the first take. The single came out on Autumn's subsidiary, North Beach, in 1966, just before the label folded.

Sylvester Stewart, a.k.a. Sly Stone, at Golden State Recorders, 1966.

The Vallejo, California–born Stewart also signed with Autumn as an artist in the mid-1960s. He recorded four tracks at Golden

State under the name Sly Stone: "Can't Turn You Loose," "I Ain't Got Nobody," "Take My Advice," and "Life of Fortune and Fame." None of these were released until much later on a Sly and the Family Stone reissue for Epic Records. Stone's career would soon explode with that ensemble, and he made appearances at several studios, one of which became his home for a while. We'll visit that "resort" in Chapter 11.

Freshly signed to Capitol Records, the Sons of Champlin recorded their debut, a double LP, *Loosen Up Naturally*, in 1969 at Golden State. They even named the lead track after its purchase order number: "1982-A." "It came from a rough mix we had of Leo [who engineered the album] going, 'Alright. Sons of Champlin, 1982-A' and then the song started," says Champlin. The record label hired a young Nick Launay (who went on to produce and engineer projects for Nick Cave and the Bad Seeds, Eric Clapton, and Public Image Limted, to name a few) to produce the album. Unfortunately, he arrived a few weeks too late. "We were supposed to wait for a month for the producer to finish up a project in L.A., but we didn't want to wait," says Champlin. "So we cut it ourselves with Leo. It was a double-album, and we cut it in two weeks, mixed in a week, and then when [Launay] came up to produce, we just handed him the finals."

One reason they could record the album so quickly was because they were such good musicians. "They were probably one of the most rigorous and well-rehearsed bands out there," recalls Frost. "They were such a complete package that when they came to the studio, they only did a couple of takes of a tune."

Secondly, they knew their way around the studio a bit after spending time at Columbus Recorders. "We'd learned so much from Randy [Steirling] that we kind of knew how to do things," says Champlin. "And we, or I, had a vision of ourselves, this 'I can do no wrong, I'm on a roll, don't slow me down with stuff like tuning a guitar!' We were just flying. There was no holding us back."

A few problems in the studio temporarily derailed them, however. "We did four sides; the last side was one song called 'Freedom,'" says Champlin. "We were doing a final mix on it and the tape snapped right in the middle of a guitar solo! Eight-track tape was flying at like 2,000 inches per second...through the air, all over the place. It was a mess. So we took a rough mix of the song and just snapped it on to the final mix and it ended up okay. It was right after a long guitar solo at the beginning of another section, so all of a sudden there was a little more bottom, a little more funk, a little less reverb. That's all we could really do. But then Leo, in order to save his ass, had us cut the whole thing again so that he could hand it back." In 1969, producer Elliot Mazer came by to finish a portion of Nick Gravenites' album, *My Labors,* at Golden State. Much of the album came from the same sessions that produced *Live at Bill Graham's Fillmore West* by Michael Bloomfield (recorded with Kulka's remote truck). Bloomfield added his guitar work to some of Gravenites' live tracks, while members of Quicksilver Messenger Service chimed in as the rhythm section on several studio tracks. Members of the Ace of Cups sat in on the bluesman's Columbia Records debut as well.

Bloomfield came and went from the studio in the late 1960s through the early 1970s. "He got along real well with Leo," says Frost. "He liked the studio, he liked the environment the way it was. It was more...rough hewn, shall we say, than places like Wally Heider Studios." One particularly titillating session came from the Mitchell Brothers, founders of the infamous O'Farrell Theater strip club and movie house. They had asked if Bloomfield would play on the soundtrack to what they promised was their "epic" film. "They tried to be real discreet about what they were doing, but it became pretty obvious that we were making a soundtrack for a blue movie," says Frost with a laugh.

Business began to slow at Golden State in the early 1970s as other facilities made their way into the city. The most notable of these was Wally Heider Recording. Musicians, fickle as they can be, wanted to record at the "in" studios with the "in" equipment, which put a dent in Golden State's business. Kulka, though, had a side venture percolating that he would soon launch, and its success kept the studio humming for many years to come. We'll revisit these developments in Chapter 17.

Leo De Gar Kulka

Leo De Gar Kulka didn't look like the long-haired musicians wandering about in the late sixties, and he didn't act like the typical introverted audiophile, yet he managed to navigate comfortably in both circles. Standing more than six feet tall, bald head shining between two tufts of hair, "The Baron," as he called himself, came to work dressed for business, complete with pressed shirt, ascot, and pearl tack. He had a big, booming voice that could startle more sensitive souls, but his hearty sense of humor and patience in the studio put clients at ease.

Born in what is now the Czech Republic, Kulka moved to Los Angeles in 1938. He served in the U.S. Army Counter-Intelligence Corps (CIC) during World War II and the Korean War. His wartime experiences with wire recorders and radio transmission sparked a passion for both recording and music. Released from his military duties, Kulka returned home and soon became a staff engineer at the famed Radio Recorders in Hollywood.

In 1957, Kulka decided to open his own studio. He founded International Sound at Sunset and Western, one of the earliest multi-track studios in Hollywood and one of the first with a stereo mastering lathe—a Neumann, VMS66 or earlier. At International Sound, Kulka recorded projects for Frank Sinatra, Nat "King" Cole, Little Richard, Herb Alpert, Sam Cooke, and Sonny Bono, in addition to running numerous mastering sessions.

Following his success in L.A., Kulka moved his operation to San Francisco and in 1964 launched Golden State Recorders. He brought his 2-track tape machine collection and Neumann lathe with him and soon found himself recording what would evolve into the San Francisco Sound. Golden State's large recording room lent itself well to wily musicians, though his engineering skills proved an even stronger draw.

"He understood sound and acoustics incredibly well," says nephew David Kulka, who worked with his uncle for three years before joining Bill Putnam's United/Western Recorders in Los Angeles. "People liked working with him because he knew how to get the right sounds. He was reassuring and funny and kept things going in a nice way."

Aside from working with acts such as Quicksilver Messenger Service, Michael Bloomfield, and Big Brother & the Holding Company at the beginning of their careers, Kulka produced acts for various independent labels that he put together. He later became involved in experimental recordings and miking techniques. Under his Sonic Arts label, he cut numerous direct-to-disc and binaural ("dummy head") recordings.

In addition to studio work, Kulka taught at San Francisco State University for more than a decade, and in 1974 founded the College for Recording Arts, one of the area's first dedicated recording schools, which he ran out of Golden State until 1994.

The same year he launched the school, Kulka teamed with a small group of local industry pros to form the Recording Academy's (a.k.a. NARAS) San Francisco Chapter (now the fourth-largest chapter in the organization), which also operated out of Golden State. A longtime Audio Engineering Society member, Kulka chaired its San Francisco Section for several terms and helped organize the 93rd AES Convention in San Francisco.

He spent the latter part of his career working on analog and digital mastering, specializing in the restoration of vintage recordings. He passed away in 1998, leaving a long line of bad jokes, good recordings, and well-trained engineers behind him.

CHAPTER 5

Early Recording Around the Bay

Circle Records

Some sources question whether or not the small spot on Treat Street (an alley street in the Inner Mission district) could, as rudimentary as it was, even be called a studio. Right after World War II, Sol and Max Weiss started Circle Records as a pressing plant, issuing tiny titles mostly for the Chinese community. However, the Weiss brothers also owned a piece of the famous San Francisco jazz club The Blackhawk, and after recording a number of shows there, the pressing plant morphed into a small jazz label. Their first artist was an Oakland pianist named Dave Brubeck. When Brubeck's recordings began to sell, they pursued their label ventures more aggressively, recording Gerry Mulligan, Chet Baker, and Cal Tjader, as well as Odetta, beat poets Lawrence Ferlinghetti and Allen Ginsberg, and comic Lenny Bruce.

"If they had facilities [on Treat Street] they weren't very good," recalls engineer George Horn. But engineer Jim Easton reportedly got his start in a studio at Circle Records and later went to work at Fantasy Records. A young John Fogerty worked in the stock room. A few years before Phil Edwards walked into Columbus Recorders for an engineering gig, he recorded at the Treat Street studio with his jazz band. "It had corrugated a tin roof that leaked and would leak into the piano when it rained," he recalls. "Their entire record inventory was in this building, along with this sort-of studio. And Sol was this odd guy who explained that you couldn't have too many mics in a room because it would suck all the audio out."

My, how much we've learned. The Weiss brothers would later take over Koronet Records, the original home of Brubeck, rechristen their company Fantasy Records, and grow it into one of the most successful independent labels in the United States. And it all started by two visionary music lovers under a leaky tin roof.

Sierra Sound Labs

Robert DeSousa's Sierra Sound Labs, located on the other side of the Bay Bridge in Berkeley, held sessions as early as 1955. These included regular visits from folklorist/producer Chris Strachwitz. Strachwitz founded Arhoolie Records and recorded albums for blues artists such as Tony De La Rosa, Sydney Maiden, Earl Hooker, Mississippi Fred McDowell, K.C. Douglas, and various projects for Prestige Records, among many others. East Bay "Record Man" Jim Moore, founder of Jasman Records, brought in Joan Adams (the singer that reportedly inspired him to start a label) and the Bay Area's beloved blues queen, Sugar Pie DeSanto, in the early 1960s.

During this time, the East Bay flourished with a scene quite different than the big city across the Bay. In Oakland, Berkeley, and other smaller communities around the area, small labels churned out folk, blues, R&B, and gospel, a lot of them with their own small recording setups. Many who didn't record in-house came to Sierra Sound to record on their custom console and Scully tape machine. The studio's solid reputation later attracted the likes of psychedelic rock pioneers Country Joe and the Fish, who recorded their Vanguard debut, *Electric Music for the Mind and Body,* at Sierra Sound in 1967. To his credit, Country Joe continued to record locally while his musical peers headed for better-equipped L.A. and New York facilities.

The late 1960s saw acts such as Lightnin' Hopkins, Stonewall Jackson, Los Tigros del Norte, and a slew of Latin and other international acts at the studio. Jef Jaisun visited Sierra Sound Labs in 1969 to record "Friendly Neighborhood Narco Agent," which became sort of a cult classic when Dr. Demento started playing it on his radio show years later. He chose Sierra Sound Labs mainly because Country Joe had recorded there. On his website, Jaisun says that he had a grand time that day recording the goofy song around the jackhammers outside drilling the new Grove Street (now Martin Luther King Jr. Way) BART line about a half a block away.

Music City, Veltone Records

Of the various labels/studios operating in the East Bay, notables include Ray Dobard's Music City Records and Veltone, an R&B label owned by Oakland producer Bob Geddins, the man who taught Strachwitz the art of record-making. Jim Moore dropped in as Geddins put the finishing touches on his 11th Street studio in downtown Oakland in 1959. As Geddins tinkered away, Sugar Pie DeSanto and her husband walked in. She had a new song she wanted Geddins to hear; when she played it for him, he flipped and organized a session for that night. She came back, and with Johnny Heartsman on guitar, recorded "I Want to Know," her first and biggest hit. The song later caught the attention of Chess Records, where she remained for seven years. "He loved the blues and he put all his life in it," DeSanto said in an early interview. "He recorded some of us that he knew really had it."

Music City Records cornered most of the market for Bay Area R&B around 1954. Guitarist Heartsman was Music City's A&R man. Some of the originators of California doo-wop and R&B came out of this label and recorded singles at Dobard's studio. For example, Salinas quartet The 4 Deuces shared a session one day in late 1954 with R&B group The Rovers, who recorded "Ichi-Bon Tami Dachi." Like The Rovers, The 4 Deuces reportedly had popular success but received no money from their label owner, called "cheap" and "tone deaf" by those close to him. Dobard released one of the two singles The 4 Deuces recorded that day: "W-P-L-J" (white port with lemon juice). The single sold at least a few hundred thousand copies, and the Italian Swiss Colony wine company offered a yellow vinyl 45 of the song free with every bottle of white port. But even though members the group wrote the song, Dobard registered the copyright in his name. The songwriters didn't get a cent.

Chris Strachwitz, Arhoolie Records

Producer Chris Strachwitz, founder of Arhoolie Records in El Cerrito, California, has worked passionately to nurture and preserve traditional American music for more than 45 years. Strachwitz and his family migrated from Germany to California in 1947. Upon landing in the West Coast cultural melting pot, the teenager became hooked on New Orleans jazz and fascinated by old-time country music, blues, gospel, jazz, R&B, Mexican, and other music he heard on the radio. He produced his first record in 1960, a 33⅓ RPM single for Texas songwriter/guitarist Mance Lipscomb titled "Texas Sharecropper and Songster." That single marked the beginning of Arhoolie Records, a longstanding independent label devoted to a vast range of folk and traditional music originating from all over the globe. Strachwitz helped acts such as Clifton Chenier, Lydia Mendoza, and Mark Savoy reach a wider audience by issuing their work on Arhoolie. Many blues, gospel, Tex-Mex, Cajun, zydeco, jazz, and old-time country artists have found a home at the label. The label also reissues vintage folk recordings from the early 20th century, including Mexican-American border music, early Mexican mariachi music, and work from Greek, Polish, Cajun, and Ukranian artists.

In 1966, he produced the inaugural Berkeley Blues Festival, as well as concerts for Bill Monroe. He helped organize tours of colleges and clubs for Lightning Hopkins, Mance Lipscomb, and Fred McDowell. In 1976 he conceived and helped fund the film Chulas Fronteras on Texas-Mexico border music, produced with Les Blank. In the late 1980s, he co-produced and co-directed *J'ai Eté Au Bal*, on Cajun and Zydeco music.

When country star Alan Jackson's 1997 recording of "Mercury Blues"—originally composed by K.C. Douglas and Bob Geddins and published by Arhoolie's publishing wing, Tradition Music Company—became a number-one hit, Arhoolie received a boost in funds that has allowed the label to continue to this day. (In the mid-1970s, too, a version of that song on Steve Miller's *Fly Like An Eagle* album had sold millions.)

In 1995, Strachwitz founded the not-for-profit Arhoolie Foundation, established to enable "the documentation, dissemination, and presentation of authentic traditional and regional vernacular musics and by these activities educate and enlighten the public as well as support and reinforce traditional community values." One of the many projects the foundation has funded is the digitizing of the Strachwitz Frontera Collection, its biggest project to date, which is still in progress as of this writing. The collection of Mexican and Mexican American recordings contains about 15,000 78 RPM recordings, 20,000 45 RPM recordings, and numerous, cassettes, LPs, and CDs. Digitized copies go to the UCLA Digital Library (http://digital.library.ucla.edu/frontera), which are available to the public to browse and listen to 60-second clips. The ongoing effort further ensures that future generations of music listeners will have the opportunity to hear some of the same music that inspired Strachwitz to carve out a long, valuable career in the Bay Area.

Buena Vista Studios

Buena Vista Studios, one of the first truly hippie-friendly studios, appeared on the scene in the mid-1960s. It was located in an old-money mansion, didn't have much space, and the acoustics weren't the best; however, its close proximity to Haight-Ashbury coupled with owner Gene Estribou's musician contacts led to some interesting sessions.

Engineer/producer Estribou learned his craft from Henry "Sandy" Jacobs, an audio wizard known for his experimental KPFA radio programs, where he often showcased his space age soundscapes, hypnotic drum loops, and other avant-garde arrangements. Estribou had also conveniently married an heiress to the Spreckels Sugar fortune. He set up his recording facilities on the fourth floor of a late 19th century mansion formerly belonging to Richard Spreckels (nephew of sugar baron Claus Spreckles), overlooking Buena Vista Park at the edge of the Haight. Estribou's room did not reflect its lavish surroundings by any means, but the bare-bones space did acquire one of the city's first 4-tracks, at a time when most engineers were still trying to get more mileage out of the 3-track.

Photographer Herb Greene introduced Estribou to members of the Grateful Dead, and he promptly invited them to his studio. They accepted, the day after a Saturday night Acid Test party at California Hall, on the fringe of the seedy Tenderloin district. Band and crew hauled massive amounts of heavy equipment up four flights of stairs to rehearse and record some of their first studio demos under their new name (putting an end to The Warlocks) for Scorpio Records in June 1966. Scorpio released two of these tracks, "Stealin'" and "Don't Ease Me In."

"We had an Ampex 3-channel instrumentation deck that Henry Jacobs brought into the studio," said Estribou in an early interview. "I had built a big horn and a studio; we had good condenser mics and spent a lot of time optimizing the board. We went down to Western Recording and used their studio for doing some tapes that ended up being on the first 45 from Scorpio Records." Other songs from these sessions came out much later, in 2003, on *Birth of the Dead,* a compilation of studio and live material from 1965 to 1966.

Bob Matthews, fresh out of high school and living on Bob Weir's bedroom floor, sat in on the sessions at Buena Vista. A voracious learner, he took in every microphone placement, every spin of the tape machine's reels, every nuance of the recording process. And on that post–LSD trip Sunday, he realized his purpose with "the tribe." "That was when I became enamored with recording as a function and a process in the legacy of any given live performance of the Grateful Dead," says Matthews, who went on to engineer dozens of live and studio recordings for the band. "I told Weir that the live performance would always be what they were about; that whatever they did in the studio would be different, and I thought it would require somebody within the family to properly create a recording that represents what takes place musically. And I was going to be that person." Weir answered, "If you have the dream, go for it!"

When The Dead weren't using the room to rehearse or record, Estribou rented the space to bands such as Quicksilver Messenger Service and Steve Miller Band, who recorded songs for the film *Revolution* at the studio. Mainstream Records' Bobby Shad, a guy that Joel Selvin describes in his book *Summer of Love* as a "practiced shyster who rummaged through the peripheries of jazz and blues, making cheap records and paying the artists as little as he could," also graced the studio with his presence.

Shad auditioned S.F. rock acts such as Wildflower and the Final Solution, both of which he signed. Big Brother & the Holding Company, featuring their new lead singer, Janis Joplin, also auditioned for Mainstream Records at Buena Vista studio, but didn't get a deal initially. After a four-week residence at a Chicago nightclub, the band got a call from Shad, who apparently pitted the group against their manager, concert promoter Chet Helms, and convinced them they would get the "short end of the stick" if they didn't sign with him. They agreed to the deal, shoddy as it was, and recorded their self-titled debut for the label in 1967. Columbia Records soon saved the group from Shad's grip by buying out their Mainstream contract.

Not much of note came from Buena Vista Studios after the late 1960s. Graham Nash bought the mansion in the 1970s, followed in the 1980s by actor Danny Glover, who performed with the San Francisco Mime Troupe before going to Hollywood. The city saved the mansion from demolition in the 1990s, when it operated as a bed and breakfast.

San Francisco Tape Music Center

At the dawn of the 1960s, San Francisco hummed with new ideas in music and other art forms. Aside from the more organic genres, electronic musicians began playing around with proto-drum machines and sequencers and putting tape recorders to work in interesting and unusual ways. To help further such developments, Ramon Sender organized the first electronic music studio at the San Francisco Conservatory of Music in 1960. Sender and fellow composers Pauline Oliveros and Terry Riley began to produce a music concert series called Sonics, which marked the beginning of San Francisco Tape Music Center, an organization whose mix of sound, film, and image set the bar for experimentation for decades to come.

In 1962, instructor Mort Subotnick, who dabbled in the medium, got involved. The group pooled together their resources and equipment to launch the Center officially—first on Jones Street, later on Divisadero. Established as a nonprofit educational and cultural center where artists could produce concerts and learn about and work within the tape music medium, SFTMC consisted of two auditoriums shared with Berkeley's listener-supported non-commercial radio station KPFA, the Ann Halprin Dance Company, and an attic studio, all of which continually expanded between 1960 and 1963. The group hosted monthly concerts with the assistance of visual artist Tony Martin, who joined the group in 1963 to maneuver light projections for the performances, and William Maginnis, who served as both technician and composer. Local painters, poets, dancers, and actors also aligned with the Center. While the concerts introduced American and European avant-garde composers to local audiences, the studio attracted the most attention. Composers, especially those from the West Coast, virtually lined up outside the door to get in.

The attic spot didn't have much in the way of equipment, but its occupants used whatever was available to reshape modern music. Oliveros brought in her tape loop and delay systems. By 1964, composers had six audio oscillators, 14 loop generators, and five tape recorders (including a 3-track Ampex) to work with, but no mixing board or similar control surface to meld it all together. The Tape Music Center desperately needed equipment to match the sophisticated music created within its four walls, and engineer Donald Buchla, who appeared at the Center around 1965, helped make this happen. A contemporary of Bob Moog, Buchla partnered with Subotnick and Sender to design the Buchla Modular Electronic Music System, the first Buchla analog synth. Not officially introduced until 1966, prototype components arrived at the tape center as they were developed. Maginnis produced one of the first pieces on the system, a composition called "Flight."

In 1965, the Center received a grant for $15,000 from the Rockefeller Foundation. The next year, Mills College, which had been a hotbed for modern experimental music for some time, offered the Center an even larger sum of grant money, but they had to move to the college to receive it. They accepted the offer and changed their name to the Mills Tape Music Center, becoming part of the Mills Center for Contemporary Music. While people either with or without academic credentials could —and did—still record at the spruced-up studio, organizational problems and the restrictions that come with operating under an educational institution took its toll. The studio continued to produce innovative music, with musician/engineers such as Patrick Gleeson (See Chapter 13) and Funky Features owner Jack Leahy getting their start at the Center, yet many believe that it never saw the same level of excitement as the San Francisco site.

Funky Features

Prior to Funky Features' official opening in 1969, Jack Leahy had built a workshop/studio in the basement of an old Victorian on Central Avenue, near the panhandle of Golden Gate Park. Originally designed for personal use only, the small space became a popular place for young bands to rehearse and record new material under Leahy's guidance. As the engineer continued to invest in his private workshop, he acquired enough gear (and spent enough money) that he opened the studio to outside clients in 1969.Preferring to work fast in order to cater to bands on a budget, Leahy's comfortable space turned out a healthy number of demos and masters, with many referrals coming from the neighbors across the street, Big Brother & the Holding Company. Producer David Rubinson reportedly brought some of his Fillmore Records acts, such as Cold Blood, to the studio. Acts such as Steve Miller, HooDoo Rhythm Devils (managed by Leahy), Country Joe McDonald, Link Wray, Terry Garthwaite, Wah-Wah Watson, Herbie Hancock, and Steamin' Freeman also spent time in the upper Haight studio.

The 20×20–foot studio had a Steinway grand piano at one end. A Hammond B3 organ with a Leslie speaker and an antique Everett upright tack piano could be rolled in as well. Leahy worked on an equally antique console comprised of Ampex and Shure mixers, recorded to 3M 8-track (he later acquired a 16-track), and listened on a pair of JBL monitors. When the HooDoo Rhythm Devils signed with Capitol Records in 1971, they reportedly spent part of their advance on a 16-input console for Leahy.

In 1979, Leahy moved his recording operation to Russian Hill to open the aptly named Russian Hill Recording, which we'll visit in Chapter 21. An odd, fan-run museum called The Jimi Hendrix Electric Church took over the lovely Victorian on Central for a few years before it reverted back to a residential space.

Roy Chen Recording

Even though he didn't open up shop until 1970, and despite the studio's three-year lifespan, Roy Chen deserves credit as a pioneer for opening the first professional recording studio in Chinatown. On Waverly between Sacramento and Washington, just a block away from the bustling Grant Street markets, stood Roy Chen Recording, then one of the few small facilities where artists "on a budget" could record with good equipment in a room with excellent acoustics. The studio contained a custom Fairchild console, UREI 1176 limiters and other outboard equipment, a 3M 16-track recorder, as well as Ampex and Scully machines. But Chen was most proud of the mid-sized room's acoustics and his microphone collection. He had a "very special" Neumann KM84, along with Neumann U57, 67, 87, the RCA 44 ribbon mic, RE 20s, and others from AKG and EV. "We just bought everything," he says. The recording room "wasn't very big but it had good acoustics for rhythm sections," he says. "It was good for recording drums. Out-of-towners said it had a Memphis sound."

While a large portion of Roy Chen Recording's business came from demo work, he also saw projects from Columbia and Elektra, as well as some early demos for Almo Irving Music. Producer Ron Haffkine produced some of Dr. Hook & the Medicine Show's earliest recordings at the studio, and Nick Gravenites and Big Brother & the Holding Company both recorded some of their first projects there. Groups such as the Pointer Sisters and the Edwin Hawkins Singers used it as rehearsal space. Esteemed engineer Roy Halee even stopped in once to cut basic tracks with Boz Scaggs for one of his albums. Chen watched him work. "He showed no expression on his face," he says. "He was steady, unperturbed…he knew what kind of sound he wanted to get out of this group. They finished the vocals at Columbia. I bought the album when it came out, and I think it's one of the best recordings we ever made."

The studio ceased operation when Chen went through a divorce. "But that didn't stop me from coming back!" he says. After a 13-year hiatus, Chen returned to the local scene as a pro audio dealer, and he continues to run a successful business covering that facet of the industry.

SECTION TWO

The Late Sixties: The San Francisco Sound and Studio Explosion

The San Francisco Bay Area has always been a place that attracted artists, rebels, and free-thinking individualists. Maybe it has something to do with being at the far edge of the American continent, perched out over the edge of the Pacific Ocean. The Beatnik scene germinated in San Francisco's North Beach in the 1950s; the Free Speech movement happened in Berkeley in 1964; and beginning around 1965, the hippie counterculture—the libertine "children" of Kerouac and Ginsburg and The Beatles and Dylan—started to coalesce in Berkeley and in San Francisco's Haight-Ashbury neighborhood, near Golden Gate Park. Rents were low then, and living communally made it even cheaper. Bands sprang up in garages and in drafty old Victorian houses. Everyone, it seemed, was trying some form of art, whether it was poetry or collage or poster-making or light shows. And the copious amounts of marijuana coming up from Mexico and LSD being manufactured locally (it was legal even until October, 1966) were helping fuel what really was a sort of Day-Glo renaissance.

According to the small circle of friends and band mates that laid the groundwork, the San Francisco rock scene was at its most fun, communal, and vibrant between 1965 and 1967, and it peaked between late 1966 and January 1967, when the Human Be-In attracted some 20,000 people to Golden Gate Park for a day of poetry, spirituality, and music by the area's best bands—it truly was, as it was billed, "A Gathering of the Tribes."

By the time Big Brother & the Holding Company, Country Joe & the Fish, David Crosby, Jefferson Airplane, Quicksilver Messenger Service, and the Paul Butterfield Blues Band took the stage at the Monterey Pop Festival in June, 1967, the mainstream press had caught wind of the curious activity in the Haight-Ashbury and declared 1967 the "Summer of Love." By that point, thousands of teenagers and young adults, all wanting to taste this freedom and to escape their straight upbringing, decided to drop out in San Francisco. As more people moved into Haight-Ashbury—many of them would-be musicians who had heard about the magical festival in Monterey and also had been turned on by the first wave of records to come out of the San Francisco bands—the neighborhood changed dramatically. "At that point, the streets became lined with panhandlers," says The Charlatans' Mike Wilhelm, who moved out of the Haight to an apartment near Japantown in 1968. "You couldn't walk down the street and say 'Hi' to anybody anymore because they'd just ask for change, or maybe they'd be hawking: 'acid, speed, lids?' The scene started to feed and imitate itself, and the music became really overblown with these huge, long, self-indulgent jams. Things started to become big business at that time."

By 1969, Jefferson Airplane, The Grateful Dead, and Janis Joplin had already reached superstar status, many of them leaving their Haight-Ashbury or North Beach neighborhoods for more spacious digs in Marin County, or in the Airplane's case, a huge mansion at 2400 Fulton Street next to Golden Gate Park. San Francisco, particularly the Haight, had become dingy, dangerous, and a popular spot for panhandlers, hustlers, and protestors. Smoke bombs flared, police sirens blared, and the local markets barred their doors. When The Grateful Dead left their Ashbury Street pad in 1968 for pastoral North Bay, much of the peace, love, and happiness of the times went with them.

However, despite its rough exterior, San Francisco held on to its reputation as the cosmic center of the musical universe. Joel Selvin writes in *Summer of Love*, "The music emanating from the city over the previous three years had captured the imagination of the world...On any given night, dozens of bands worked ballrooms and small clubs around town."

The Musician's Switchboard, a not-for-profit crossmatching and referral service that published job opportunities and a directory of active musicians, listed more than 500 bands and 2,000 musicians in the summer of 1969, with more coming in at a rate of 10 or more a day. Since the release of Jefferson Airplane Takes Off in 1966, more than 15 albums by San Francisco artists had hit the upper reaches of the *Billboard* charts. Others who stayed closer to the San Francisco underground still sold albums by the truckload. Creedence Clearwater Revival earned its first national hit in 1969 with "Suzy Q" and consequently turned its small label, Fantasy Records, into the most successful indie in the U.S. during that time. Just about every record company sent out talent scouts who prowled the dance halls in search of the next big psychedelic rock band.

Funny, the bands that founded this scene didn't start playing with the intention of getting signed, but for the sheer fun of it. Technical chops weren't required, which was good, because not many of the early musicians had 'em (at least at first)! With some exceptions—Jerry Garcia, Jorma Kaukonen, Mike Bloomfield, Bill Champlin, and Steve Miller among them—the level of musicianship was somewhat lacking, and the level of music-business knowledge was pretty low as well.

"When I arrived from New York in 1969, there were no managers, and very few that understood recording technique," says producer David Rubinson, who started a small school at Pacific Recording in San Mateo to teach music-business topics and basic audio principles to the community, for free. But did the fans care? No. The scene was about getting together, the spirit of community, and digging the bands uncritically. Crowds packed the Avalon Ballroom and the Fillmore West because it was Saturday, or Tuesday, or whatever, not necessarily because of a certain headliner. If a local band butchered an old Muddy Waters tune at the Avalon, it didn't really matter. The enthusiasm, positive spirit, and infectious love for the music usually won out and even won over a few of those label reps, too.

As a result, the few local studios in town stayed booked literally around the clock with demo recordings and record label projects for primarily local artists. For one of the only times in San Francisco studio history, demand exceeded supply, studios overflowed with business, and the engineers worked their derrières off. Many of the industry's most revered recordists, including Elliot Mazer, Glen Kolotkin, Jim Gaines, Dan Healy, mastering engineers George Horn, Paul Stubblebine, and many others either earned their wings or greatly expanded them within the late 1960s San Francisco studios.

In an effort to accommodate the rush of new music, a number of new studios opened in 1969 and 1970 alone. The arrival of Wally Heider Recording in 1969 caused the biggest stir by bringing some high-profile local acts out of the L.A. studio market and moving San Francisco up to a new level of professionalism in recording.

CHAPTER 6

A New San Francisco Coast

Maybe part of the reason Bill Putnam didn't seem too concerned about keeping Coast's Bush Street space technically up to date or funneling much money into extensive acoustical renovations had to do with the long-range planning that went into his next—and most significant—move. The Bush Street locale ultimately would not work as a professional studio unless Putnam wanted to tear down the building and start from scratch. As cool as it was with its stage and chandelier, the live room had all parallel walls—certainly not ideal for a recording studio, as it leads to standing waves, which leads to, in short, odd acoustics. To redo the room would have meant extensive renovation; one of the walls in question was a load-bearing wall, which meant the whole building relied on it. Rather than undertake such a job, Putnam found a vast, vacant warehouse space downtown, at 827 Folsom Street, in the dicey South of Market neighborhood. Planning, design, and construction took three years, but when finished, Putnam realized his vision of providing San Francisco with "the finest technical and engineering facility within an attractive and creative environment to serve the needs and desires of all our clients," as he described in a United and Affiliates newsletter. In the process, Putnam also created the beginnings of a "one-stop shop" business model, with tracking, mixing, and mastering facilities all operating under one roof. However, the shop changed hands almost as soon as it opened.

The new Coast on Folsom Street.

Universal Audio Archives/David Kulka

Initially, it seemed Coast aimed to attract all facets of the audio community: music, film, and broadcast. Right off the bat, they rented their second floor to the up-and-coming filmmaker Francis Ford Coppola, who used the warehouse-like space for his American Zoetrope company. Coppola had recently finished *Rain People,* which was presented at the Mexico City and Bahamas Film Festivals in June and released nationally in October, 1969.

Putnam also acquired accounts and substantial ad agency business from Commercial Recorders, Inc. In addition, co-owner Lloyd Pratt joined Coast as its director of agency recording. This arrangement seemed to be a "win-win" for Pratt, who had full entry into record production. This was an avenue he had been interested in pursuing since his Page Cavanaugh days.

"An increasing number of national radio and TV music tracks for commercials are being recorded at Coast," he said in an October 1970 United and Affiliates newsletter. "We have the facilities, the engineers, and the know-how, and more and more clients are coming to us rather than taking the more time-consuming and expensive route through Hollywood or New York. Agency work is a large part of our business and we will continue to do our utmost to serve these valued and important clients." CBS-TV brought recording and voiceover work for many of their network shows to Coast, including the voices of Charlie Brown, Linus, Lucy, and the gang for various *Peanuts* specials. They also brought jazz pianist Vince

Guaraldi's music for the programs, which he began working on over at the Bush Street space.

The mid-sized Studio B on Folsom Street went online first, with its debut live session taking place on June 23, 1969. Prince Albert in a Can, a new Mercury Records signee for the Phillips label, recorded the song "Fall Out" with producer Frank Morin during a four-hour "shake-down" session. Studio manager Walt Payne and mix engineers Stan Agol and Jim Economides took turns at the mixing board.

Coast's new Studio B.

Universal Audio Archives/David Kulka

Once Coast completely moved out of the 960 Bush Street space in August of 1969, Doug Weston, who owned the Hollywood folk-rock venue The Troubador, opened Troubador North there. After its short run, club manager David Allen, who previously managed the Hungry i, assumed the lease and launched The Boarding House, incorporating Coast's old sound baffles into its décor. The Boarding House was considered one of the finest clubs of San Francisco's rock era: It was the site of many a historic show by the likes of Steve Martin, Oakland's Pointer Sisters, Bob Marley & The Wailers, Patti Smith, Talking Heads, Neil Young (who recorded *Rust Never Sleeps* there), Willie Nelson, Waylon Jennings, Emmylou Harris, and Jimmy Buffett, among many others. Despite the stellar track record, however, the club continually lost money. In 1980, even after a huge fundraising concert generated $50,000, Allen was forced to move, pushed out by aggressive real-estate developers. He never found a new venue, and the 960 Bush Street building was torn down to make way for condominiums.

Back on Folsom Street, Coast Recorders' new facility celebrated its grand opening in November 1969. Putnam's United and Affiliates spent more than $200,000 on the new Coast—almost half of the $500,000 total they invested that year on all of their operations.

The largest of the rooms, Studio A, contained a custom 20-input Bushnell console with matrix switching, built-in EQ, filtering, limiting, and compressing. "UREI built the modules and Bushnell built the consoles," says Horn. There was an Ampex 16-track recorder along with the 3M 8-track the studio had purchased just before their move. Playbacks were heard through an Acoustic Power Contour Control monitor system. The large studio area contained one iso booth, a smattering of gobos, and had acoustic materials lining the walls and suspended from the ceiling. At the time, United and Associates seemed especially proud of accoutrements such as fluorescent lighting with red, blue, and amber filter options and dimmer switches, electric stop clocks for the control room, and extra large doors for the moving of props (for potential film and television shoots) and large pieces of equipment.

The inaugural Studio B mirrored Studio A in terms of equipment and control-room size, though the décor in the live room was created to appeal to the new crop of young, hip San Francisco rockers, aiming for a warm, inviting feel as opposed to the more clinical studios that existed previously. Newly available acoustic materials combined with bold colors and textures to set a creative mood. Above an Alaskan gold wainscot were white Monocoustic Fiberglas wall backgrounds. Overlaying this background on one end wall were free-form designs of natural birch, each outlined by a wood-burning process. Collages from psychedelic posters and two huge overlapping oval paintings (created on premises by Gordon Halvorson) continued the psychedelic motif.

Another shot of the B Room, groovy murals in full view.

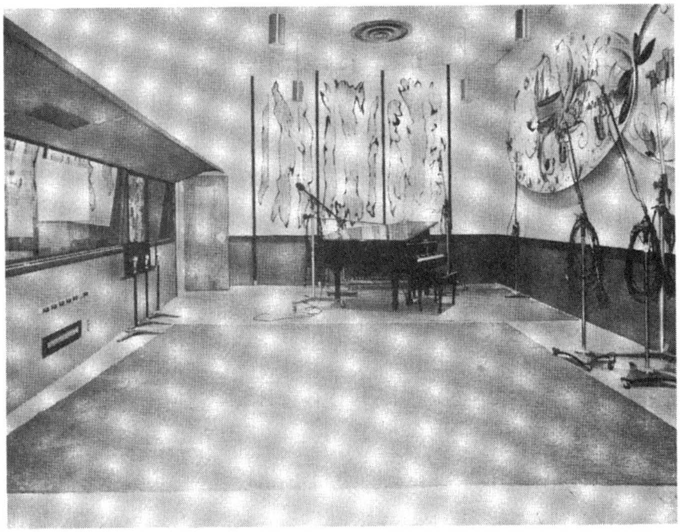

Universal Audio Archives/David Kulka

Studios A and B both had access to Coast's *five* echo chambers and EMT reverb plate. One dual (stereo) chamber was normalled to Studio A, another was assigned to Studio B. The other three chambers and EMT plate could be used with any studio.

Studio C, the smallest of the Coast studios, offered a mid-sized control room and a separate voiceover booth. Most of the advertising work took place in Studio C, which worked well for narration or dialog recording. Music and sound-effects libraries were available for those who needed them.

Aside from the control rooms, clients could hold meetings or just chill out in the client conference room. Coast called the room "comfortably furnished"; furnished, yes, with bare walls and sofas that resembled large bricks with legs.

Studio D, the mastering room, offered monaural disc cutting and either mono or stereo tape editing. Equipment included a Scully mastering lathe and Westrex 2B cutting system and heated stylus for reference dubs or master lacquers. Equalization, filtering, and limiting facilities were offered, and reverb could be added while cutting. Studio D also housed a master control switching center, which permitted use of any combination of reverberation devices and chambers with any studio as well as sending and receiving between Zoetrope's facility and/or any of the other studios. Coast's Magnefax high-speed reel-to-reel tape-duplication equipment lived in Studio E, offering duplication of material in monaural or 2-track ¼-inch stereo.

Phil Edwards, who first got Coast's attention by engineering a few advertising spots from clients that had jumped ship from Coast to Columbus Recorders, joined the staff in 1970. He made the move after once again successfully "faking his way through" a session. This time, he had more tracks and a higher profile artist to improvise with. "I got a call from Lloyd Pratt, saying, 'Can you do a date over here?' I said, 'Sure, what do you want me to do?' He says, 'We want you to do Duke Ellington. Do you know how to work a 16-track machine?' There were a total of two in Northern California at the time, and Coast had both of them. I said, 'Sure! I can do that.' I didn't know what I was doing," he laughs. "So I go over there, and there's Duke Ellington. The band was on salary, and Duke used to record with Bill years before, so any time they were in town and not doing anything, they'd go over and just record stuff. A 16-track was like rockets to Mars, nobody knew what to do with all that stuff, and I didn't know any better so we just lathered up stuff with tracks, and we recorded some stuff and it was all of no consequence. Just standards of 30 years before. I don't think they had any intention of releasing any of it. But I guess Lloyd was sufficiently impressed, because he offered me a job on the spot and a sum of money that left me speechless."

Coast's clientele remained essentially unchanged: radio ad spots, jazz clients, and, of course, a smattering of local bands, who seemed to be multiplying by the minute. A few found success; others fell into obscurity, leaving behind only demo reels to be unearthed decades later by hard-core Sixties' rock fans. For example, the flamboyant, caped manager Matthew Katz (pronounced "Cates") brought a couple of bands to Coast. Katz was notoriously ineffective as Jefferson Airplane's and Moby Grape's first manager. He's reputed for stunts such as failing to tell the rest of Jefferson Airplane that drummer Skip Spence was taking a trip to Mexico, which led to the band firing and replacing him with Spencer

Dryden. He later caused Spence's next band, Moby Grape, to miss a photo shoot for *Look* magazine because he got the time wrong. He's also known for tying up the court system for more than 20 years with legal wranglings between both bands. Katz shacked up at Coast for weeks on end producing two new acts: Tripsichord Music Box and Indian Puddin' and Pipe, a Seattle band who migrated down around 1967.

"Indian Puddin' was sort of a mystery band," recalls Edwards, who engineered what seems to be their first and only album, which never got released and whose masters were lost until a few years ago. They're now assembled on a CD and sold through CD Baby and eBay. Edwards continues, "Turns out I was the fifth of five engineers to work on this project. They had totally wiped out all the others. I didn't know this, so I went in and worked on this stuff. They were totally tripped out, stoned out people, and this was my inauguration into the world of pop music! These guys would spend maybe half the time getting loaded and, as the term was, they'd send a guy to go out and 'score a brick.' Which is like a kilo or two kilo, so they'd bring this enormous thing back, and Matthew would spend his time sifting through this stuff, pulling out stems and flowers, and the band would come in and smoke these bombs and go crazy; we'd spend 12-hour days or more recording this stuff. At one point the guitar player disappears, and nobody knows where he is. He was high on mescaline somewhere. They finally locate him and get him to come back and finish the record. We finally finish the record and the label, Janus Records, has an album party. The band plays and we record what they're doing in the studio. And Matthew Katz's wife bakes brownies. So she's passing these brownies around, and they're not regular brownies, you know. The office manager of Coast, who's very straight laced, [unknowingly] takes one. They had to send her to the hospital and pump her stomach. The flour-to-weed mixture was 50/50—just loaded! They had other people who were getting sick and passing out on this stuff. Then at 2 or 3 a.m. the party finally fizzles down, and I'm left by myself trying to close this huge facility. I remember having to literally drag somebody out of the room, off on the street, so I could lock the building up."

Despite their ambitious efforts with groovy painted walls and dimmer switches, Coast never really caught on with the rock community. There were a few exceptions, such as our puddin' pipe friends and random one-offs, such as The Shades of Joy with producer Frank Morin, and artist Norman Greenbaum, who recorded his million-seller "Spirit in the Sky" with producer Eric Jacobsen and Coast engineer Walt Payne. Bernie Krause, then president of Parasound Inc., installed the first Moog synthesizer at Coast Recorders in April 1970 and promptly used the refrigerator-sized electronic device on a Warner Bros. recording titled *In a Wild Sanctuary.* He produced the recording with Paul Beaver, using 80 percent Moog-created environmental sounds and 20 percent ducks swimming around the Palace of Fine Arts and animals from the San Francisco Zoo. Aside from Krause's endeavor, though, the first two Moog sessions at Coast were for radio and TV commercials. Other activity came from the land of television.

Synth pioneers Bernie Krause (left) and Paul Beaver of Parasound Inc. try out Coast Recorders' newly installed Moog synthesizer, acquired in 1970.

Universal Audio Archives/David Kulka

The Coast landscape would change considerably on September 15, 1970, when another one of Putnam's deals made behind the scenes—this one with one of the record industry's heaviest hitters—would finally come to be. We'll save that visit for Chapter 12.

CHAPTER 7

Pacific *High* Recording

Peter Weston, who started his career working in audio in the Midwest, moved to the Bay Area and became involved in the folk scene. In the late 1960s, Weston combined his technical knowledge and passion for acoustic music to launch Pacific High Recording. The first incarnation of the studio appeared in Sausalito in the early to mid 1960s: Look for the sign with the big red sun. In 1969, he moved PHR to a former plastics factory at 60 Brady Street in San Francisco, a short alley littered with random industrial buildings just off of Market Street and only a few blocks away from the Fillmore West: Look for the purple door. Ring the buzzer, and if they let you in, pass through pillows of pungent-smelling smoke to explore a quintessential San Francisco studio—proudly independent, experimental, and laid back.

Many from the San Francisco rock scene dug Pacific High. Certainly one of the more hippified studios in the city, PHR hovered on the avant-garde in terms of technology and ethos. It was independently owned—hippie-owned, actually—which, for the anti-establishment crowd, made it more appealing than corporate-owned facilities. Richard Olsen, bass player for The Charlatans, managed the studio and used both his musician contacts and street cred to get bands in the door. Bandmate Dan Hicks usually played the studio Christmas parties. And if the guys from Quicksilver

Messenger Service weren't in session, they'd come over to noodle around with whomever else might be hanging out in the studio that day. "It really was an experimental place in that sense," says Phill Sawyer, who came up from L.A. to take an engineering job at PHR after a stint as an evening traffic manager for Putnam's United Western studios. "The atmosphere was really conducive to that world...a natural organic exhibition of the behavior of the times."

Richard Tauber

Former Charlatan and PHR studio manager Richard Olsen (left) and engineer Phill Sawyer at the custom console, 1971.

Just as many PHR inhabitants liked to experiment with mind-altering substances, Weston liked to mess around with equipment. In the process, he came up with a few hits, misses, and left-field modifications. When PHR opened, it contained a Scully 12-track machine, reportedly the first in the city, which would later get passed on to a couple of other studios. According to Bob Shumaker, who joined PHR in the spring of 1969 to work in the shop before moving on to second and first engineer, "[The Scully] was this odd-ball weird machine that was comprised of a 1-inch tape deck, the electronics from an 8-track that went with the 1-inch, the electronics from a ½-inch 4-track, and [it] had a 12-track head-stack and all of that [was put] together. That didn't work so well." They later purchased a Stephens 16-track, another unusual (but good) machine and easier to deal with than the Scully.

To complement the 12-track, Weston custom-built the studio's console with Electrodyne parts. "He had an innovation which, at the time, was unusual," says Shumaker. "He had a completely separate input section for mic pres and feeding the tracks, and then a separate set of mixdown modules that served as the monitor for what you were recording. In those days you would primarily monitor off of some funny little mixing bus, while the main console was being used to feed the tape recorder. But with Peter's [board], you were always monitoring through what was actually going to be the mixdown console. It didn't have any EQ on the Record side of the board, but you could plug in outside EQ: we had Pultecs and little bit of outboard gear. But conceptually it was a pretty good board."

"Weston's concept included the use of a new innovation offered by Ray Dolby," adds Sawyer, "His device reduced audible noise generated by devices such as transmission lines, amplifiers, and, most usefully for us, audio tape. By having a Dolby device on each channel of a multi-track tape recorder, Peter realized the concept of recording unprocessed signals on multiple tracks of a tape, and only subsequently adding any processing or other manipulation of the signal. He made tape noise reduction the key to retaining the natural dynamics of the music performance."

The custom recording equipment, combined with a large 50×60–foot main room, fell in line with Weston's vision to build a studio suited for acoustic music—a place where he could get accurate sound on those instruments without a lot of hiss and not a lot of processing. Colored burlap sheets served as decoration, acoustical treatment, and camouflage for the Fiberglas that covered three of the tall, wide walls. Certainly not the ideal space and by no means acoustically correct, the recording area was considered too big and too live by some; however, some engineers found a workable solution by creating "sub-areas and screening off the rest of the room with portable acoustic panels," says Sawyer. "But unless you close-miked, you would always run into problems that took some experimenting to resolve."

In other words, "No matter what speakers you used, theirs or your own, the room was just terrible," says engineer Bob Matthews, who worked on a few Grateful Dead albums at PHR with studio partner Betty Cantor. "Nobody could ever get a good sound out of it. When we went in there, we isolated, used baffles, and made it work. We had to go in thinking 'What do we need,' not 'What do we have.'"

Weston had the foresight to build a stage at the far end of the room, which became the site for Ralph Gleason's *Go Ride The Music* documentary, centered on Jefferson Airplane, that aired on the National Educational Television Network (now known as PBS) in 1970. A couple of years later, in 1972, DJ Tom Donahue used and abused that rectangular piece of wood during his popular KSAN live radio broadcasts, recorded in quadraphonic sound direct from Pacific High. Everyone from the Doobie Brothers, Elvin Bishop, Clifton Chenier, Dr. Hook, Loose Gravel (featuring former Charlatan Mike Wilhelm), and Jerry Garcia played on those shows, while Phill Sawyer got it all on tape and a crowd of some 200 to 300 people gathered inside. Fire marshal? What fire marshal?

Peter Weston, testing a mic in PHR's vocal booth prior to the first KPFA quadraphonic broadcast in 1971.

Richard Tauber

Dan Healy came to Pacific High on occasion, working in both its Sausalito and San Francisco locations. He brought Quicksilver Messenger Service to the Brady Street studio to record a few tracks and mix their album *Shady Grove*. It was the first studio album Quicksilver recorded locally, having done their self-titled debut at Capitol Studios in Los Angeles and its follow-up, *Happy Trails,* live at The Fillmore East and West, with one song recorded live at Golden State Recorders.

Capitol Records extended two of its most financially substantial contracts to two San Francisco "psychedelic" acts: Steve Miller Band and Quicksilver Messenger Service. Steve Miller Band signed a deal with Capitol that was equally generous in terms of artist rights. In exchange for a five-album commitment, the band received a $50,000 advance and retained complete ownership of publishing and artistic control. The label also reportedly gave both acts the freedom to choose their own producer, engineer, and studio, with no time limits. Such freedom would theoretically allow for unlimited creativity, which Capitol saw as a greater chance for a hit. It worked for Steve Miller, but Quicksilver's album only made a brief chart appearance. "Because of their contract, there were times when quite literally, the kilo would show up and I'd be rolling joints on the clock for four hours," recalls Shumaker, who served as Healy's assistant engineer on the sessions. "It wasn't exactly tough duty, but that kind of excess would go on, because it didn't matter to Quicksilver. Ultimately they didn't make any royalties, because they spent the money in the studio. Their sales weren't great anyway, but they were a great live band."

By the time *Shady Grove* was released in December 1969, Quicksilver's starpower had waned. Nicky Hopkins, an ace session keyboardist fresh off a stint with the Stones, had joined the group, while guitarist Gary Duncan left to work with Dino Valente in a group called The Outlaws. Healy recorded the group on the Ampex MM1000 16-track machine owned by Alembic, the Dead's sound company, who parked the recorder at PHR and rented it out to other bands when the Dead wasn't using it.

Shumaker recalls watching Cipollina play a Danelectro six-string in the control room like a lap steel, using a kitchen table knife as the slide during an overdub. To eliminate the hum pickup from all the equipment, the guitarist had to play facing a blank wall. Shumaker heard Cipollina's guitar work—with and without butter knife—over and over for 12 hours a day, six days a week during the *Shady Grove* sessions. In the studio world, 12-hour days are common, almost standard, but they take their toll, especially when the workday ends during most people's morning commute. "For basically three summers in a row, I'd go to work at four in the afternoon and drive home with the sun coming up," Shumaker recalls. "That was my life. I saw nobody. I had no social life except for the studio. The band had friends and family coming around and it was a party to some extent, but I learned a lot, as well."

When Sawyer joined PHR in April 1969, he crossed that curtain of smoke to find the Grateful Dead wrapping up mixes for their third album, *Aoxomoxoa,* which had been recorded at Pacific Recording in San Mateo. Bob Matthews and Betty Cantor mixed the album after much experimenting with the 8- and 16-track machines at Pacific Studios. Keyboardist Tom Constanten comments on the mix, "Even when it didn't sound loud, it sounded dense, and the VU needles were bouncing off the pins. The mixdown became a performance in its own right, with three or more pairs of hands on the soundboard, minding their cues."

After checking in on his extended family, The Dead, Healy joined The Charlatans to record and mix their first and only long-player, a self-titled release for Mercury Records. Again, Shumaker assisted. This wasn't their first Pacific High experience, however. In its Sausalito days, the group recorded three songs—"Stepping in Society," "East Virginia," and "I Got Mine"—with the intention of releasing a three-song LP. "We were going to have music on one side and this embossed artwork on the other," says Wilhelm. "We'd seen 78s that looked like that. We would sell them ourselves as a souvenir thing for our fans. But [Mike] Ferguson left, then Hicks left, and then George [Hunter] left…so that never happened." The Charlatans forged ahead, replacing Ferguson with keyboardist Patrick Bogerty, adding Terry Wilson on drums, and carrying on as a four-piece until entering PHR.

Though still relatively inexperienced as an engineer, Healy claims those sessions inspired him to develop a direct box. "Richard Olsen had this really cheap bass—like a Sears or something—with these really rinky pickups," he recalls. "I wanted what's called a buffered direct box. I wanted to be able to take a direct sound without representing any visible load to the pickups. So I commissioned Carl Countryman to build me a transistorized direct box that would use phantom power like a microphone and would represent zero load or infinitely high impedance load to the pickups, so the instrument would sound like it sounded when it was plugged into your amp. That became the Countryman direct box."

Meanwhile, the band had its own issues to deal with. With regard to the album, the band had to cut basic tracks pretty quickly, before their drummer, Terry Wilson, left to serve prison time for marijuana possession. "We were still trying to keep some of The Charlatans mystique," says Wilhelm of a band struggling to keep it together. "We had Darryl Devore on piano, a bebopper from Kansas City who was into free jazz. It was pretty psychedelic. Most of the tunes were written while stoned on acid."

The Charlatans served as something of a long detour for Healy, a revered figure in Grateful Dead circles as a live engineer. Even when not on the road, he often dropped into Dead sessions as sort of a supervisory figure. But for the nine-day *Workingman's Dead* sessions at PHR in the winter of 1970, Matthews and Cantor worked on their own, armed with new knowledge since the *Aoxomoxoa* experience. They had spent a lot of Warner Bros.' money on *Aoxomoxoa,* and the label wondered out loud how they would get it back. Both the band and their engineers made good on *Workingman's Dead.*

The band rehearsed the songs for the album for a month. About halfway through, Matthews and Cantor brought them to PHR and recorded a rehearsal that included every song intended for the album. They spliced together a 2-track tape with all of the songs sequenced in the order they were to appear on the record, and each band member walked away with a cassette that served as a rough sketch of the album, "so when they came into the studio to record, everybody had a vision in their mind of what the album was going to be like, how it was going to flow from one song to another, what was on the beginning of side one and side two...everything that we'd learned about how the Beatles made albums. And it worked. We recorded the album in nine days. When we presented the bill to the label, they couldn't believe it!" Instead of $200,000, the band spent around $20,000, Matthews and Cantor got production credit, and the band came out with an album of relaxed, traditional sounding tunes.

In an early interview, Garcia notes, "*Workingman's Dead* was our first true studio album, insofar as we went in there to say, 'These are the limitations of the studio for us as performers; let's play inside those limitations.' That is, we decided to play more or less straight-ahead songs and not get hung up with effects and weirdness. For me, the models were music that I'd liked before that was basically simply constructed but terribly effective—like the old Buck Owens records from Bakersfield. Those records were basic rock and roll: nice, raw, simple, straight-ahead music, with good vocals and substantial instrumentation but nothing flashy. *Workingman's Dead* was our attempt to say, 'We can play this kind of music—we can play music that's heartland music. It's something we do as well as we do anything.'"

When the Dead weren't working at PHR, the studio filled itself with pieces and parts of various projects, including Commander Cody & His Lost Planet Airmen and Joy of Cooking, engineered by Sawyer. He also engineered and mixed the Jefferson Airplane single, "Mexico," the B-side of "Have You Seen the Saucers," the last single of the classic Airplane lineup (with Marty Balin in the group) and a fitting sendoff tribute to two of their favorite dealers.

All was on the up and up as the "Mexico" sessions got underway: The Stephens 16-track machine was properly aligned, and the Scully stereo mastering machines, LA3 and UREI 1176s, Pultec EQs, Allyson EQ modules, and other items were all in working order. The initial tracking session went off without a hitch. But when it came time to work on a few overdubs, something went very, very wrong. It was one of those situations that you think will never happen until it does. Like having your car break down in the middle of the Bay Bridge during rush hour (which happened to me). Or erasing a Jefferson Airplane master tape (which happened to Sawyer and Shumaker), with Grace Slick and Paul Kantner watching in the next room.

"Grace was out in the studio with a [Neumann] U47 in front of her, headphones on, waiting for us to get prepared," recalls

Shumaker. "The guy doing tech work was finishing the alignment, was going to slap on the master and off we would go. And I looked at what he was putting the tones on to align the machine, and realized he had just erased the master. It was gone. It was a set of tones over an Airplane master. I was dying, I told Phill, and he immediately said, 'Well here's what we gotta do' and he got up, walked out in the studio where Grace and Paul Kantner were waiting and he said, "I'm really sorry to tell you this, but we've accidentally erased your master." And Paul just kind of went, 'Huh; How 'bout that,' then goes into the control room and calls Jack Casady and says, 'You know that thing we've been worried about in the studio ever since we started? It finally happened. Can you get down here?' And he got the band back together, and they did the tune again. They weren't thrilled but they weren't uptight about it either. They were very relaxed and very gracious about it. Believe me, there are many people I've worked with who would have gone totally ballistic. But they were great."

Kantner even came back in 1970—this time to mix one side of his solo project, *Blows Against the Empire*, which featured members of the Airplane, the Dead, David Crosby, Graham Nash, and various others. They had done most of their work at Wally Heider Recording (the subject of Chapter 8), but toward the end of the session, they lost their muse and thought that a change of scenery might re-ignite a creative spark. Weston and crew had just finished remodeling PHR's control room and had added a new stereo echo chamber designed by Scott Putnam, son of Bill and carrier of the excellent acoustician gene. By this point, Kantner had built a positive rapport with Sawyer and mentioned that he wanted a cool sci-fi intro and couldn't find the right sounds. Sawyer had just the ticket, in the form of some old sound effects he had assembled while working at a cartoon factory years before. It fit so well, Kantner gave Sawyer composer and producer credit on the album. Later, in the newly modified PHR control room, "The three of us spent at least two days trying to figure out how to mix the thing because...they recorded in very sloppy ways," says Sawyer. "There was a lot of postponing of decisions in those days. The phrase 'We'll fix it in the mix' was still sort of new, and it was a luxury to say. So the tracks didn't seem complete. We created some more sound effects at PHR, and then Graham got the blend of the voices and guitar in a way that I couldn't have. He had a nice authority with Paul. He could say what he wanted and Paul wouldn't object."

Van Morrison, who arrived to the Bay Area in the early 1970s but left for his native Belfast, Ireland in 1973, made a couple of brief stops at Pacific High—first, to record "Listen to the Lion" and "Almost Independence Day" from his 1972 release, *Saint Dominic's Preview.* Ted Templeman, a label-approved producer, and Donn Landee, a label-approved engineer, came up from Los Angeles for the sessions. Shumaker, who assisted on those sessions, recalls that Morrison entered the picture late in the rehearsal process. Pianist Jeff Labes and saxophonist Jack Schroer taught the songs to the rest of the band. Once the band had the songs well-rehearsed and backing vocals down, Morrison came in to add his lead. Singing through a hand-held Neumann U87, Morrison nailed the tracks in one or two takes, and that was that. The interesting thing was, Shumaker notes, "When Van came into the control room to listen to a track, Landee walked out. He would not be in the control room with Van. Obviously they weren't getting along. He just put up a rough mix and walked out." He later came in with full band in tow to record "Jackie Wilson Said (I'm in Heaven When You Smile)" for the same album at PHR.

Joan Baez, Steve Miller, It's a Beautiful Day, Judy Collins, and a number of others visited PHR as well, but despite its coolness, most acts seemed to make only brief passes: an overdub here, a mix there, a few songs during a break on tour. The meat of the work, as much as some hated to admit, still went to L.A. Jefferson Airplane recorded their first three albums in Los Angeles, the Dead cut their first two, and Janis Joplin with Big Brother & the Holding Company recorded most of their catalog there, save for some live tracks. Some of these acts brought their business to San Francisco more often in late 1969 and 1970, but most of it went to the newly opened Wally Heider Recording, considered the city's first professional multi-room music-recording studio.

Struggling to keep up with increased competition and changing technology, Pacific High's legacy ended in 1972. "When you're going for the people with the biggest budgets, you have to have the latest equipment and keep upgrading," says Shumaker. "We just couldn't make enough money to keep things going, unfortunately." As a silver lining in their story, Alembic took over the studio in 1972 and put it through extensive renovations, including redesigning the studio space. They laid down a new floor and tore down the burlap—good riddance!—and added movable panels to change the size and acoustics of the room. They even rolled in a Pong video game next to the pinball machines. Stephen Stills, New Riders of the Purple Sage, Gordon Lightfoot, Johnny Winters, Santana, The Doobie Brothers, and the Youngbloods all passed through Alembic's doors, as did the Grateful Dead. Coincidentally, the custom PHR console went to Mickey Hart, who purchased it for one of his early home studios. In 1974, Alembic sold the studio to Elliot Mazer, who christened it His Masters Wheels, which we'll visit in Chapter 17.

CHAPTER 8

Wally Heider Recording

San Francisco's recording landscape experienced a seismic shift on April 27, 1969, the opening date of Wally Heider Recording. Heider's already established reputation as a producer, engineer, and owner of a popular professional studio in L.A. suddenly gave many San Francisco bands a reason to record in town. Before Heider's arrival, nearly all major local acts recorded at their respective label studios in Los Angeles or New York. The Grateful Dead recorded their first album at Warner Bros. in L.A. Jefferson Airplane holed up in RCA's basement studios for their first five albums. Quicksilver Messenger Service's debut came out of Capitol Studios in Hollywood and Creedence Clearwater Revival did their first three there. Big Brother & the Holding Company and Moby Grape tracked at Columbia Studios in New York. As young artists, they often didn't have much choice in the matter, although that was slowly changing as artists gained more power in the industry. Plus, it worked to the labels' financial advantage to keep their artists—their products—in-house. But even if a big-name band wanted to record in their home city, the facilities available in early 1969 couldn't compare technically or acoustically with the facilities available at or near label headquarters. So off they went, until a piece of L.A. moved up North.

Wally Heider oversaw an L.A. studio deemed *more* than acceptable by label standards. A former attorney turned engineer mentored by Bill Putnam, Heider likely saw an opportunity to create a substantial recording center in San Francisco based on the overflowing talent pool there at the time, and he had more than enough connections to make it happen. Laurel Canyon boys David Crosby, Stephen Stills, and Graham Nash recorded their groundbreaking debut *Crosby, Stills & Nash* at Heider's Studio 3 in 1968 before moving north to join San Francisco's community. Famed producer/engineer Al Schmitt, a Tom Dowd protégé and Grammy-winning engineer since 1962, also worked at Heider's L.A. studio regularly. Both would both go on to become some of Heider's first San Francisco clients.

A longstanding passion for music brought Heider into the recording business and, on more than one occasion, to San Francisco. He had played saxophone in a big band but, as he readily admitted to his staff, he was such a bad player that the bandleaders made him turn *away* from the mic. Recording other musicians seemed a more logical choice. He recorded a number of Woody Herman shows, following the group around in a station wagon with an Ampex 351 in the back. After moving to Los Angeles from Oregon in the late '50s, Heider went to work for Bill Putnam at United Recording Studios as a part-time apprentice. He worked his way up to engineer, then moved again to serve as chief engineer at Putnam's Las Vegas studio. While there, he leased his remote recording equipment to United and managed that end of United's business, as well. About 18 months later, he left Putnam's expanding umbrella, moved to Hollywood, and opened a small studio in 1965. In 1967, he launched Studio 3 of Wally Heider Recording, which he then sold to Filmways a year later. He remained actively involved in both his L.A. and San Francisco studios during the next decade.

The same year he opened Studio 3, he drove one of his popular remote trucks to the Monterey Pop Festival, an event that may have given him the impetus to open a studio in San Francisco. His other work as a live recordist may have also influenced his decision to expand to S.F., right down to his choice of address. Heider leased an old building near the corner of Turk and Hyde for the new Wally

Heider Recording site. That building, 245 Hyde Street to be exact, previously housed film offices, screening rooms, a soundstage, and storage for 20th Century Fox, and it sat across from the legendary Blackhawk nightclub (see Chapter 5), where Heider recorded some Miles Davis performances for CBS. The hot jazz club was long gone when Heider moved to the neighborhood. In its place was a methadone clinic.

The Tenderloin district was raw, on its way to becoming seedy, when Heider sent Dave Mancini, owner of Devonshire Sound Studios in L.A., to design and build the new rooms. Studio C would come first, with a total of four rooms running by 1971. Heider hired Mel Tanner away from Coast Recorders to serve as general manager, with studio manager Ginger Mews, chief tech Harry Sitam, and staff engineer Russ Gary rounding out the original staff.

Measuring roughly the size of Studio 3 in L.A., Studio C offered EMT plates, tape delay units, and access to live echo chambers. The recording room was covered with odd-looking, square midrange/diffuser-type objects that were popular at the time. While engineers have described the studio area as everything from "great-sounding" to "crackerbox," not many criticized its equipment. Possibly influenced by mentor Putnam, Heider installed custom DeMedio equipment throughout his facility, most notably a 24-channel console for Studio C equipped with passive Universal Audio EQs on their way to United Audio plug-in line amps. It had eight buses and Gotham linear faders that had a resolution of 2dB steps. It was a workhorse of a board, nearly indestructible. Outboard gear included four UREI 1176s, two Teletronix LA-2As, Altec and Lang EQs, and two portable Pultec EQs.

The monitoring system featured Altec 604-E loudspeakers with McIntosh 275 power amps, which cranked loud enough during playback to satisfy most of the rock and rollers. They also had an amply stocked mic closet and two of the finest tape machines in town—an Ampex MM1000 and a 3M 56 16-track—both as new to the city as the studio itself.

Thrilled at the idea of getting away from RCA's watchful eyes and corporate hassles, not to mention recording in a new, independently owned studio and sleeping in their own beds at night, Jefferson Airplane booked Studio C to record their sixth album, *Volunteers,* months before the room was even finished. They didn't care that they had to pay for studio time—about three months total—for the first time. Freedom, comfort, and making the record they wanted to make took priority over money, which they had more than enough of anyway. Grace Slick probably enjoyed driving her new Aston Martin to the studio. She parked it out front in the "No Parking" zone so she wouldn't have to walk through the sketchy neighborhood, and after the sessions, she made the short drive home to the Airplane mansion on Fulton Street, thus avoiding much of the hassle of recording in L.A.

The group brought up Al Schmitt from L.A., who had recorded their previous three albums, to produce the sessions. Heider, in his typical fashion, went out of his way to tend to his clients: he made sure Schmitt had a nice place to stay and even loaned him his car while he was in town. The Airplane worked Monday through Friday. They usually started in the afternoon, took a break for dinner at a nearby restaurant—sometimes at Original Joe's, an old-time steak and spaghetti place at Taylor and Turk—then resumed work at Heider's until 3 or 4 o'clock in the morning. Friday night, Schmitt would catch a midnight flight to spend the weekends with his family. They took their time in the studio, giving this album more attention than any of their previous works.

While Heider's crew finished up final tweaks to Studio C, Jefferson Airplane would come in as a unit to record basic tracks. Aside from putting Jack Casady's bass amp in the still-unfinished Studio D, Schmitt kept the recording process simple. He didn't experiment with any off-the-wall recording techniques; he just wanted to capture their latest collection of songs as best he could while ironing out some minor kinks on the brand-new DeMedio board.

Throughout the recording of basic tracks and overdubs, frequent visits from friends and fellow musicians added not only to the relaxed vibe but to the album itself. Jerry Garcia added a pedal steel part to "The Farm." Nicky Hopkins took a break from his Quicksilver Messenger Service duties to play piano on several tracks, and many other friends came by to listen, smoke a joint, or just hang out. "We were always having visitors," recalls Schmitt. "Janis [Joplin] would come by, Big Mama Cass...David Crosby would stick his head in every so often. Anytime anyone was in town they'd drop by the studio. A big part of the day was socializing, which was one of the reasons records took as long as they did [back then]. And my job was to keep it all going, because me and [Airplane manager] Bill Thompson were the ones getting all the calls from RCA!"

Calls to Schmitt became even more frequent and heated after he turned in the record. With the recent election of President Richard Nixon and the unrest on college campuses over the Vietnam War dominating the news, Kantner voiced his own views on "We Can Be Together" and the title track, which he wrote with Marty Balin. RCA nearly rejected the record. "When they heard 'Up against the wall motherfucker' [on 'We Can Be Together'] they almost died!" says Schmitt. "They were *not* going to put this record out. They said, 'No way. You have got to change that.' And I said, 'You know what, you're going to have to talk to them because they're not going to change it.'" And they didn't. Jefferson Airplane did not give in, but the label did, and released the album as is, (although the offending word was written as "Fred" on the lyric sheet). Chalk up one for the Airplane and a big one for Wally Heider Recording; which, by the time the group left in the summer of 1969, had become the most popular game in town.

Not long after Jefferson Airplane took off, Steve Miller Band came by to record *Your Saving Grace*. They emerged in November 1969 with an album that would hit number 38 on the album charts, despite the recent departure of Boz Scaggs and with the addition of keyboardist Nicky Hopkins. Producer Glyn Johns made a more subdued appearance than on Miller's previous effort, *Brave New World,* where he engineered and added guitar, percussion, and backing vocals. Make no mistake, though—Miller never gave up control of his music and would go on to set a precedent for artists' rights. "They were great musicians," adds engineer Stephen Barncard, who assisted on this project. "They would spew forth as if spontaneously, and perhaps it would be the first time it would be recorded, but Miller was prepared. There weren't a lot of accidents."

Miller also got actively involved in the technical aspects of recording, which was rare, if not unheard of, in the late 1960s.

Amongst visits from Blue Cheer, Sly and the Family Stone, and others, Miller and band returned to record a follow-up, but disagreements among band members hastened Hopkins's and bassist Lonnie Turner's departure in 1970. Bassist Bobby Winkleman was added to the fold, but the group headed to Nashville's Cinderella Studios to resume what would become *Number Five*.

Creedence Clearwater Revival came in for an extended stay during Heider's early years, beginning with sessions for their third album, *Willie and the Poor Boys*, engineered by lead staffer Russ Gary. For this album and the next three—*Green River, Cosmo's Factory* and *Pendulum*—all recorded at Heider's, CCR took the day shift, while Crosby, Stills, Nash, and Young worked at night tracking and mixing their anticipated second album, *Déjà Vu*, with engineer Bill Halverson. Barncard helped out on both.

Barncard had barely enough time to unpack his bags before Heider gave him a job—with a salary ($10 an hour!) that left the young engineer stunned. But in 1969, the engineers hadn't become celebrities. They were technicians who happened to work around celebrities. In addition, studio owners expected even assistant engineers to come in with a solid knowledge of basic electronics, know how to align a tape machine, navigate a console's patchbay, and most importantly, have an instinctual understanding of studio etiquette, more of an inherent personality trait than a learned skill.

Barncard met these requirements, plus he had the long hair and Lennon specs that allowed him to blend in with the musicians. He was "one of them." After only a couple weeks, he was working double duty: Creedence Clearwater Revival during the day, *Déjà Vu* at night. He recalls very little magic during those initial CCR sessions, with John Fogerty playing most of the instruments while the band waited around on the sofa. "He would have loved Pro Tools," Barncard says wryly. "Russ would do these ¼-inch splices on the two-inch master tape—he was fixing the drum beats, doing what they do now in Pro Tools, but it took hours and hours, just to get the perfect drum tracks."

The scene at Heider's changed dramatically when Crosby, Stills, Nash, and, on occasion, Young came in to record. Many songs became keeper tracks after one pass, maybe with an overdub on the vocals. Listening to their gorgeous harmonies, it's obvious they worked hard on the vocals. Despite a sky-high level of musicianship, *Déjà Vu* had problems. When the group entered Wally Heider Recording in late 1969, they had, with only one album to their name (as CSN), achieved astounding success. They should have been overjoyed with their lives and good fortune, but personal problems overshadowed their joy. David Crosby had just lost his girlfriend Christine Hinton—the love of his life—to a tragic car accident. Nash's relationship with Joni Mitchell had just fallen apart. Stephen Stills' relationship with Judy Collins was on the rocks, and Neil Young had other personal problems to deal with. To make matters worse, they all stayed together at the Caravan Lodge Motel. Miraculously, they made it out in one piece. Their new staffer, often the silent observer in the back of the control room, saw Crosby take out his frustrations on those closest to him: his bandmates. Engineer Bill Halverson instructed Barncard to keep the mics off during private conversation; otherwise, record everything. They usually recorded until 3 a.m., with Stills often tinkering around until 8 a.m.

Young came in for one of the first tracking sessions, "Country Girl." He usually came in to sing scratch vocals and would then finish tracks at his own studio. Jerry Garcia, quickly becoming a Heider's regular, broke in the newly completed Studio D when he laid down a steel guitar part for "Teach Your Children." The arrangement allowed Halverson, known for his speed especially when punching in and out on a tape machine, to complete an overdub without tearing down the existing Studio C setup.

Wally Heider Recording remained steadily booked through the early seventies. CSNY closed out 1969, but acts such as Big Brother & the Holding Company, Norman Greenbaum, Seals and Crofts, War (who reportedly cut two albums worth of material in two days), Cliff Coulter, Clifton Chenier, Bill Evans, Paul Butterfield, and Brewer and Shipley, who recorded their *Tarkio Road* album there, which features their only Top Ten, "One Toke Over the Line," kept the studio busy.

In the midst of all of this activity, which was split between Studio D and late nights in Studio C, a highly prolific Creedence Clearwater remained parked in Studio C to record their aforementioned four albums between 1969 and 1970. They racked up many of hits in the process. When the group pulled out of Heider's to work in Fantasy Records' impressive new in-house studio (funded primarily by their record sales), Gary also left and joined Fantasy as an in-house producer/engineer for CCR and other Fantasy artists. Heider recruited Memphis engineer Jim Gaines, who got his start working on Stax Records demos. Mallory Earl and David Coffin rounded out the engineering staff during this time.

Vance Frost, an assistant at Golden State Recorders, moved over to Wally Heider Recording after a few instances of "We don't have enough work for you this week" (in other words "We don't have enough money to pay you this week") at his former workplace. "I'd be the Heider's rep when people like Jefferson Airplane would bring up the RCA engineer," explains Frost. "Those guys would usually start around 10 or 11 at night and work until 5 a.m. I'd bring a sleeping bag to the studio!" But he only endured that schedule for about a year. In 1971 he returned to Golden State as manager and chief engineer, replacing Mike Larner, who accepted a very good offer at CBS/Columbia Studios. Barncard left the staff in 1972 to work as an independent producer and mixer. We'll revisit the Wally Heider saga, and its revolving door, in Chapter 14.

CHAPTER 9

Pacific Recording

Before we launch into the nuts and bolts of Pacific Recording, a mid-size studio with a larger-than-life history, let's back up a bit to cover the circumstances that motivated producer David Rubinson and his engineering partner, Fred Catero, to relocate from New York to San Francisco and settle for a short time at that location. The duo brought high-caliber acts to this particular facility, although plenty of other clients also produced great music there. Rubinson and Catero would go on to work at Wally Heider Recording and various other spots before settling into a more permanent home in the mid-1970s.

Initially, Rubinson tried to persuade Columbia Records, the label he worked for as a staff producer in New York, to open a studio in San Francisco. They balked. They already had operations in Los Angeles, a city they had helped establish as a music-industry and recording center, so they preferred to send their San Francisco bands down to those studios, just as with any other pop act. And if one of their East Coast reps discovered an S.F. band, they might bring them to their New York City facilities. Rubinson, strong willed and barely in his 20s, argued with his superiors, "You don't understand the mentality there," as paraphrased by Fred Catero. He continued, "These people don't want to move to L.A. and record in a big corporate establishment. They're already protesting about enough stuff! What you have to do is open a studio in San Francisco and make it San Francisco–friendly. Put up the tie-dye, let 'em smoke dope, do whatever's required to get them comfortable. Then bring them in and record them and capitalize on their talent." CBS's "counter-creative" union rules, which prohibited producers and other non-union personnel (engineers and artists included) from touching any recording equipment, further complicated matters and would continue to do so for some years to come.

The Columbia execs didn't get Rubinson's S.F. studio idea initially, but then they didn't completely "get" Rubinson, either. In 1963, when he was 20 years old, Rubinson produced *The Cradle Will Rock*, a left-wing, Obie Award–winning off-Broadway musical. Leonard Bernstein signed on as musical consultant after Rubinson cold-called him from a pay phone. Goddard Leiberson of CBS Records bought the show and later hired Rubinson as a producer—in the classical music department. In the mid 1960s, the self-described "company freak" got assigned such gems as Phyllis Diller, the Clancy Brothers, "America's polka king" Frankie Yankovic, and—best of all—pop singer and former orange juice saleswoman Anita Bryant, a notoriously religious right-winger and anti-gay crusader. Definitely *not* a San Francisco–friendly lady. Needless to say, Rubinson decided to find his own talent and presented Columbia with country blues legend Taj Mahal, San Francisco band Moby Grape, and folk group the Chambers Brothers, whose Rubinson-produced album *Time Has Come* yielded their biggest hit, "Time Has Come Today." This single reached Number 11 on *Billboard*'s Hot 100 in 1968. "I built my own artist roster because I couldn't stand what was happening," he says. "I couldn't mesh with the corporation. I tried. I bought some suits and I bought some ties; I really tried my ass off to fit in. But the culture there was white, authoritarian, and to them the music was [secondary]. They were about selling a catalog number and how to make more money. It was very straight. They threatened to fire me if I participated in any more political demonstrations! I had to leave."

Rubinson had a couple of irons in the fire that would allow him to leave Columbia as an employee, one of which came from S.F. club impresario Bill Graham, a fellow New Yorker whom Rubinson had met in 1965 when Graham managed the San Francisco Mime

Troupe and Rubinson produced their live appearance at New York's legendary Town Hall. He made several trips to San Francisco after that, mainly to seek and sign his San Francisco finds. Rubinson also produced Tim Rose's album *Hey Joe,* a sizable hit in S.F. He and Graham worked together to bring Rose to The Fillmore in 1966. Graham made frequent trips to New York, especially around the launch of The Fillmore East in New York City. A solid working relationship was already in the works when the two began discussing an official partnership.

By 1968, Graham was already the most successful concert promoter in S.F. He had both a management company and booking agency, Shady Management and The Millard Agency respectively, that represented clients such as The Grateful Dead, Santana, and It's a Beautiful Day, among others. Rubinson had scouted the latter two bands and recommended their signing to Clive Davis for Columbia. He produced the first Santana recordings, both live and in the studio, in late 1968 and early 1969.

Entertainment attorney Brian Rohan, who had negotiated deals with most of the big names in town, had been urging Graham to start a label, but he resisted prior to piquing Rubinson's interest. As a producer, Rubinson excelled at recognizing and developing raw, young musicians. "Give him raw talent and he's a genius at developing that talent," says Catero. "Columbia offered him Streisand and he turned it down. He said, 'Well, what am I supposed to do with her? I'm just going to be a yes-man. I'm not going to be able to involve myself."

He didn't always have a sense of what would sell a lot of records (although many of his acts did sell well), but that wasn't his primary concern. He cared more about originality. "I wanted to find not only talent, but unique talent. I really didn't care about commercial potential," he says. "I was really famous for picking off-the-wall people. So most of the people I chose to work with were unique and had a point of view and a way of processing music that was very different from anybody else."

Graham was a triple Type-A personality known for working fourteen-plus hour days and wearing two wrist-watches—one set to California time, one to New York time. To him, Rubinson, with his major-label and music-business knowledge and passion for San Francisco music, seemed to be the missing link that would make launching a record label not just feasible, but lucrative.

While Graham pondered his new enterprise on the West Coast, Rubinson's frustrations with the corporate Columbia environment mounted, especially because he knew there was so much untapped talent out West. When he realized the label couldn't see the logic behind a San Francisco studio, much less an office, Rubinson quit. He would move to San Francisco, he informed them, start the record label with Graham, and sign and produce acts under the guise of Fillmore Records. But the relationship didn't sever completely. Fillmore Records signed a distribution deal with Columbia, which gave him the best of both worlds: some of the power of a major, the creative control of an indie, and an ongoing, reasonably positive business relationship.

He then gave word to his studio partner, Fred Catero, who already had a long tenure with Columbia. Catero, a native of New York raised solely by his mother in Harlem, had just had his first home built, in Long Island, and he and his wife had only lived there a month when Rubinson made him an offer. "He came to me and said, 'Fred do you want to join us and be our chief engineer?' I said yes, I thought it would be a great idea," explains Catero. "I had gone up as high as I could go [at Columbia] without being an executive. And I didn't want to be stuck behind a desk. I wanted to be with the music. So I went with him." "He pulled up everything to come with me," Rubinson adds. "What belief he must have had to go and do that."

Rubinson made huge sacrifices as well. The amply-paid staff producer, his wife, and two-year-old son lived in a beautiful, spacious apartment in New York City. All issues aside, he had a great job—a dream job for a 27-year-old—and his wife and son were both happy. But he, like Catero, saw an opportunity to achieve something great. So they took the risk, ripped up their comfortable lives, and moved. A wild ride and some long, rocky roads lay ahead, but their presence would dramatically alter the local recording community for the next two decades.

Upon their arrival in 1968, Rubinson and Catero indeed joined forces with Graham and Rohan to form The Fillmore Corporation, with Fillmore Records and San Francisco Records operating under that umbrella. Rohan struck two separate distribution deals: Fillmore Records with Columbia, San Francisco Records with Atlantic. On paper, the company had powerhouse potential: The city's top promoter would book their artists in the hottest concert venues; the hit record producer and engineer would give them a killer-sounding album and big names on the liner notes; and the successful music attorney would help them gain major label distribution, higher advances, and royalty points, and make sure everything stayed on the up and up. The inaugural roster for Fillmore Records was supposed to consist of Santana and It's a Beautiful Day. Rubinson had produced some of Santana's first sessions in 1968. They spent ten days recording at Columbia Studios in Los Angeles, with lackluster results. More artistically satisfying was Rubinson's 1968 live recording of the group's debut at The Fillmore West (the band headlined the club before ever releasing an album), which sat in the vault for 30 years until Columbia/Legacy put it outas *Live at The Fillmore 1968.*

Rohan jumped the gun, however, and signed the two groups to Columbia before The Fillmore Corporation's other half had time to load the moving vans. In their place, Graham and Rohan chose blues guitarist Elvin Bishop and blues-rock trio Aum as their flagship acts. This significant lineup change proved to be only the first of a string of disagreements to surface within The Fillmore Corporation. On the upside, Cold Blood, a smokin' combo led by petite singer Lydia Pense, as well as Tower of Power and Lamb, would later join the roster.

In addition to signing and recording his own acts, Rubinson continued to produce for Columbia. In 1968, the label still wasn't interested in opening a studio in the Bay Area and San Francisco's supply of both quality session musicians and studios fell far short of the resources in both L.A. and New York. "There were very few multitrack studios that could really record a room full of people," says Rubinson. "There were some 4-track studios in the city, but the only 16-track studio in the area was Pacific Recording in San Mateo. And that was because the studio was only a couple of miles from the Ampex headquarters. Ampex agreed to put the [MM1000] machine in and supply tape, so they would have this ongoing lab." Granted, Catero honed his craft making 3-track recordings, but for late 1960s–era bands with horn and percussion ensembles, multiple guitars, and complex, multi-layered instrumentation, extra tracks were almost a necessity. The music was there, but the technology to support it wasn't. "Sixteen-track was an incredible blessing," says Rubinson. "It meant you could record the drums, string, horns and background vocals in stereo—natural stereo—and make choices by having alternate takes and combining them. There were finally enough tracks to really do what you wanted. Being able to put bass drum on its own track was a real breakthrough."

Though he has since been widely disparaged by many who worked with him, Pacific Recording owner Paul Curcio presided over what was reportedly the third 16-track studio in the U.S. and certainly the first in the Bay Area. The bare-bones studio, called a "hole in the wall" by some, had two recording rooms, including the 50×25×20 Studio 1, where most of the tracking sessions took place and the smaller 20×15×15 Studio 2, used mainly for vocals and occasional voiceovers. The tracking room offered a custom Quad Eight console with 20 inputs, while the B room contained a custom 16-input Electrodyne console.

Some clients complained that the ceilings were too low, making it a dead-sounding room. (In a few years, clients would want that!) But for the highly skilled Catero, who could probably get great sounds out of a shoebox, the room proved adequate. He bought a home nearby, which allowed him a little bit more time to spend with his family...after sessions ended at 4 a.m. Curcio had worked out a pretty sweet deal for himself with Rubinson as one of his primary clients. Rubinson kept the room booked with quality acts, brought up some of L.A.'s top session musicians to play in his studio, and other successful producers drove down to the South Bay from San Francisco based on Rubinson's name alone. Unfortunately, Curcio's poor management skills led to a string of heated encounters with Rubinson and Catero, leading to their exit in 1973. Catero, a strong man, had nearly ripped Curcio apart one day after being pushed too far. He ripped the front door off hinges its instead. Another time, Rubinson reportedly backed his car through the front door when Curcio failed to show up to open it. It was day two of a session, and Rubinson had booked a full band of L.A. session players, billing A-rate union scale. On day one, Rubinson drove up to the studio to find Catero and the musicians sitting on the front steps, locked out. Curcio "forgot" to open up. The clock was ticking, the band was billing. When the same thing happened on day two, Rubinson, typically an intense personality known for shot-putting ashtrays on a bad day, decided to open the studio himself…and backed his car in the front door. They had the session nearly up and running before Curcio, and later the police, showed up. Needless to say, they weren't welcome back, and they soon relocated their business to Wally Heider Recording.

After their initial sessions with Rubinson in L.A. didn't work out, Santana arrived at Pacific Recording in 1969 to record their self-titled debut with friend Brent Dangerfield, who ran sound for the Straight Theater on Haight Street. Dangerfield had never engineered, much less produced, a record before, which seemed perfectly okay to Santana. By this time, Santana had changed their sound and personnel significantly, adding a real timbalero and moving musically more toward East Coast salsa influences. The mind-boggling cast of players—all unknowns at the time—included drummer Michael Shrieve and percussionist Jose "Chepito" Areas, plus the core lineup of bassist David Brown, vocalist/keyboardist Gregg Rolie, conga drummer Michael Carabello, and Carlos Santana, who drove the band with his lyrical guitar work. The album reached the Top Five and remained on the charts for two years.

Another New Yorker, Elliot Mazer, who, among other achievements recorded and produced several albums for Neil Young, as well as classics by Big Brother & the Holding Company and Bob Dylan, made his first San Francisco visit in 1968 to work with both Janis Joplin and Michael Bloomfield. The first Bay Area studio he saw was Pacific Recording. "Fred Catero had engineered records for me in New York, and when he moved West. I was excited to see him and work in his studio," he recalls. A band he had founded, played in, and produced out of Nashville, Area Code 615, booked a few sessions there in 1969 while they were in town to play The Fillmore. Members of this Music City band, a 10-piece comprised of ace session players Charlie McCoy, Wayne Moss, Kenny Butrey, Norbert Putnam, David Briggs, and Bobby Thompson, among others, dropped into Pacific to play on *Secret of the Bloom*, the debut album from Victoria, a folky, Judy Collins–inspired singer/songwriter signed to San Francisco Records. Rubinson and Catero worked on this one. The supergroup also cut a few tracks for Linda Ronstadt's career-launching *Silk Purse*, produced and engineered by Mazer. "*Silk Purse* was recorded in L.A., San Francisco, and Nashville," says Mazer. "It was her first real solo album and her first substantial hit. She was very particular and exacting in what she wanted to accomplish."

Pacific Recording is also where Grateful Dead engineers Bob Matthews and Betty Cantor first worked together. They teamed up for *Aoxomoxoa*, the Dead's first recording without an outside producer, the first physical manifestation of the Jerry Garcia/Robert Hunter songwriting partnership, and their first foray into 16-track experimentation. Matthews already knew the studio from working with Brian Rohan, who would hire Matthews to record demos and then try to sell the bands to Mercury Records. "We did at least a dozen," he recalls. "Maybe a third of them became anything." The Dead found out their friend Matthews was working at this studio, and that it was cheap, so they decided it would make a good place to fool around, "which is really what it was all about—exploring and learning how to do things ourselves, especially after having a Hollywood producer shoved down our throats in a studio in L.A."

The Grateful Dead entered Pacific Recording during a period of transition. The band's music was becoming more complex, and harmonica/keyboardist Ron "Pigpen" McKernan and rhythm guitarist Bob Weir were having trouble keeping up with some of the directions being forged by Jerry Garcia and bassist Phil Lesh. So at a band meeting at Pacific Recording, manager Rock Scully fired Pigpen and Weir. The decision didn't seem to hold much weight, however, as neither member left, and the group commenced recording in September 1968. They spent about four months recording Dead classics "St. Stephen," "China Cat Sunflower," and a bizarre nitrous oxide-fueled experiment called "What's Become of the Baby," among other songs, on Pacific's new Ampex 1-inch 8-track. They were just getting ready to mix when the chief engineer, Ron

Wickersham, rolled in the new Ampex MM1000 16-track, one of the first off the assembly line. Wickersham worked in various capacities at Ampex during the day and was instrumental in fostering the relationship between the two companies. "We took one look at [the MM1000] and Jerry said, 'Okay. Now we're going to do [the album] again the *real* way," says Matthews. They used simple technology, but the combination of recording and re-recording cumbersome, overwritten material, as Garcia readily admitted in old interviews, led to an unsuccessful and expensive album. The record label was not impressed, especially after learning the album cost around $200,000. "It was our first adventure with 16-track, and we tended to put too much on everything," Garcia said many years later.. "We tried to use up every track, and it came out mixed by committee. A lot of the music was just lost in the mix."

Pacific Recording continued for some years with Curcio at the helm. In the early 1970s, he received a visit from Bruce Cohn, who had just started working with a San Jose band called the Doobie Brothers. He and his brother Marty came in to produce the demos that would lead the group to a deal with Warner Bros., and later to their new producer, Ted Templeman.

CHAPTER 10

Mercury, Columbia, and the Launch of The Automatt

As much as the record labels loved the profits coming in from the San Francisco rock bands, some executives (and engineers) at these straight corporations were less than thrilled about having to work with musicians they believed were probably tweaked out from LSD, zoned on marijuana, or loaded on that ol' studio favorite: alcohol. It wasn't unusual for San Francisco musicians to start at dinnertime and have nothing on tape until after midnight.

For a few years, the record industry had flirted with San Francisco but didn't make any bold moves until 1969. By the late '60s, the famously hedonistic city was thick with promising unsigned musicians. In addition, some of the majors' key artists lived in the area. By setting up shop locally, the thinking went, they could keep a close eye on these bands and theoretically pick up a few more. Their efforts at the latter, however, yielded less than stellar results.

In an aggressive effort to establish a presence in San Francisco, Columbia Records and Mercury Records both set up offices and studios there. They operated for only short time, but their influence would affect the community for years to follow.

It's also interesting to note that as much as the labels tried to keep a short leash on their acts, they were slowly losing control.

First off, they gave away some of their power to the highest selling entertainers on their payroll, a lot of them young, floating through their fantastical lifestyle on inflated egos and mind-altering substances. When these artists asked for a purple sofa in the studio instead of a brown one, for example, the label usually said yes. When these same artists began requesting particular producers and engineers instead of accepting the labels' choice, they often said yes to that, too.

Those union rules mentioned earlier didn't go over well in San Francisco. The fact that an artist couldn't even touch a microphone, according to strict union contract with CBS and RCA, turned off many an artist and frustrated the emerging crop of independent engineers and producers. The union engineers, who had to follow these rules, often didn't gel with the Bay Area bands, either. Oftentimes, the labels would send one of their staff engineers for sessions. They'd listen to a band's unconventional ideas and think they were strange, while the band labeled the engineer "square"; the band would then make life miserable for the engineer day in and day out until he quit. Another engineer would take his place and the cycle would begin all over again until the band got what it wanted—usually an independent it already knew.

So, the pool of independent producers and engineers started to grow, many of them sympathetic to the creative mindset. Rather than waste time and money as their artists wore out a long line of staff engineers, the labels would hire the laid-back independents. Second engineers and tape ops would still change shifts if a session ran late, per union rules, but not if the producer wanted to keep him or her around a bit longer.

When Columbia and Mercury opened their local shops, they both brought in staff engineers, some of them considered the best in the business. These studios existed primarily to serve their own acts, with outside clients making only random appearances. The barriers between union and non-union, musician, producer, and engineer were crumbling, brick by brick.

Mercury Studios

Mercury Records, whose San Francisco roster already included Doug Sahm (Sir Douglas Quintet), Dr. Hook & the Medicine Show, The Charlatans, and Mother Earth (featuring blues belter Tracy Nelson and guitar whiz Michael Bloomfield), knew the city's studio landscape reasonably well, as they sent many of their local acts to such facilities as Columbus Recorders.

Through the mid to late sixties, a handful of record labels scouted the city for talent, but Mercury was the first to take a more active role in establishing a presence there. In late 1969, they set up a satellite office in San Francisco and opened Mercury Studios at 1340 Mission Street. George Horn, who had worked on several Mercury projects at Columbus, joined the company as its chief engineer and manager. The local engineers deemed Mercury's equipment adequate; both control rooms contained Bushnell consoles that mirrored the Coast boards, and had access to a 16-track tape machine. The main recording room, Studio A, received high marks from Horn. "It was superb sounding," Horn recalls. "It was a pleasure to work in and we always got good sounds."

The studio went online in January 1970 but, despite its good facilities, never fully took off, much to the disappointment of all of the local acts with big dreams of getting signed. Local DJ Abe Kesh, known as one of the first to play "hippie" music on his KSAN radio show "Lights Out San Francisco," produced a few projects at Mercury as an independent. Records for Fifty Foot Hose and Blue Cheer came out of this facility, but the label never really established the foothold it wanted in San Francisco. Plus, "They weren't really interested in the studio," says Horn. "They were interested in the San Francisco rock scene and wanted to sign [bands], but that never really happened."

At the time Mercury shuttered its San Francisco studio, the company was in the process of merging with Deutsche Grammophon to become PolyGram, so financial issues played a key role in their decision to close. An abundance of bands but a lack of hit songs probably factored into the equation as well. On the other hand, the local musicians' general aversion to recording in a "label studio," was yet another reason that Mercury never became a hotbed of activity like nearby Wally Heider Recording. In general, the rock and rollers didn't feel comfortable in the corporate studios, deeming them too sterile, and, ironically, too commercial. They didn't want to be watched. Hence, not much more than a bunch of unreleased demos came out of this facility, and in October of 1970, less than a year after opening its doors, Mercury Studios packed up and left. Typical of San Francisco's incestuous studio relationship, the 1340 Mission Street space would live to see better days, which we'll talk about in Chapter 12.

Columbia Studios

While David Rubinson and Fred Catero went about their business as one of the top producer-engineer teams of the late 1960s and early 1970s, Columbia Records, the label they had severed contractual ties with in New York, had a change of heart about San Francisco. Columbia realized that former "company freak" Rubinson had been right about San Francisco all along. Columbia president Clive Davis, already enamored by the city and the top-draw artists he had signed from the area—Santana, Janis Joplin, Herbie Hancock, Taj Mahal, Boz Scaggs, and Sly Stone—spearheaded a mission to shake up the local scene by opening studios and A&R offices in San Francisco. With the studio, Davis hoped to create a facility less regulated by the union rules that stifled so many artists and engineers. The A&R office would not only handle the administrative tasks for its existing local roster, but sign new acts as well. George Daly ran the A&R office initially, later replaced by Ellen Bernstein. They achieved these goals with only minimal success.

From L to R: Boz Scaggs, Mike Hart of the band Little John, and Clive Davis at Columbia Studios' grand-opening party.

On September 15, 1970, Columbia Records, a division of CBS, took over the majority of Coast Recorders on Folsom Street. On March 3, 1971, they celebrated their "official" opening with a grand party, which was attended by Bill Graham, Mike Bloomfield, *Rolling Stone*'s Jann Wenner, and several Columbia staff members, including Davis. Under the long-term lease agreement, Columbia gained exclusive use of Studios A and B, the mastering room, maintenance shops, and offices. Coast then converted some of the building's unused space into a quadraphonic "dubdown" room, new offices, and work areas. As much as Coast tried, with its "groovy" murals and dimmer switches and all, it had little luck attracting the San Francisco Sound crowd—the large converted warehouse just wasn't bringing in the business Putnam had hoped it would. Coast's broadcasting business did well, but Coast-on-Folsom as a hip rock studio would not come to be.

"We were always doing advertising; our expertise was commercials," says Steve Atkins, who would later manage Coast Recorders. "We tried to get the San Francisco bands...it was a period where everyone wanted the San Francisco sound." Not everyone got it. It's possible the musicians could sense something uncool about the "vibe" of the place. Coast had the atmosphere of a jingle studio, which is very different from a rock room.

The presence of Columbia and its powerful roster had the potential to alter that vibe and bring in a lot of regular business. So, with Coast continuing work in its small corner of the world, CBS installed a custom 36-input 16-track console—one of its own workhorses sent from New York—equipped with UREI's then-new 1109 preamp, designed by Erik Porterfield, director of Columbia's electrical engineering, research, and development. They stocked the studios with cherished tube electronics such as old RCA compressor/limiters, Pultec EQs, and, giving a nod to Mr. Putnam, UREI 1176 compressors. The microphone selection was equally first-rate: at least 10 Neumann M49s and 10 U67s, along with multiple KM84s and AKG C-12s for string dates.

In addition to great equipment, Columbia sent two of its top New York studio personnel: revered producer/engineer Roy Halee, known for his work with Simon & Garfunkel and Blood, Sweat &

Tears, would run the operation and serve as head engineer, and Roy Segal, who joined Columbia in 1958, worked his way up to engineer, and had already worked on albums for locals Sly Stone and Big Brother, would supervise the facility and engineer. "Clive Davis basically told me I could build the studio and do whatever I wanted out there," Halee said in an interview with *Mix* magazine in October 2001. Davis may have thought that Halee's experimental recording techniques, which clearly conflicted with union rules, would go over better in S.F. "If you wanted to do something really strange with a lot of machines, they didn't like it," said Halee, known for putting speakers in elevator shafts and other interesting techniques. "If I had four or five tape machines running with echoes and reverbs—because you didn't have digital delays in those days, of course—I'd line 'em up in the hallway of the studio, and the union didn't like that. [They'd say] 'What do you need all those machines for?'"

Right behind Halee and Segal came engineer Glen Kolotkin from Columbia in L.A. Kolotkin got his start in New York, had worked with Halee, and coincidentally had mixed Rubinson's hit album for the Chambers Brothers. Then, when Mercury packed up in October, George Horn moved over to run Columbia's mastering department. While at Columbia, he made the decision to focus solely on a mastering career (he previously worked as both a studio engineer and mastering engineer) and still masters records today.

Coast Recorders kept the Westrex cutting system in Studio D. Horn commissioned that lathe and mastered most of the Columbia projects that came through the door during its first few years, in addition to taking care of maintenance issues. Engineers Mike Larner from Golden State Recorders, Mike Fusaro from Coast, and Tom Lubin joined the staff during the first year.

"When Columbia moved here, because of David [Rubinson] and Bill Graham and one or two other producers who had vision, the industry had really grown in S.F.," says Catero. In a United and Associates newsletter, Halee said, "There's a wealth of talent abounding in the area, and a lot of unknowns with whom I'm anxious to work. I find this opportunity very challenging…to really build something here. The prospects are pretty much untapped at present and I think much can be done."

Kolotkin agreed. Of his decision to join Columbia's San Francisco staff, he says, "[San Francisco] was where all the great music was coming from. It was, like, the flower children days, and this was Clive Davis' personal venture, and he was the man! And Roy Halee would be heading it up, and we were friendly. It was a chance to get in on the ground floor of something really big, which was very exciting."

The level of engineering talent was also pretty exciting. Halee is considered one of the greatest engineers of all time, and his partner, Segal, was known as a superior engineer as well as an excellent organizer. Larner and Lubin were both geniuses at designing and maintaining equipment, and Kolotkin was already regarded as a top mixer and was on his way to becoming an equally skilled and efficient recording engineer. "Kolotkin was one of the fastest engineers I'd seen," says Paul Stubblebine, who joined the staff in 1973. "It was amazing how fast he could get a sound, whereas Halee liked to take his time. Halee would do days of preparation and would spend typically three days just getting echo sounds before he ever started to mix."

Despite all the hype and buzz and the presence of kingpin Clive Davis, the studio got off to a slower than expected start. Most of the "name" acts in 1970 gravitated toward the independently owned and wildly popular Wally Heider Recording down in the Tenderloin district. To feed Davis' new baby, Halee brought in his own Columbia artists, and Davis shuttled in acts from the New York, L.A., and Chicago offices to record. As one of the most powerful labels in the industry, they had little difficulty filling the new studio with their own kind. Blood, Sweat & Tears christened the room, recording *B.S. & T.4* in the studio with Halee producing and engineering. He then went on to record Paul Simon's self-titled solo debut in 1972, a million-seller that he recorded, at Simon's request, "in a sparse, almost homemade way; almost like a demo," said Halee. "No big arrangements or big flourishes; just straight ahead, his voice way out in front." His former partner, Art Garfunkel, followed suit in 1973.

Segal, meanwhile, engineered Big Brother & the Holding Company's second Columbia album, *How Hard It Is* (he recorded their debut at Columbia Studios, New York) and several other projects during his first year in S.F. This was followed by *Fresh* from Sly & the Family Stone and portions of Dr. Hook & the Medicine Show's *Sloppy Seconds*, with "Cover of the Rolling Stone" as the album's brightest spot. Kolotkin and David Brown engineered on the project, as well.

Several albums and a couple of breakups into their career, Clive Davis took an interest in The Sons of Champlin and signed the group to his label. Armed with a new rhythm section that gave the group a deeper R&B groove, the group entered Columbia Studios to record *Welcome to the Dance* with Roy Segal co-producing and engineering and staffer Mike Fusaro assisting.

"We had tried to do it ourselves, so I went with an engineer into a studio in Berkeley, and we did demos of the whole record," says Bill Champlin. "Then we re-cut the whole thing with Roy, and he did a bang-up job. He's the guy who told us, 'You see this stuff?' pointing at the equipment. 'This stuff ain't here for a hobby!' which meant we better record some hits!"

David Brown began work on *Santana III* in 1971, but made the classic mistake that others have made so many times through the years: He called in sick. It's hard to avoid catching the flu on occasion, but unless you're working with a very loyal client, that healthy fill-in—in this case, Kolotkin—could very well take over your project. "It just so happened it was a full session with the whole band," recalls Kolotkin of his first day subbing for Brown. "I just did my normal thing, and their road manager called the band's manager and said, 'You gotta come down here right away. I've never heard the band sound like this!' So from that point on, I worked with Santana. I felt bad and said, 'David, I didn't mean to steal your band,' and he says, 'Believe me, it's a pleasure! I've had it with those guys!' Their entourage consisted of the Hell's Angels, and they used to bring their motorcycles right through the hallway. I was amused by all of it, but it drove Roy Segal crazy!" The good-natured engineer would go on to record nine more albums with the band, though *Santana III* remains his favorite.

To make matters worse as far as Segal's blood pressure was concerned, Santana had secured a special contract that granted them free studio time after selling a certain number of records, which meant the studio turned into their second home. "They used to book the studio by the year!" Kolotkin recalls. "They'd just book the studio until they went on tour, move in a refrigerator and stock it every day, and we'd record all the time."

But maybe one reason for the ongoing studio lockout stemmed from Carlos Santana's recording style. He was, and still is, the polar opposite of a one-take guy. "We'd punch in a lot and we might work on a solo of his for hours at a time, maybe a day," Kolotkin recalls. "He just wanted to get everything perfect. I like to record live, get the best feel, and not plan out each solo, but Carlos would learn those solos and play them identical each time they were on the road—the exact solo—because he had perfected them in the studio."

One day, Santana got a bit of competition from young guitarist Neal Schon, then relatively new to the group. The song "Toussaint L'Overture" became a contest between Schon and Santana. "We were working with Carlos's guitar solos and Neal comes in and says, 'Oh let me try one!' So Carlos let him try one, and it was great! Then Carlos would do a solo, and Neal would come in the next day and try to better it. We had 16 tracks back then, and we were just about filled up when one night, Neal came in with a bunch of his friends and wanted to do his solo over. I said, 'Are you kidding? That solo was incredible!' He really wanted to do it, but in order to [re-record his solo] we had to erase the original, so that's what we did. To this day, I think we erased the best solo he had on that album. But it's my word against his, and he swears the new one's better."

Kolotkin continued working with Santana as he explored his spiritual path and a jazz-fusion direction, beginning with *Caravanserai*. When the original lineup disbanded in 1973, Santana collaborated with guitar virtuoso John McLaughlin on *Love Devotion Surrender*. The guitarists shared Sri Chinmoy as a guru but possessed very different recording styles. "John did all of his solos in 45 minutes," Kolotkin says of the album, recorded in New

York and San Francisco. "John played thousands of notes, and then when it came time for Carlos to record, it took him three days! But when we were mixing, we listened to John's solos, and at the end of each one there'd be this 'gonk.' Carlos said, 'Well we can't leave those gonks in there.' So we spent two more days hand-erasing the gonks! So John might have done all of his solos in 45 minutes, but it still took us three days to work on his parts."

Like most studios, every day was full of surprises at Columbia, some of them magical, like the day Paul Simon sat down with Kolotkin and Roy Halee in the studio. He wanted their feedback on some new songs he had just written. "Kodachrome" was one of them. Kolotkin recalls Simon asking them, "You know, I've known both of you for a number of years, what's your true opinion of these songs?" Their response was the verbal equivalent of falling out of the chair.

The studio continued to operate full speed ahead for a solid half-decade. Halee brought in as many Columbia acts as he could to fill Studios A and B, while Coast kept its remaining C room booked with commercial spots and film and television projects. One of the highest profile ones came from New York, down on *Sesame Street*. In only its third season in 1970, The Children's Television Workshop program began incorporating the now-famous number and letter cartoon spots—i.e., "sound like…the letter 'I'!" Imagination Inc., a film-production company based in San Francisco, played an integral role in many of these spots and booked heavyweight talent to get them done. The company brought Grace Slick and jazz musician/composer Denny Zeitlin, who worked with Imagination Inc. producers Walt Kraemer and producer Mike Felix. For numbers 1 through 20, Zeitlin composed and played music on an intricate electronic panel, while Slick improvised vocal and scat singing. For letters E and O, Dan Hicks and his Hot Licks performed to music by Great Society's Darby Slick. Bud Luckey put together animation and music and sang for numbers 2 through 6. Music for the animated spots was recorded on Coast's 16-track, as was another television campaign, the stick-in-your-head-for-days jingle "A is for Apple, J is for Jacks" for Kellogg's Apple Jacks cereal.

Engineer Walt Kramer (seated) and executive producer Mike Felix confer on a Sesame Street track at Coast in 1971.

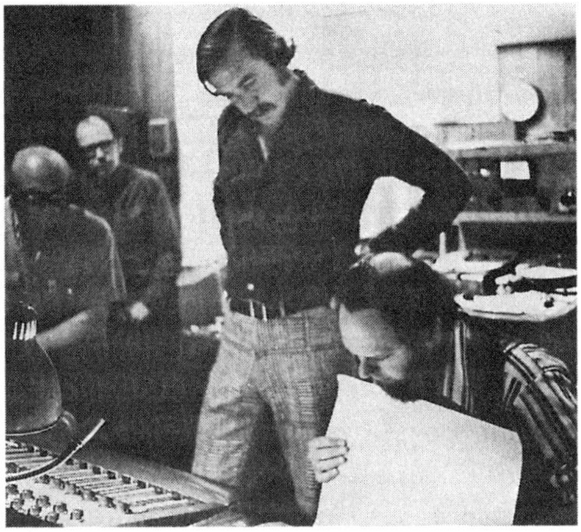

Universal Audio Archives/David Kulka

Steve Atkins, longtime partner of Lloyd Pratt, who oversaw Coast Recorders, came over to Folsom Street after Pratt passed away. "I was on the road, and by the time I came back in 1970, Lloyd had merged with Coast. I had been working at my tiny studio when they called me the day after Lloyd died and asked me to babysit Coast on Folsom. So I did; I was with Coast for about three or four months, then they made me manager. I stayed with the company until 1993."

George Horn, who served double duty as both chief tech and lead mastering engineer, handled much of the mastering for the studio, including most of the in-house work as well as outside clients. To accommodate the influx of business, he trained engineer Phil Brown, who soon joined him in the mastering department. In the early 1970s, Columbia was the only place in town that could cut stereo lacquers, so anyone who wanted their album mastered in stereo and didn't want to travel to L.A. to do it brought their business to Columbia. As an aside: at the time, one of the only independent mastering houses *period* was Doug Sax's Mastering Lab in L.A., which opened in 1968. The Lacquer Channel opened in Sausalito in the mid-1970s and even then, it was a rare bird, and rarer still in a "B" market such as San Francisco. Even now, the city maintains a limited number of indie mastering rooms; Stubblebine owns one of them.

Horn recalls mastering a Neil Young album directly from 16-track, without going through a mixdown stage. Producer Elliot Mazer, who had opened his own studio, His Master's Wheels, in the old Pacific High Recorders space in 1974, had a Neve 8016 desk with a Neve Melbourne sidecar, along with a couple of Ampex MM1000s. "His idea was to work out all the mixes with automation and transfer them directly onto multitrack tape to the lathe and bypass the 2-track tape," recalls Horn. "It was quite an undertaking but it worked." Horn couldn't recall the name of that particular Young album; he remembers catalog numbers, not album titles.

A young Paul Stubblebine began his mastering career at Columbia in 1973. He joined the staff as an intern, worked his way up to second engineer, then joined the mastering department where he learned from both Brown and Horn. The studio had two shifts, so once Horn trained Stubblebine, he would work the first shift while Brown took the second shift, or vice versa. The team of three collectively handled everything from the Paul Simon, Art Garfunkel, and other Columbia projects to classics such as Bob Dylan's *Blood on the Tracks* and The Grateful Dead's *From the Mars Hotel*, "which not everybody knows because there were hardly any credits on the album," says Stubblebine. "George Horn got credit on the LP, but only because he asked."

The studio held its own until 1975, when a convergence of events led to its eventual downfall. One, the goal of signing up new talent on par with its existing roster didn't happen. With the exception of Journey, which released its self-titled debut with Columbia in 1975, the acts signed later, such as the Rowan Brothers, Pamela Polland, Grootna, Masters of the Airwaves, and Les Dudek didn't sell well, either because, in label parlance, "the hits weren't there," or because they got buried under company bureaucracy. Their field reps could take part of the blame, as the label passed on locals The Tubes, Earth Quake, The Doobie Brothers, Jefferson Starship, Tower of Power, and Graham Central Station. "All those acts were in CBS Studios and made demos there and CBS passed on every one," wrote San Francisco *Chronicle* music critic Joel Selvin in 1976. "They were pioneering and everyone else adopted a wait-and-see attitude while Clive flopped around. That failure justified the end of the San Francisco explosion."

Strict union rules didn't help matters, even though Segal and Halee didn't run the studio the way CBS ran its facility in New York. Drugs were used in the Columbia studio as they were everywhere; you just weren't allowed to smoke in the control room. As the only union studio in town, however, it had nearly 20 people on payroll and an expensive lease, both factors hugely detrimental in an industry where it is hard turn a profit.

The biggest blow, however, happened in 1975, when CBS fired Clive Davis. It was Davis' vision to open the studio and branch office in the first place, so with him gone and the local roster waning, the studio didn't really get much support from New York. That same year, Halee took a position at ABC in Los Angeles, where he had been working more frequently anyway. "I eventually got really tired of it, because I had to keep bringing musicians in from L.A.," he said of San Francisco. "I tried using Bay Area players. I brought in San Francisco Symphony players a few times. And there were a few horn players. I brought in Jerry Garcia a couple of times, which was nice. But Hal [Blaine] was down in L.A., and so many of the regular musicians I liked to use were down there, and then I got involved with Albert Hammond and I was spending more time there than in San Francisco, so I figured I'd go back down there. I just couldn't find the musicians I needed to help me."

Though he stayed in San Francisco a few more years, Glen Kolotkin followed Halee's lead and left the studio to work as an independent engineer/producer. "It came at a good time for me," he says of Davis's departure, which led to the end of Columbia Studios. "I'd thought I wanted to be on my own more, and I was interested in doing more producing, and I did." Even as an independent, he continued to bring acts to the studio until it closed. During Columbia's final year, he allied with the eccentric Matthew Kaufman (self-proclaimed "reigning looney," known for claiming that Reverend Ike and marijuana were his greatest life influences), who brought in the band Earth Quake, dropped from A&M Records after two unsuccessful albums. Kolotkin recorded these initial tracks and offered to help Kaufman get them a deal. Kaufman wanted his own label instead and promptly formed Beserkley Records with partner Steve Levine. The band's first single, "Sitting in the Middle of Madness," sold more than 3,000 by mail-order and grassroots efforts, which gave Kaufman the funds needed to move forward. Kolotkin stayed on board as a producer and engineer and worked with the entire original Beserkley roster: Greg Kihn, Earth Quake, Jonathan Richman, and The Rubinoos. He recorded Richman's *Rock & Roll with the Modern Lovers* in Columbia's echo chamber—the whole *band* in the echo chamber. He continued to work with Santana, as well, through his 1977 release *Moonflower.* Kolotkin then moved back to New York not long after, but he and Santana would reunite in San Francisco many years later to work on his mega-mega Platinum release, *Supernatural,* in 2000.

Mathew Kaufman (left) and Glen Kolotkin, going Beserkley in Columbia's Studio B control room, circa 1976.

Photo courtesy of Glen Kolotkin

In the midst of all of these developments on first floor of 829 Folsom Street, David Rubinson took over the upper two floors (which had been occupied by Francis Ford Coppola's American Zoetrope enterprise) for offices and rehearsal space as well as Studio C, the small studio used mainly for voiceovers by Coast. By this time, Coast had moved what was left of its Folsom Street business to 1340 Mission, former home of Mercury Records, which it acquired in late 1970. The Coast-at-Mission chronicles continue in Chapter 12. When Rubinson began negotiations with Cal Roberts, CBS vice president in charge of recording operations, he needed his own studio badly. His lease with Heider's, for which he paid for about 3,000 hours a year in advance in exchange for a discounted rate, required him to work during its off-hours, which usually meant a lot of nights and weekends. He also worked in Los Angeles quite a bit, often working in both cities the same day. He produced the lion's share of his work at Heider's, and therefore felt justified in asking for a few modifications to the studio: a 4-channel headphone cue system and monitor section mute switches and automation for the console. This feature was just beginning to make its way on the market. Filmways, the company that owned Wally Heider Recording at the time, refused, further reinforcing the quest to find a permanent home.

The Automatt

The time had come for Rubinson to secure his own studio, and an opportunity to reconnect with his comrades at Columbia seemed like an ideal choice. Under the agreement, Columbia would provide the room, maintenance, parking, reception, and microphones—basically, all of the extras—and Rubinson would provide the console, machines, his ace engineer Fred Catero, an assistant, and lots of clients. Again, he offered to pay by the year. Agreements were made, papers were signed, and in the fall of 1976, Rubinson hung the shingle for The Automatt, a combined reference to an old New York fast-food chain and the advanced technology that would grace his small studio.

David Rubinson in The Automatt's Studio A.

Kaz Tsuruta Photography

He installed a custom Harrison 4824 (Harrison had just come into the market in 1975) console with programmable mute keys on every module and brought in a decent selection of outboard equipment: an Eventide Harmonizer and Omnipressor and various limiters, EQs, and machine sync equipment for the MCI 24-track, Scully 8-track, and MCI 2-track machines. Monitors included the popular Altec "Big Red" system driven by Mac 75 power amps.

Mike Larner, who came on board as Rubinson's engineering consultant, put together a computer-accessed automation storage and retrieval system that interfaced with The Automatt's Harrison 4032. The Allison Memory-Plus Automation System had the ability to store more than 65,000 separate functions. With the Zilog Z-80 computer system, automatic recall of a mix became possible. Another Larner invention, Autopunch, interfaced the Allison programmer with the MCI 24-track, thereby automating all of its tape-recorder functions, including motion control, record, and playback.

Another Automatt first was Larner's 4-track earphone cue system, which let each musician mix his or her own cue balance. Today, most studios have up to 16-channel headphone cue systems. At the time, the Automatt system was revolutionary and a huge benefit to the musicians, who could now hear only what they needed to hear without affecting the other musicians' mixes or relying on the engineer's headphone mix. With The Automatt, Rubinson got everything that Heider's wouldn't provide and then some, and he began touting The Automatt as the city's first fully automated studio.

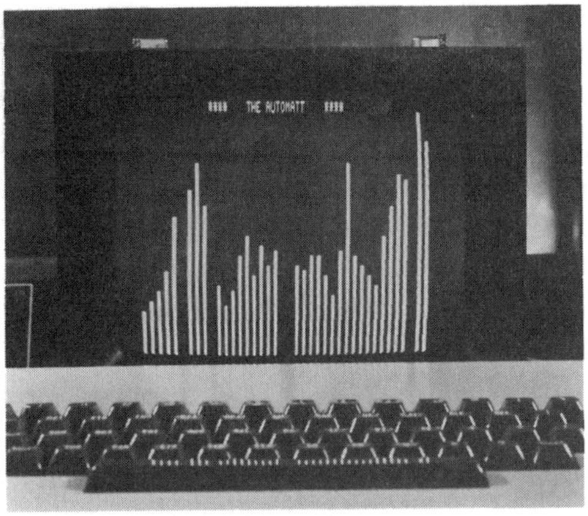

In picture #1, a graphic representation of the mix is displayed on the video screen.

In picture #2, the visual display depicts current console settings alongside the "frozen mix" (represented in picture #1). The three unmatched bars indicate that the current console settings do not match the previous mix.

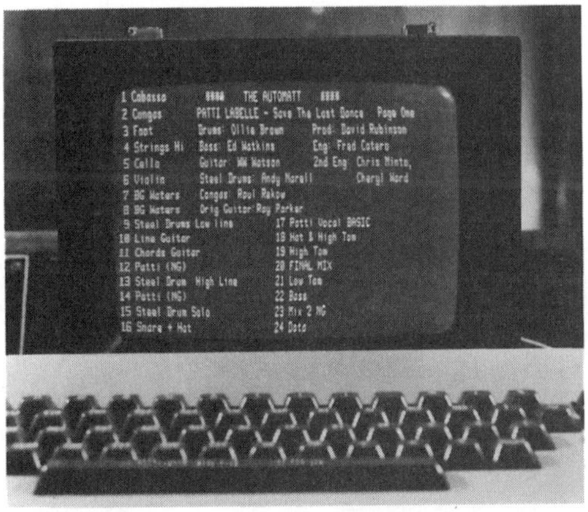

In picture #4, we see an example of the capability of this unique interface of systems to store any desired text along with the console automation data on the tape. Automatically re-called, the text pictured here includes information regarding track assignments, musicians, artist's name, title of song, and recording personnel.

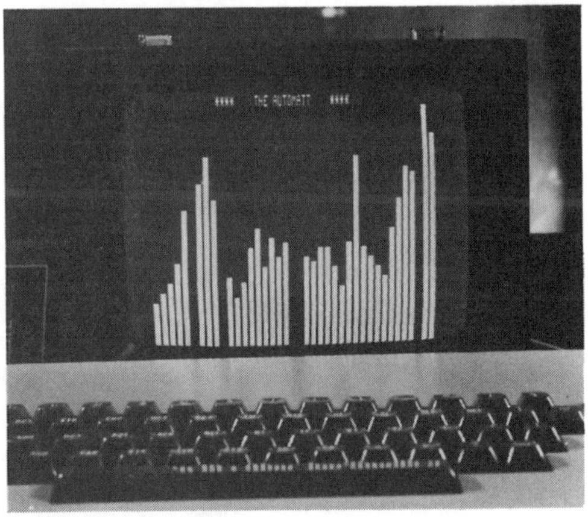

In picture #3, we see that the console settings have been adjusted to match exactly the previous mix — what normally would take hours accomplished in a matter of seconds!

The Automatt interface of the Zilog Z-80 (microprocessor) Computer System with the Allison 65K Automation System creates many new technological capabilities never before possible in the art of recording. One of the capabilities of this newly interfaced system is the almost immediate recreation on the console of a previous mix, as shown in the first three photos of the series above (clockwise from top left).

THE AUTOMATT

AUTOMATED RECORDING STUDIOS IN SAN FRANCISCO

Kaz Tsuruta Photography

A sheet from The Automatt press kit explaining their Allison automation system.

In 1977, Rubinson brought Patti Labelle to his relatively new studio to record her self-titled solo debut. Prior to the session, he and his A&R man, Jeff Cohen, selected about 40 songs (some of which Cohen co-wrote) to take to Labelle in her native Philadelphia. She had also written several songs for the project, and together they narrowed down the list to an album's worth of material. Next came rehearsals at The Automatt with Labelle. The band included musical director/pianist Bud Ellison, drummer James Gadson, guitarist Ray Parker, Jr. (of later "Ghostbusters" fame), and bassist George Porter and guitarist Leo Nocentelli from The Meters, who had just come up from New Orleans the week before to record a Meters album with Rubinson at The Automatt. According to a 1977 feature in *Modern Recording,* Catero used a "standard, basic set-up" that included Neumann U-87s on the guitar amps, bass and Fender Rhodes recorded direct, two U-87s on the acoustic piano; on the drums were U-87s, Shure SM56s, and Sony C-22s. For Labelle's powerhouse vocals, Catero used a Shure SM56 for the "live" cuts. If the lead vocal was overdubbed, he used a U-87 with Labelle singing close to the wind-screen. "Patti's voice is so strong and clean she could telephone in her part and it would come out sounding great," he said.

Patti Labelle and David Rubinson, preparing for another spot-on vocal.

Labelle and the band recorded "You Can't Judge a Book By the Cover" completely live, and they built up "Dan Swit Me" from the ground floor, writing and composing the song in the studio. Rubinson notes that Labelle, as with most singers he worked with, always sang live with the band—that interaction was crucial in these creative moments—with a few "fixes" made later, if need be.

For "Dan Swit Me," they laid down a foundation with one of Roland's first rhythm machines, with drums, bass, piano, and guitar and background vocals added on top. Labelle reportedly wanted to add her own backing vocals, but Rubinson advised against it; her voice was too powerful for backgrounds, even her own! The experience led to a solo album that would ultimately send the singer down a new path of high-charting success.

Herbie Hancock first came to the burgeoning Automatt to listen to the mix of *V.S.O.P.*, the live album from the reformed Miles Davis Quintet (minus Miles, but with Freddie Hubbard on trumpet). Hancock reportedly didn't like the amount of echo he had requested from Rubinson on the piano track. He wanted to change it. Had Rubinson owned the average manual board, the remix would have been quite tedious and costly. But with Allison Automation on board, Catero could simply recall the original mix, tweak the EMT on the piano, and save the new mix. They were able to make the change without altering the levels on another client's album being mixed on the Harrison at the time.

The president and chairman of Columbia listened to the final mix of *V.S.O.P.* during the official grand opening party for The Automatt. A who's who of San Francisco's recording scene came out to celebrate the occasion, and Rubinson was thrilled to raise a glass to his new recording home, which was already booming. "They walked out the door, everybody was feeling great, and the announcement came the next day that they were closing the entire studio complex, including The Automatt," Rubinson remembers. "Closing! I signed the paper! I gave them a lot of money! I was depending on their ass, and they announced they were closing the San Francisco studio. I called them up and said, 'You were just in my studio. I signed the lease with you guys, what do you mean you're closing? My machines are in there. My whole life is in there. I've got projects booked for the next two years. You can't *close*.'"

CBS/Columbia forbade Rubinson to record any Columbia acts until they settled a nasty dispute that arose with the engineer's union as a result of their closing. But The Automatt wasn't a union studio, Rubinson protested. Couldn't they keep recording?

They locked the door.

SECTION THREE

The Seventies: It's Party Time

The music business in the 1970s got off to a booming start, especially in San Francisco. In fact, in 1972, a demographic survey of the city listed the music industry, including nightclubs, concert halls, record labels, and recording studios, as the second-largest industry in the city, after tourism. Records sold well, and a select group of San Francisco bands made themselves and their labels sacks of money. Building on the recording industry established in the late 1960s, several new studios opened in the area, but they played by different rules than their predecessors did. The Record Plant brought the concepts of the resort studio and the lockout to the city, as well as a steady stream of L.A. clients. Other new additions, Different Fur and The Automatt among them, existed primarily as a workspace for their producer and/or musician owners, while also welcoming outside clients. Recording equipment was still too expensive for the average Joe to open a decent home studio, but artists with above-average royalty statements—Neil Young, members of The Grateful Dead, and Steve Miller, among others—created studios of their own. Both of these types of entities, the project studio and the home studio, would rapidly develop as the years and technology advanced.

Inside the studio, the glass wall between the artist, producer, and engineer broke down in the early 1970s as artists became more involved in the production process. Producers could freely get their hands on the console (union rules wouldn't let them before), engineers offered up their opinion on a song's structure, and artists could sit in on their own mix and have a voice in the process. As keyboards and synthesizers became more commonplace, even these moved into the control room. Tracks increased from 16 to 24 early in the decade, which further fueled the "We'll fix it in the mix" dilemma. Some bands saw this as a way to get out of rehearsing their material, while others who could play multiple instruments, sing, and engineer, such as Sly Stone, produced innovative work by building tracks one instrument at a time. Recording consoles, which had progressed from custom jobs to manufacturer-designed desks, improved to offer more bells and whistles, most notably computerized automation, which allowed engineers to recall an earlier mix more quickly.

As engineers and studio architects learned more about acoustics, studios began adding more isolation booths and such features as movable panels to change the reverberant qualities of a room. In the early 1970s, the concept of the "dead" room with virtually no echo came to be. Yet, as the rooms became deader, the décor became louder! Red and orange carpet and low lighting often replaced the fluorescent lights of the more utilitarian facilities from the 1960s.

By the mid 1970s, however, the fortunes of the industry had plummeted. Nationally, music had become a $3 billion industry, but the music coming out of San Francisco wasn't selling as much anymore. The local club scene suffered because "Bands forgot that people liked to dance," recalls one producer. The fans that rocked out at the Fillmore Auditorium and the Carousel Ballroom didn't necessarily know what to do to with bands like Fleetwood Mac and Yes, except retreat to their bedrooms and zone out by the speakers. The rock clubs went through a slow time right along with the recording studios.

Soon enough, though, the need to dance begat a resurgence of funk and the emergence of disco that peaked toward the end of the decade. At the same time, punk rock and new wave drew an entirely different young audience to clubs and concerts. Meanwhile, Marin County still had its hippie music scene, thanks in large part to the enduring Grateful Dead family. Some of the originals from the S.F. psychedelic scene either altered their sound to become more "commercial" or bailed and moved to L.A to earn good income as session players or sidemen.

No, San Francisco never did become the major music center that some hoped for, but the city would continue to attract and bring forth a strong and diverse talent pool. More L.A.–based artists found their way up north, even though they gravitated toward a few elite studios. The rest of the facilities around town got along by catering to a primarily local client base, enhanced by occasional out-of-towners and creative, multi-tasking owners.

CHAPTER 11

The Record Plant: Magical Seeds

Halloween Masquerade Ball

Studio Opening

Dancing BYOD

October 29

6 p.m. to 2 a.m.

RSVP 415-332-2755

In the fall of 1972, the who's who of the music business in L.A., New York, San Francisco, and beyond received this invitation on a slab of California redwood from Chris Stone and Gary Kellgren, owners of The Record Plant studios in Sausalito, California. John Lennon and Yoko Ono showed up dressed as trees, their presence a clear indication of the level of clientele The Record Plant's Northern California outpost (they also helped launch The Record Plant's L.A. and New York facilities) would attract. As the grand-opening bash raged through Sunday morning, word spread fast that this new studio across the Bay was a party getaway for the rich and famous.

With its Jacuzzi, guest houses, organic chefs, and rooms with waterbed floors—not to mention the laughing gas masks hanging from one control room ceiling and two fake walls leading to an escape route in case of a drug bust—The Record Plant reflected the excess of the times in grand, glitzy L.A. style. It also brought to San Francisco one of the industry's first "resort" studios: one that would offer good equipment and better times. It was one of the first independently owned studios in town with the cache to bring in top-tier talent. At Sausalito's "living room" studio, clients could take an extended vacation from label-town recording, stay in a beautiful city, and record in a high-end studio that offered as many or more perks as a four-star hotel.

Stone, armed with an MBA and the ability to "make money from water," and Kellgren, a respected engineer who had crafted albums for Bob Dylan, the Velvet Underground, Jimi Hendrix, and the Mothers of Invention, had already established themselves in the studio world with successful New York and L.A. studios, both with the same living-room feel and elite guest lists. They hadn't planned on opening a Northern California outpost until one of their Bay Area clients planted the seed.

KSAN's Tom Donahue often brought former Band of Gypsys drummer and solo artist Buddy Miles down from San Francisco to record at the L.A. Record Plant. Often during their stay they would plead with the owners, "There are no *really* hip studios in San Francisco, please come up here."

Donahue promised a live radio program if they agreed, which they did, deciding to settle in sunny Sausalito on the north side of the Golden Gate. Unintentionally, they beat Wally Heider to the area. Knowing that many of his San Francisco studio clients had moved to Marin County and had a hard time leaving their pastoral surroundings, Heider had drawn up plans for a second facility and even found a spot nearby in Mill Valley's Tam Junction before The Record Plant came in, speedboats and all. Heider had trouble getting the proper sewer permits, so the studio never happened.

Stone and Kellgren had better luck with a plain-looking building on Bridgeway Avenue owned by real estate developers Sasaki Walker

Associates. When the company decided to relocate, they leased the space to Stone and Kellgren, who proceeded to tear it apart and turn it into their two-room, multi-accessorized Bay Area headquarters. They recruited Tom Scott from Wally Heider Studios in L.A. to help them erect the Sausalito Record Plant and later serve as its chief maintenance engineer. Tom Flye, one of their top engineers at Record Plant New York, moved west to serve as chief engineer as Studio B neared completion. The two Toms already knew each other from working on the road with The Record Plant's two remote trucks and had become friends. Once Flye heard that Scott had relocated to join the new Record Plant staff, he accepted the lead engineer job and relocated as well. They even moved to the same neighborhood in Marin County and bought houses on the same dead-end street—three doors apart—where they both still live today.

The core Record Plant lineup—Stone and Kellgren, Flye, and Scott—two teams united by friendship and a passion for music and recording, created a cozy hangout for clients who wanted to escape the L.A. scene. "Gary decided that the most important thing was for the artist to think that he was in a living room," says Stone. "The greatest compliment that an artist could pay us was, 'Hey man, I don't want to leave!'"

Lots of Record Plant clients did stay...for a very, very long time. The studio originated the lockout concept, offering clients a weekly or monthly rate with all of their usual perks, including housing. "That way, the record companies would know they were going to stay on budget, with the exception of extras," says Stone. "We were careful to abide by the company's wishes in that regard."

Whether the act paid by the week or the month, they usually received red carpet treatment. "The San Francisco market was very limited," says Stone. "The majority of our business came from outside the Bay Area. In particular, we once flew George Harrison over from London, picked him up at the airport in a limo, brought him to Sausalito, where he worked for three or four weeks and nobody ever even knew he was in the states!" The studio limo, owned by Stone, had the license plate "DEDUCT." The license plate on Kellgren's purple Rolls Royce read "GREED."

The two guesthouses, next door to each other and within minutes of the studio, each had multiple bedrooms, providing ample accommodations for large entourages. "We had a retired American Airlines stewardess as the house mother," adds Stone. "We were able to offer each group virtually anything they wanted...organic cooks, whatever they wanted we would provide." Flye and Scott conveniently lived down the street. "So if the hot tub conked out at 1 a.m., there'd be a knock at my door," laughs Flye.

When they wanted to record a vocal at 2 a.m., they called Michelle Zarin, who joined the Record Plant Sausalito in early 1973 as an assistant to studio manager Ginger Mews. In short order, Mews moved on, and Zarin got promoted and became the missing link in the studio team. She developed close relationships with record labels and clients alike, running a smooth-sailing ship despite its zany passengers.

Their marketing plan and strong customer service certainly boosted business, but their success didn't solely stem from organic chefs, a basketball court, or limo service. It came from the triumvirate of Stone's business sense, Kellgren's engineering talents and creativity, and studio designer Tom Hidley's trendsetting plans, as well as a skilled and dedicated staff who understood that The Record Plant was a 24/7 job, and that was okay. The fact that Record Plant L.A. fed them a lot of business didn't hurt, either.

The Sausalito Record Plant modeled much of its interior, including the sculpted redwood hallways, after Frank Werber's popular local jazz club/restaurant, The Trident. Combined with stained glass and skylights, the studio had a warm, country feel—until you got past the lobby. The conference room originally had a waterbed floor—one of Kellgren's crazy ideas—but it caused so much water damage that they ripped it out, only to replace it with five thick layers of carpet and no chairs. Outside the conference room was the Jacuzzi, a perk made famous in L.A. "Gary wanted to build a swimming pool and I wouldn't let him," says Stone. "So we installed the Jacuzzi. When we built Sausalito he said, 'Okay Stone. There's no room for a pool so I'm not even going to ask, but we are going to have a Jacuzzi.' It was a popular place to be."

Studios A and B, located to the left and right of the reception desk, mirrored each other in acoustics and equipment, but had very different décor. Studio A came with a sunburst pattern on one wall of the studio and white fabric that resembled tents on the ceiling, which were hung to help eliminate reflection. Studio B had swirls of colors and a mural on the walls and different colored cloths hung in layers on the ceilings. Equally colorful gobos could be rolled into either room. "Studio A was more…sedate if you can use that word with The Record Plant," says Stone.

API consoles resided in both control rooms, as well as ample EQs, limiters and compressors, and Yamaha grand pianos. Tape machines included a 3M 16-track and Ampex 2-, 4-, 16-, and 24-track machines. The mic closet came stocked with Neumann, AKG, Shure, Sennheiser, Sony, RCA, and ElectroVoice models. Large monitors from JBL and Hidley's newly formed Westlake Audio flanked both control rooms. Clients in either A or B could also dial into the studio's own FM transmitter, which allowed engineers to broadcast from the control room so that artists could listen to rough mixes from one of their favorite reference points: their cars. Studios A and B incorporated Hidley's acoustical concept of the "dead" room, which incorporated heavy amounts of trapping as a way for rock bands to get a large room sound in less space.

The Record Plant's Studio A, circa 1972.

Photo courtesy of Chris Stone

"Traditional recording studios were large rooms; in a city, that's very expensive real estate," explains Flye. "So studio owners learned from Tom Hidley that you could have small piece of real estate and make it sound big with reverb chambers, which everybody used anyhow, to help with leakage problems. A small room sounds bad, like a Holiday Inn room, just terrible. And [Hidley's concept] works; you can make it sound tight or cavernous, as long as you have control."

"At that point in time, the rock and roll bands were so loud; they could always add brightness, but brightness wasn't always what they were after," adds Stone. "So we deadened the room knowing that we could brighten them up with wood gobos or with LA2As and other outboard, but to deaden it, you have to have that in the walls."

While most engineers either liked or adjusted to the idea, it didn't win everyone over. "It was horrendous; the room was so dead it just sucked up all the sound!" says engineer Betty Cantor-Jackson. Her engineering partner Bob Matthews proposes, "The idea was that they could have two rock bands playing at full tilt 130 dB and still have isolation." The Grateful Dead's *Wake of the Flood* album was recorded at The Plant in 1973, with Dan Healy working as principal engineer on the project. It's rumored that the band took full advantage of the gas masks.

When clients weren't working, which at The Record Plant was sort of a relative term anyway, a speedboat docked at Gate 5 could take them to Tiburon or Fisherman's Wharf or for a quick joyride around the Bay. Want company? There are probably some teenage groupies hanging out in the lounge. Or you could hire a pro. At a time when The Record Plant's market—the top ten percent of rock and roll—had unlimited budgets, those "miscellaneous expenses" could mean just about anything. The rock and roll elite could spend months in the studio writing, recording, and, well, partying, on their own time table, and the labels often didn't question the bill. "It was that era where you found your favorite eight bars and stayed on it for maybe 36 hours," former Pablo Cruise frontman Cory Lerios said in a 1998 interview with *Pulse* magazine. The band recorded "the better part of four albums" at The Record Plant. "It was a great time, no question."

"You had to have a major-label budget to afford places like The Record Plant, with all of the perks—the Jacuzzi, the décor, the psychedelic atmosphere—and everybody was high as a kite," says artist/songwriter Bob Welch, who played guitar in Fleetwood Mac from 1971 to 1974 before going onto other ventures. "A lot of great records got made. Most of them could have cost half of what they did, but a lot of that budget went for...other stuff."

Yes, The Record Plant was a great place to party, but its owners aimed to create a worry-free environment where the artist "had no choice but to make the best music possible," says Stone. "There was no way out. You've got a good acoustical environment, we'll set the monitors the way you want them, you've got housing, food...now go make your music. And they think, 'Oh shit. I have to perform.'" And they did, sometimes for a couple of days straight, aided by their chemical of choice, but regardless, the studio regularly churned out Gold and Platinum sellers, the evidence of which can be seen now by the RIAA-certified plaques that line the walls.

Kicking back in The Record Plant's pre-production room, 1972.

Photo courtesy of Chris Stone

The same guy that broke in Wally Heider Recording, producer/engineer Al Schmitt, christened The Record Plant in 1972 with a band called Finnigan and Wood. Donahue lived up to his word, and in 1972 the inaugural "Live from The Record Plant" show aired on KSAN, Jive 95, on Sunday nights at 11 p.m., with Jerry Garcia, Fleetwood Mac, Bob Marley and the Wailers, and Bonnie Raitt as some of its early featured performers.

Flye alone kept Studio B booked solid. The first project he engineered at the studio, *Adventures of Panama Red* from the New Riders of the Purple Sage, went Gold. Subsequent left-coast Record Plant visitors such as Stephen Stills, America, Commander Cody,

Joe Walsh, Three Dog Night, Yes, Marvin Gaye, and Tower of Power continued the hit streak in The Record Plant's first few years.

Sly Stone, who would later become a permanent resident, made his first appearance at the studio while he still had the Family Stone behind him. Considered the group's and Sly's final masterpiece, *Fresh* was recorded mostly in Sausalito by Tom Flye. With their previous album, *There's a Riot Goin' On* (recorded at CBS' New York studios by Don Puluse), the band had all but moved away from recording live and instead recorded one instrument at a time. Once known for their groundbreaking integration of black and whites in one ensemble, the group had devolved to separation in the studio. They recorded this way partly because of Sly's unpredictable behavior: his cocaine addiction had gotten the better of him, and he often showed up hours late for gigs or missed them altogether. Furthermore, by this point, Sly Stone wrote, arranged, and produced most of the material and played the majority of the instruments anyway. He became an innovator in the overdub style of recording, tracking one instrument at a time, usually beginning with a rhythm track. "Usually he started out with a Maestro Rhythm King. We called it the 'Funk Box,'" says Flye. "That was the original drum machine. It could only do real simple stuff, but it gave him a foundation to work on, and then he'd build his record. But sometimes he'd put the drums on last. Sometimes he'd put down an organ track first, and that would tell you the chord changes. Then he'd go into whatever idea he had next. So there was no set way of working." Flye also credits Sly Stone as one of the first to use a drum loop. "We were working on 'Babies Making Babies,' and every time we'd get to one section, he'd go, 'Now that's funky. Those four bars, boy I wish it all sounded like that.' So I made 24- to 24- copies of it and cut 'em all together and that became the track."

By this time, drummer Greg Errico had left the group and bassist Larry Graham had moved on to form Graham Central Station. Not so coincidentally, Flye recorded most of Graham's albums as well, mostly at The Record Plant, and some of them simultaneously with Sly Stone. "It was right after the group had broken up, so it was a little weird," says Flye. They even recorded in the same room, with Graham usually coming in when Sly Stone was out of town.

Larry Graham

Dig that funky bass line? Thank Larry Graham, the originator of the percussive slap/pop electric bass style that defined 1970s progressive funk. In fact, you can partially credit Graham for the term progressive funk, as Sly Stone, his bandmate from 1968 until 1972, coined the phrase to describe the music of Sly and the Family Stone.

Born in Beaumont, Texas, but raised in Oakland, California, Graham started taking piano lessons at age 8; by his early teens, he knew guitar, bass, harmonica, and drums and had a three-and-a-half octave vocal range. He joined his mother's lounge act, Dell Graham Trio, at 15 and worked the San Francisco club circuit. He first met Sly Stone, then known as Sylvester Stewart, on one of those nights.

After backing R&B and blues artists such as John Lee Hooker, Jackie Wilson, and Jimmy Reed and the Drifters, Graham joined Sly and the Family Stone in 1968. His deep baritone and thick grooves defined their sound and brought Bay Area funk into the mainstream spotlight. He stayed with the ensemble through their heyday, contributing to now-classic albums such as *Stand!* and *There's a Riot Goin' On,* as well as such singles as "Dance to the Music" and "Everybody Is a Star," among others.

He resigned to giving Sly the spotlight throughout those heady years, but his talent as a musician and songwriter deserved one of its own. Not completely by his own doing, Graham exited the group in 1972. He joined a group called Hot Chocolate (not the U.K. band who had the 1975 hit "You Sexy Thing"), renamed them Graham Central Station, and with an equally red-hot ensemble, released several funk albums through the 1970s before disbanding at decade's end. As a solo artist, he reached another peak in the early 1980s with *One in a Million You.* The title track became a Top Ten hit. The following albums, *Just Be My Lady* and *Sooner or Later,* had success as well, though his next two albums, *Victory* and *Fired Up,* essentially fizzled.

He worked steadily as a songwriter and sideman for several years, led the nine-piece Psychedelic Psoul in the early 1990s, then re-formed Graham Central Station in 1993, this time with Cynthia Robinson and Jerry Martini of Sly and the Family Stone. They received a substantial boost from Prince, a longtime fan and supporter, when he asked Graham and crew to serve as the opening act on his Jam of the Year tour in 1997.

As the 1970s progressed, Sly Stone became one of The Record Plant's best clients. He loved recording, so he naturally spent ample time at the studio. His name alone brought more business to the studio. When he asked for his own room in the mid-1970s, Chris Stone and Kellgren obliged, which led to the design of The Pit, a one-of-a-kind studio that incorporated one of Kellgren's crazy ideas with Sly Stone's specs. Like the other two rooms, The Pit had an API console and 3M 16-track, but they resided in a sunken-in area about 10 feet deep. The musicians stayed at ground level on a ledge that went around all sides of the control room below. The entire place—the floors, ceiling, walls, and stairway—was covered in plush carpet for absolute deadness, and psychedelic murals and embroidery added to the very 1970s vibe. "The actual recording area was a full story above in this padded, carpeted room where there was absolutely no echo. There were no reflective surfaces at all, and the engineers were blocked form the live sound because they were a floor below and they had this cowling that came up over, like a windshield on a convertible that was also carpeted, so the engineers could monitor at pretty high volume and still not get any leakage."

Nobody ever imitated The Pit, probably for good reason, but it sure supported the hot-tub-loving Kellgren's idea of super-decadence. "So you're laying on this carpeted floor, guitars on your lap, pillow under your head," recalls Welch, "I remember watching [Rolling Stones bassist] Bill Wyman doing his vocals laying down with a bottle of brandy and a mic jack stuck in the wall. It was the concept of the times. I think people like to work more efficiently now."

When Sly Stone recorded in The Pit, he recorded *in* The Pit. He liked to record in the control room, and he recorded keyboards (he always had a Hammond B3 in the control room), vocals, and anything else he could get away with down below.

Flye once recorded the Tower of Power horns in the control room, standing in the doorway. "I'd line the room with plywood, so they wouldn't overblow," says Flye. At one point Sly wanted to move the drums in the small control room, but that's where Flye drew the line. Drums stay out!

Oddly enough, real sessions did happen in The Pit. Welch and numerous others came in to play on Bill Wyman's solo album, *Stone Alone,* which materialized in The Pit in 1975. "It was totally out of control," recalls Welch, who added guitar parts. Other guests included Dr. John, Van Morrison, Joe Walsh, the Tower of Power horns, former bandmate Ron Wood, and Tom Johnston of the Doobie Brothers, among others. "Bill Wyman was very straight. He didn't touch any drugs, but everybody [else] was stoned out of their brains. We didn't know what time of the day or night it was, it was completely ridiculous. I remember Stephen Stills taking an hour and a half to tune a guitar, sitting under the piano…it was wonderful! I'd never want to repeat the experience, but it was very unique."

Welch's hard rock group Paris, which included former Jethro Tull bassist Glenn Cornick and former Nazz drummer Thom Mooney, recorded their debut album there with producer/engineer Jimmy Robinson, around the same time. Welch recalls the setup in the unusual room: "The musicians were on a ledge looking down. We baffled off the drums and set them up somewhat further away so he couldn't actually see down into the control room. The rest of the musicians were on top and if you wanted to, you could peek over the ledge and throw spitballs at the engineer. Most people preferred to go off in a far corner. The isolation was really pretty good, and of course you monitored yourself with headphones like you usually do. The lack of the glass wall didn't seem to matter."

In between the occasional outside client, Sly Stone often spent weeks at a time in The Pit. So Kellgren built Stone his own apartment, complete with small office, lounge, bathroom, and bedroom. The loft bed, accessed by climbing through a huge pair of bright red upholstered lips—designed as a parody of Sly Stone's big, wide grin—had mic input jacks on the headboard, so you could theoretically do your vocal part from bed.

While Sly Stone hibernated in The Pit, the rest of the facility hummed with activity. During one season of 1977, for example, Al Kooper came in to produce Massachusetts' Chris Morris Band with staff engineer Bob Edwards; Allen Blazek produced and engineered a live album for Elvin Bishop; Tom Anderson mixed a Supertramp album for A&M.

Fleetwood Mac, accompanied by producer/engineer Richard Dashut, came in to record *Rumours*. The album, released in 1977, became one of the best-selling of all time, arguably their greatest achievement, but they knit it together during one of the most traumatic periods of their lives.

John and Christine McVie faced divorce, and the relationship between Lindsey Buckingham and Stevie Nicks' was unraveling. Mick Fleetwood's marriage was on the verge of collapse as well. Personally, the group was falling apart, but professionally, they were at the height of their career. "Rhiannon," the second single from the band's self-titled 1975 album, sprinted up the charts as the *Rumours* sessions got underway. They were on a roll and didn't want to screw it up.

But the strained male-female relationships created a tense studio environment, even at the party studio by the Bay. "It took two months for everyone to adjust to one another," Dashut said in the band's biography, *The Fleetwood Mac Story: Rumours and Lies* by Bob Brunning. "Defenses were wearing thin and they were quick to open up their feelings. Instead of going to friends to talk it out, their feelings were vented through their music. The album was about the only thing they had left."

To take the edge off, they did what any pressured musician would do: They partied. A typical day would start around 7 p.m. with a big feast, then party until 1 or 2 in the morning, and somewhere down the line, they would start recording. Van Morrison, Rufus and Chaka Khan, Jackson Browne, and Warren Zevon often hung out, some of them working down the hall. Sometimes the band would listen back to what they thought was last night's masterpiece, only to find that it sound terrible, so they'd start all over again. "It was the craziest period of our lives," Mick Fleetwood told Brunning. "We went four or five weeks without sleep, doing a lot of drugs. I'm talking about cocaine in such quantities that, at one point, I thought I was really going insane."

Fleetwood tried to keep everyone happy and even took the clocks off the wall so that no one would worry about how much time had passed. They entered the studio with no demos; the album happened in the studio. After a long drought, McVie wrote continuously one day; resulting in four and a half songs on the album. She also requested piano tuning every hour, as opposed to the standard daily piano tuning. Meanwhile Dashut, who had worked with Buckingham and Nicks since before joining Fleetwood Mac, and Caillat, whom Dashut had brought up from Wally Heider Studios in L.A., worked to get near-perfect sounds for every instrument. They spent ten hours on a kick drum sound in Studio B, then moved to A, built a special platform for the drums, and *finally* got what they wanted. For "Don't Stop," assistant Cris Morris sat between Fleetwood and McVie in the studio, because his drums and her piano were angled in such a way that they couldn't see each other. Morris acted as conductor so they could stay in time.

Morris cites recording "Gold Dust Woman" as one of the sessions' great moments, according to the Brunning book. "Stevie was very passionate about getting that vocal right. It seemed like it was directed straight at Lindsey and she was letting it all out. She worked right through the night on it, and finally did it after loads of takes. The wailing, the animal sounds, and the breaking glass were all added later." She did the first take standing up, the studio fully lit. Several takes later Dashut dimmed the lights. She then sat down on the floor, wrapped in a cardigan to keep warm, and nailed the vocal on the eighth take.

An estimated 3,000 hours—six months of tracking, five months editing and mixing—ended up on the 24-track masters. In order to preserve some of the clarity, they transferred the overdubs to a safety master "We had no sync pulse to lock the two machines together, so we had to manually sync the two machines, ten tracks by ear, using headphones in twelve-hour sessions."

The fact that Caillat recorded most of the parts separately made the process even trickier. "Virtually every track is either an overdub or lifted from a separate take of that particular song," said Dashut. "What you hear is the best pieces assembled, a true aural collage. Lindsey and I did most of the production. That's not to take anything away from Ken or the others in the band—they were all very involved. But Lindsey and myself really produced that record and he should've gotten the individual credit for it, instead of the whole band."

One other significant album that came out of The Record Plant during this era was Steve Miller's *Book of Dreams*. Though by the mid-'70s Miller was doing most of his work in the Pacific Northwest, he recruited the Bay Area's Jim Gaines to be his principal engineer after Gaines had helped him complete the multi-Platinum *Fly Like An Eagle*. For *Book of Dreams*, Miller and Gaines cut most of the tracks in Seattle, but finished up at The Record Plant.

Unlike *Fly Like An Eagle*, which developed through a lot of experimentation with sounds and re-working previously recorded tracks, Gaines says they recorded *Book of Dreams* in a more "professional" manner, Later in the process they had to work around Miller's busy touring schedule.

But wait a minute. This is The Record Plant! Party central! "The only thing was," Gaines says "even though we were there to work it still felt like a party situation." They had Rick James, who actually lived in the waterbed room for a time, working next door. "He'd come out in the mornings with just a towel around him and just accidentally let it drop in front of all the women. Crazy stuff like that."

About two months after *Book of Dreams* hit the record stores, on July 20, 1977, Gary Kellgren drowned in a Hollywood swimming pool. His death devastated the industry so deeply, *Rolling Stone* ran a black box obituary on Kellgren, coverage rarely given to an engineer. As his partner and one of his best friends for more than a decade, the news hit Chris Stone hard. They had met years before when Stone's wife Gloria had just had their son, and Kellgren's wife was seven months pregnant with their daughter and scared to death of childbirth. Mutual friends put the couples together, and the husbands suddenly had a few hours to themselves while the wives talked about having babies. When they met, Stone had never been inside a studio, but the straight guy and the artistic guy found they had a magical partnership. With Kellgren gone, Stone lost his verve for the Sausalito studio. "Without Gary's creative genius it just didn't make sense anymore," he said. He hung on for a few more years, but knew it was time to move on.

CHAPTER 12

Concord Records: Past and Future

Coast at Mission

In August 1970, Bill Putnam signed a lease-purchase agreement for Mercury Records' Sound Studios West facility at 1340 Mission Street. Mercury Records had decided to close its San Francisco operation after less than a year, and with CBS occupying the majority of Coast's Folsom Street facility, it needed to put its clients somewhere. They christened it The Annex, or Coast-at-Mission (CAM for short).

Soon after assuming the lease, Putnam redesigned the rooms, and they remain structurally the same to this day. Studio A featured a 20×22–foot control room equipped with the same Bushnell 24×12 console from the Mercury days. The Studio A recording room, an adequate 30×40 feet, became one of the best-sounding rooms in the city and is now the last-remaining Bill Putnam room in San Francisco.

"Bill Putnam's rooms were never splashy; they were never overly live," says Dan Alexander, who would take over the facility some years later. "But it's a room where stuff sounds really good; very nice and neutral and spectacular."

The smaller Studio B, which was not designed by Putnam, offered a 15×20–foot control room, also Bushnell equipped, with an equal-sized live room suitable for a guitarist/vocalist, soloist, or small combo. Studio B worked well as a voiceover room for Coast's advertising clients.

George Horn, then chief tech at Mercury, became chief engineer for Coast's Folsom and Mission Street facilities. Mark Harman came in as a producer/mixer for the Mission Street studio, followed by Phil Edwards, Steve Atkins, Sol Weiss, and Bob Lindner, all of whom joined the team as engineers in the early to mid 1970s, though most bounced between the two Coast facilities. Mercury Records continued to send some projects through the building, and Coast brought over some of its jingles and jazz clients from Folsom Street.

Edwards, who moved to CAM not long after it opened, formed a good working relationship with Concord Records, a leading independent jazz label founded by Carl Jefferson. Edwards recorded *Jazz/Concord* and *Seven Come Eleven*, the two sequential and classic releases from the 1973 Concord Summer Festival featuring Herb Ellis, Joe Pass, bassist Ray Brown, and drummer Jake Hanna. Dozens, if not hundreds, of Concord jazz albums were either fully or partially recorded at Coast through the 1970s, including ones by Tito Puente, Cal Tjader, Mary McCartland, and Rosemary Clooney, among many others, with Edwards handling most of them.

To deal with the large volume of work, which usually involved a live remote recording at an out-of-town club or jazz festival, Edwards opened his own two-room post-production facility right next door to CAM, which he held for about 10 years. "At one point we had as many as 40 album projects a year," says Edwards. "There were sessions going night and day. We'd go back and forth between the Mission Street Coast facility and my place. We'd often track at CAM and bring projects to my place to mix."

Not long after moving to CAM, Edwards engineered portions of *Gandharva,* a Paul Beaver and Bernie Krause collaboration featuring their Moog, organ, and keyboard work. The project included guests such as Michael Bloomfield, Ray Brown, Ronnie Montrose, and dozens more. The record also became one of the first ½-speed mastered records issued. Edwards remembers introducing the iso-booth concept to crooner Mel Torme at CAM in the mid '70s, when it was still a relatively new idea. Meanwhile, back on Folsom Street, Coast Recorders continued to churn out its ad work. Its portion of the building included the smallish Studio C, a voiceover room, a combination edit/maintenance room, and offices. In 1976, they moved their entire operation to Mission Street. Atkins added studio manager to his duties. They operated in this capacity until 1989, when another owner took the reins. We'll return to CAM in Chapter 22.

A Private Fantasy

Fueled and funded primarily by Creedence Clearwater Revival's multi-Platinum record sales (total sales of over 100 million up to this point), the group's label at the time, Fantasy Records, expanded its catalog as well as its two-story building at 10th and Parker in Berkeley. They built an impressive in-house studio, nicknamed "The House That Creedence Built," and equipped it with DeMedio consoles for Studios A and B and an API in Studio C. They built the studio to accommodate their growing roster, which remained primarily and most successfully jazz, with adventures in rock, soul, and disco. Label president Ralph Kaffel negotiated the purchase of several jazz labels during the early '70s, including Prestige and its many subsidiaries, as well as Riverside and Milestone. The latter two were founded by producer Orrin Keepnews. (He launched Riverside with partner Bill Grauer.) Interestingly, Fantasy Records, one of the most prominent jazz labels in the U.S., would join forces much, much later with previously mentioned Concord Records. Details to come in Chapter 25.

The boost to the Fantasy catalog in the 1970s led to an extensive reissue program for the work of Miles Davis, Thelonious Monk, Bill Evans, John Coltrane, and the Modern Jazz Quartet, among others. At the same time, the label brought in Keepnews to oversee its expanded jazz roster. Anticipating an influx of musicians who often record live-to-tape, they built large recording spaces for each room, with Studio A offering the most square footage. (See Chapter 19 for specifics.)

By 1973, Cannonball Adderley had joined the Fantasy roster by way of Keepnews' Riverside label. Although Keepnews had produced dozens of albums for the legendary sax player, he gave the reigns for *Inside Straight* to Dave Axelrod. Keepnews then went about the business of organizing a special live-in-the-studio recording, giving the artist the benefit of Fantasy's exquisite acoustics, as well as the energy of an audience. "The particular bright spark of an Adderley performance always seemed to glow at its best when an actual audience is breathing (and hollering) around it," writes Keepnews in the album's liner notes. "So, why not bring the club to the studio?"

He goes on to describe the scene: "An overflow crowd of friends, well-wishers, Fantasy staff, a sprinkling of press and DJ representatives…and the expected quota of folks who just heard about the session. Fantasy's very large Studio A converted (by the addition of a band-stand, a public address system, tables and chairs, and a stocked bar with bartender) into one of the cleanest nightclubs you ever saw. I've previously noted that I had nothing to do with the record, but that isn't entirely accurate. Somebody had to supervise such vital creative functions as removing the dangerously fancy candles from the tables, substituting some standing room for some of the furniture, and keeping some of the too many people waiting patiently outside for a while."

Considering Fantasy's longstanding reputation as a premier jazz label, their success with Creedence seemed like a fluke. In a way, it was. Fantasy dabbled in media outside of the jazz genre, with mostly moderate success. Local stalwart Country Joe McDonald joined the roster in the mid-'70s and had a hit with an album called *Paradise with an Ocean View*. He also led a Country Joe & the Fish reunion album on Fantasy, which was a commercial disappointment. Other Bay Area acts to come on board at Fantasy included Terry Garthwaite, Toni Brown, and the Hoodoo Rhythm Devils. All of these acts achieved only moderate success. Fantasy worked with Stanley Turrentine, Patrice Rushen, and Bill Summers until other labels stole them away, and it assembled a quality group of soul acts, including The Blackbyrds, Pleasure, and Fever.

In this midst of these acts, disco pioneer Sylvester, who signed with Fantasy in 1976, shone like the big, bright glittery star he was. One of the most individualistic, talented, and successful artists to emerge from the dance/disco movement, Sylvester became a mega-star in his hometown first, adored not only in San Francisco's heavily gay Castro District but by the city at large. He was so special that then-mayor Dianne Feinstein declared March 11, 1979 (the date he recorded the *Living Proof* album, recorded live at a sold-out War Memorial Opera House), "Sylvester Day" in San Francisco.

He arrived in San Francisco from Los Angeles in 1967 admittedly to do nothing: take drugs, have fun, enjoy the lifestyle. Then he joined a transvestite cabaret act called The Cockettes and later signed with Blue Thumb as a solo artist and released three rock-leaning records. It wasn't until he teamed with producer Harvey Fuqua and joined the Fantasy roster in 1976 that he became king of the dance floor. His first album for the label, *Step II,* contained the A and B sides to his hit single, "Dance (Dance Heat)"/"You Make Me Feel (Mighty Real)," which certified Sylvester as one of the first disco stars. Playing synthesizers behind Sylvester's powerful falsetto was Patrick Cowley. Within five years, Cowley would team with Marty Blecman, an employee of Fantasy Records, to form Megatone Records, a small independent label taken under the wing of a well-known San Francisco producer who owned a very well-known San Francisco studio. We'll visit them in Chapter 15.

Through the 1970s, Fantasy Records held onto its reputation as one of the top U.S. jazz labels, and its studio evolved into one of the finest in the Bay Area. Keepnews continued to produce volumes of work during his tenure at the label, working on albums for Sonny Rollins and McCoy Tyner, among others, plus dozens of reissues. By 1977, he had become a VP and partner, but in 1980, Keepnews left the label to continue work as an independent producer. "By that time, I had discovered there was a limit on how long I could make myself work for someone else, even in the best of circumstances," he says. He would go on to found another label, Landmark, in 1984.

Meanwhile, Fantasy engineer Bruce Walford, who had worked with The Sons (and would again) before joining Fantasy, worked on reissue projects for Kenny Burrell, Cal Tjader and Bill Evans, among others. A young Phil Kaffel, son of label president Ralph Kaffel, had worked his way up from the warehouse to the control room and was mixing a Bill Evans album by 1977.

As the decade closed, Fantasy began construction on its building yet again; this time building up five more floors to accommodate its growing catalog and expanding its studios in preparation for a new phase in its business.

CHAPTER 13

Different Fur

A homegrown studio at heart, but on a larger and more professional scale, Different Fur grew to a fully functioning studio by 1971. This was due in part to cofounder Patrick Gleeson's reputation as a composer and synthesist and for having an attractive collection of rare synthesizers on hand. Through the years, the facility became a magnet for independent and independent-thinking artists who came for the equipment but came back because of the family feel and efficient service.

Gleeson had messed around with recording before Different Fur became a "serious" studio. In 1968, he quit his day job to pursue his first love: music. He had played piano since childhood and dabbled in music through the years, and he finally realized he would wind up a frustrated "angry alcoholic" if he didn't follow his true path. He had been experimenting with electronic music at the Mills College Tape Music Center (see Chapter 5) and gradually built a reputation as an electronic musician even though he had few professional musical credentials.

As the 1960s closed and free love blossomed, he and friend John Vieira came up with the idea to start a commune of musicians. They found a group of friends, including Gleeson's then-girlfriend whom he later married, Patty; Vieira's wife Susan, a harpsichordist;

and a couple of jazz musicians willing to join in. Everyone would contribute equally to rent, share meals, and live and work in the same space. "But we didn't all sleep together," laughs Gleeson. "We weren't *fully* hippies." The inaugural group assembled, Gleeson and Vieira sought and found a suitable space for their live/work activities: a three-story warehouse made of heart redwood in the Mission district of San Francisco. "In those days it was dirt cheap!" he says. "We paid $25,000 for the building. It had three floors, and each floor was about 1,875 square feet. The first two had 12-foot high ceilings, and on the top floor, the ceilings were about 20-feet high."

Now that they had a place, their confab needed a name. They found one with the help of beat poet/playwright Michael McClure. "I had assembled a collection of poems that [Charles E. Merrill] published as *A First Reader of Contemporary American Poetry* [1969] and wanted to put together a cassette of the poets reading their material," says Gleeson. "So Michael—a dramatic guy whose imagery was furs and jewels and female body parts and stuff—was in my kitchen one day when I was recording him for the project. I told him I was starting this recording studio, and he says, 'Well, what are you going to call it?' I said, 'I want a name that's really different.' And he says, 'That's a great name! Really different.' Then he looks out the window, reflecting, and says, 'Really different...fur.' Then 'Really different fur...trading company.' The rest of the commune didn't like the 'really.' Actually everybody but me and Michael hated the name, but we settled on Different Fur Trading Company."

Now they needed some business. Gleeson invested about $10,000 to enlarge Vieira's Moog synthesizer (one of the first in town) and started seeking session work. An ad agency hired Gleeson to produce music for a commercial. The first try sounded like a "dying whale." The second version won the company an advertising art directors' award. In 1970, Gleeson was hired to deliver a Mellotron to some of the Jefferson Airplane crew at Wally Heider Recording. "The Mellotron broke, as they were wont to do," he had said earlier, "so I suggested they use a synthesizer. 'A what?' they said." Gleeson brought in the Moog and ended up contributing tracks to Paul Kantner's *Sunfighter* and *Blows Against the Empire* projects. Gleeson soon found plenty of work for the developing studio.

Vieira and Gleeson started getting *really* serious about the studio at this point. Consequently, the commune disbanded. Plans involving hauling sheetrock and long days of manual labor didn't sound like much fun to the rest of the group. "John and I had such a strong vision of what was going to happen that we didn't understand that that wasn't everybody's vision," says Gleeson. "It was getting to be too heavy duty for most folks. But Patty [who managed the studio] and Susan were still on board."

They continued building anyway, fashioning a recording area and constructing their own console; Gleeson handled soldering, Vieira designed. The 16-in, 4-out console used Spectrasonics modules (not to be confused with today's sample library company). Bob Moog sold them a rare MRI (Magnetic Recording Industries) 8-track tape machine, reportedly the first servo-controlled tape recorder, which was, as Gleeson describes, "cheap and beyond unreliable. It was an invention of Bob's; eventually he built some of these for NASA. They went up in the early rockets and were used as logging recorders. We would want to record at 15 ips, but sometimes it would just take off at a different speed! A little later we bought a Scully 16-track." And they still had their old 8-track and the Moog as well.

By the time the studio officially opened, Gleeson had finished his work with Kantner and set his sights on Herbie Hancock, who had just signed on with David Rubinson for management and producing. Gleeson, a huge Miles Davis fan, began buttering up Rubinson to let him work with Hancock and invited Rubinson to see the studio. It took a few tries, but Rubinson finally accepted Gleeson's offer and sent Hancock over with the tapes of *Crossings*. Rubinson apparently told his client that Gleeson was more of a "knob-twister," but he could set up the Moog so that Hancock could play.

When Hancock showed up to Different Fur in 1971, tapes in hand, the two began talking about the sounds Hancock was looking for and where he wanted them in the tracks. Gleeson played a few parts that sounded interesting, so Hancock asked Gleeson to work out his ideas some more, and he would come back later to see how he was doing. "He didn't come back for two days and I didn't sleep for two days!" Gleeson says. "By the time he came back I had overdubbed the entire side of one album!" Three days later, Herbie brought him the other side of the album. Gleeson's work on that album essentially defined the jazz synthesizer sound, and he proceeded to tour and record with Hancock for two years.

Photo courtesy of Dr. Patrick Gleeson

Herbie Hancock (rear) and Pat Gleeson at work on Hancock's Sunlight *album at Different Fur, around 1975.*

Fred Catero, who engineered several Hancock albums, including *Crossings, Sextant,* and the groundbreaking *Head Hunters,* worked at Different Fur during its early years. He offers one side note about the studio, something he noticed before he ever stepped into the building. "The studio is in the back, so at the front door there was a button to push, and they'd buzz you in. Well, the buzzer was deep inside the wall, in a hole, and the hole was all covered in fur. The idea was to feel the fur, then all the way inside was the buzzer, but the fur had festered from moisture, so they had to *remove* the fur button!" Catero laughs. "I think it only worked for a month or two."

Gleeson breaks into a huge laugh when he hears Catero's story about the fur-encased door buzzer. He adds that the armrest of their custom console was covered in fur, too. "Until someone said, 'Hey isn't this how you generate static electricity, by rubbing on this?' Then we thought, 'Well, maybe this isn't such a good idea.'" The control room was completely covered in equally audacious red velvet. "It would exhaust you just to be in that environment," Gleeson says.

While Gleeson's touring and recording relationship with Hancock helped bolster both his career and the studio, it also marked the end of his partnership with Vieira. They were going in different directions. Gleeson had become fascinated with bringing avant-garde electronic music techniques to pop and jazz recordings. When Hancock fired his entire band, Gleeson poured himself into his own work, playing on nearly 100 records in one year, as well as arranging and/or producing a dozen or so albums and launching a solo career with Mercury Records. Throughout the ensuing years, he was involved in hundreds of other sessions as a synth sideman.

Photo courtesy of Dr. Patrick Gleeson

Pat Gleeson with his E-mu modular synth, reading the score for his solo album The Planets.

A few years into Different Fur, Gleeson became fascinated with acoustics, and determined that his 25×35–foot studio could sound better. He called John Storyk—then of Sugarloaf View Inc., now of Walters Storyk Design Group—for advice. Since Gleeson couldn't afford a complete Storyk workover, the designer agreed to put together sketches of the redesigned room so that Gleeson could do the work himself, which he did. "We ended up rebuilding the room three times while I was there, but we always retained Storyk's design."

Through the 1970s, the studio brought in a wide range of acts: Neil Young and Van Morrison hashed out ideas and recorded demos there. Album projects partially recorded at Fur include the Hancock releases, Con Funk Shun's *Love Shine* and *Candy*, Pablo Cruise's *A Place in the Sun*, and others from Dinah Shore, Stevie Wonder, and Patti Labelle. In between, Gleeson worked on his own projects.

By the late 1970s, Gleeson had replaced the custom console with a Harrison 4032 console that included Allison 65K Automation. He sold all of his analog synthesizers for a Synclavier, the first one in town. "I didn't want to keep relying on what I knew," he says. At this time, the 17×15–foot control room offered pairs of JBL 4310 studio monitors, Altec "Super Reds," Crown and Spectrasonics amps, and Auratones. Outboard gear expanded to include the EMT 240 Goldfoil Stereo Echo Chamber, AKG BX echo unit, an Eventide Harmonizer, and their recording options included both 16- and 24-track MCI machines.

Armed with the new automated console, Different Fur brought in clients from both in and out of the city. Akron, Ohio exports Devo came to the studio to record a couple songs that appeared on their Warner Bros. debut, *Q: Are We Not Men? A: We Are Devo!*, engineered and mixed by Gleeson. Al Di Meola came to Different Fur in 1976 to record parts of *Land of the Midnight Sun*. He had heard about the studio, but had never recorded there before. When he walked in, Gleeson says, he looked around and said, "Is this it? This is what I came all the way out from New York for?" Apparently, he expected something bigger.

The Harrison would come in handy again during the recording of Francis Ford Coppola's *Apocalypse Now* score, on which Gleeson served as lead synthesist and recorded all of his parts at his studio. (See Chapter 15 for more information on this project). At Different Fur, Gleeson used a 16-voice E-mu, a 4-voice E-mu, and two 10-voice Prophets tied together in a convoluted analog/digital setup for the project, while the other synthesists—Bernie Krause, Nyle Steiner, and Don Preston—used a mix of Moog and E.V.I. devices. "The beginning sequences, where the helicopters are flying over

Vietnam, those sounds were created by Pat's E-mu Synclavier," says studio manager Susan Skaggs, who came on board in 1977.

There was a point in this long, politically plagued project when Coppola asked Gleeson to mix the music for the film at Different Fur, much to producer David Rubinson's surprise. Rubinson, understandably, protested, arguing that the project needed an objective producer who could take all of the music composed at different studios by different people with different styles and make it sound cohesive. He did indeed mix the project in the end, at The Automatt, with Coppola and Gleeson at his side.

Patrick Gleeson

He hasn't necessarily received as much publicity as contemporaries such as Bernie Krause and Paul Beaver, but Pat Gleeson—or, Dr. Patrick Gleeson to be proper—was a synthesizer pioneer and helped bring the instrument more prominently into modern music, all the while carving out a successful career with the instrument as a sideman, solo artist, studio owner, and designer.

A late bloomer in some regards, Gleeson kept music as a hobby through his 20s and early 30s, choosing an academic path instead. He got his Ph.D and a job at San Francisco State College teaching English literature, which satisfied pretty much everyone else but Gleeson. In his spare time, though, he messed around with the Buchla synthesizer at the Mills College Tape Center and edited his 2-track tapes at home. He later gave a few concerts of his multi-channel tapes even though he considered himself an amateur, with no training in music theory or credentials as an artist.

As the 1960s came to a close, he quit his secure teaching gig to pursue music full time. He dove into his new trade. He teamed with friend John Vieira, who had a Moog, and together they began planning and building Different Fur. Meanwhile, Gleeson took the Moog about town for sessions. He composed music for an advertising agency; the first version bombed, but on the second go-around, Gleeson synthesized a small soul band, and the end result was deemed first-rate by the advertising community. He took the Moog to Wally Heider Recording for a couple of Paul Kantner's collaborative albums and took his ARP 2600 to various live dates, both of which stirred up interest in Different Fur. When Herbie Hancock walked in to work on his *Crossings* album, he not only used Gleeson's synth parts, but kept him around for *Sextant* and brought him into his touring band.

After two years with Hancock's band, Gleeson submersed himself in his craft yet again, playing on dozens if not hundreds of sessions through the years, including Lenny White, Julian Priester, Eddie Henderson, Narada Michael Walden, and Sammy Hagar.

He also continued to engineer and produce several projects, mostly at Different Fur, which he owned until 1985. He arranged and produced Gustav Holst's *The Planets* (which earned a Grammy nomination for Best Classical Album in 1976). He served as master synthesist for the *Apocalypse Now* soundtrack. He later produced an album for new wave band Crime, released a solo album titled *Rainbow Delta*, and engineered Devo's 1978 debut.

Now based in the L.A. area, Gleeson works as an arranger and studio designer, designing mid-level facilities—mostly in the $100,000 to $150,00 range, he says—suitable for the composer who works privately.

In the early 1980s, Gleeson's career continued to prosper, and his studio continually evolved to match the industry's rapidly developing technology. In 1980, much to his loyal clients' horror, he and Patty Gleeson put Different Fur through a complete acoustic and electronic redesign, with Patty Gleeson affectionately naming the revamped studio Super Fur.

Retaining Storyk's original design and adding one of his new concepts, the amped-up Fur featured Time Delay Spectometry and LEDE (Live End Dead End) construction, which reportedly eliminates sound coloration and phase cancellation so what is heard in the control room is the same as what is heard in the studio. The Gleesons redesigned the control room to make it more efficient, allowing the engineer to accomplish more tasks with minimal movement. Compressors and delay racks were mounted on movable racks that could be fanned out around the engineer's chair for easy access. Monitoring expanded to include three sets of speakers: JBL 4311s and 4313s and Auratones. They acquired a Lexicon 224 digital reverb unit (one of the hottest pieces of outboard gear at the time) and, inspired by The Automatt, headphones with individual studio cues. They boosted noise reduction to 28 channels each of dbx and

Dolby A and kept the Harrison console, Westlake monitors, and MCI tape machines.

Sound-absorbent material covered with grey fabric lined the studio walls—a big step up from the red velvet control room—while folding shutters scattered intermittently about the room added brightness if needed. The Gleesons also added private artists' quarters with full kitchen, showers, sauna, and a living area with beds. The entire renovation took a total of ten weeks and $150,000—more than triple the time and cost of what they had initially estimated. To compensate, Pat and Patty took on a lot of the work themselves, handling everything from basic wiring to woodworking.

The hard work obviously paid off, as Different Fur remained busy through the 1980s. Brian Eno and Kronos Quartet stopped by not long after the redesign, followed by Gene Clark, Phil Collins, return visits from Pablo Cruise and Con Funk Shun, The Whispers, Jonathan Richman, and many others. With a few exceptions, Different Fur didn't generally attract the "lockout" client. Those who visited Fur didn't always stay long, but they came back often, a good sign of a well-run operation. "It was more of a working-class studio, but some people liked it better for that reason," says Gleeson.

In 1982, they upgraded again by purchasing a Studer A80 24-track and A80 2-track, as well as a computer for the office. George Winston came in often during the 1980s, usually with producer/engineer Howard Johnston, who had become a regular visitor by this time. Under the Windham Hill label, located just a few miles south in Palo Alto, the artist-producer team recorded *Autumn, December, Summer, Winter Into Spring, Linus & Lucy: The Music of Vince Guaraldi,* and others. Johnston believes that the studio's Yamaha C7 grand piano lured label founder Will Ackerman to the studio, though it could have been the acoustics, which had improved greatly with the redesign. Others, such as Eno and David Byrne, who recorded *My Life in the Bush of Ghosts* at Different Fur, and local eyeball mask–wearing, synth-based group The Residents likely found the Synclavier and other electronic instruments attractive.

Early in his career and before the Oakland rap scene became nationally known, Too Short came over from Oakland to record some cassette demos that he could sell himself. Johnston helped him out. "They'd just roll in and plug in their synthesizers and drum machines, and we'd sit there and make music. They'd sell sometimes thirty to forty thousand out of their trunk. The whole genre was that way, before it got huge."

In 1985, Gleeson sold Different Fur to one of his most loyal clients, Johnston, and his equally loyal studio manager, Susan Skaggs. Skaggs had worked at both Wally Heider Recording and The Automatt before joining Different Fur, and she was ready for a step up. Gleeson, however, wanted to step out of the studio business. "It was interfering with my music," he says. "There aren't many things that I'm intensely interested in—my family and my music. I love composing, that's all I wanted to do. The business was distracting me. So to get into the composing business, I had to sell the commercial studio."

He got out for two-thirds of a million dollars. Johnston became head engineer, in addition to partner, and Skaggs became VP of the company. "We had a good CPA who helped us with our deals and found us an investor who leased us the console with no money down," says Skaggs. "Somehow we got everything with no money down—the building, the business, and the console."

Gleeson's lawyer thought he was nuts. "He said, 'Pat, you don't realize how important you are for the success of the studio. When you leave it's going to go downhill and the clients are all going to leave,'" Gleeson recalls. But he never doubted Johnston and Skaggs' ability, and it turned out that he was right. They never missed a payment. In an attempt to replace Gleeson's draw as a musician, Skaggs brought in Pete Scatturo as "resident synthesist," and Gleeson leased his Synclavier to him. He never missed a payment either.

Shortly after acquiring Different Fur in 1985, the new owners installed an SSL 4056 console; again, it was the first in the city. They also purchased one of the first ½-inch 2-track machines in the city, the popular mixdown machine in the 1980s. Their Lexicon 224 held title as an in-demand piece of outboard gear. They would later continue their trend of firsts with the first digital sessions with both 3M and Sony multitracks and the first Sonic Solutions workstation.

The studio also continued its trend of smart management with Skaggs, who some consider one of the best in the business. Her philosophy: "Never say no," as she said in a 1997 interview with *Mix* magazine. "And never give no for an answer —that's something I realized when I became an owner. If I had to rent a piece of gear, or I needed something and people told me they couldn't get it for me, I'd find a way to get it. And once you have that mind set, it's really not that hard."

Their business remained steady as a result, though competition was tough. Toward the end of the decade, Starship came in with producer Tom Lord-Alge to work on *Love Among the Cannibals.* At the end of the workday, Skaggs remembers grabbing drinks with some of the group at neighborhood bar, The Chatterbox. "Over the bar hung a petrified cat that the bar owner had found in the Presidio," recalls Skaggs. "It was everyone's favorite bar…and cat."

CHAPTER 14

Wally Heider Recording Hits Its Stride

As Jefferson Airplane transformed into Jefferson Starship, the various members occupied Wally Heider Recording to help Paul Kantner record his sci-fi Starship escapades and to crank out side projects from Grace Slick and from Jorma Kaukonen and Jack Casady's new band, Hot Tuna. They also brought in a smattering of new acts under the guise of their newly formed Grunt Records, a subsidiary of RCA. To accommodate the activity, Heider rushed plans to complete Studio A, designed to replicate a room he built at Bill Putnam's United Western in Los Angeles. It had a spacious isolation booth and the city's first Quad 8 console. It became Grunt Central for many years.

Hot Tuna's debut came out in May 1970, just before Grunt's formation, and was recorded in September 1969 at a Berkeley coffee shop called New Orleans House. Owsley Stanley ran sound at the club, and under his guidance, the band played two nights of old folk blues to tremendous response, with producer Al Schmitt brought in to produce for the pending live album. Thanks to an Owsley merry prank, he didn't get much producing done. "I got an apple juice at the bar, then I went into the [remote] truck to get my notepad and all of a sudden—wham!—the acid kicked in! He had spiked my apple juice!" Schmitt laughs. "I turned to [engineer] Allen [Zentz] and said, 'Allen—you're on your own,' and just sat back and enjoyed the trip."

The scene was no less sedate back at the studio, where engineer Fred Catero came in to engineer and co-produce, with Carlos Santana, Santana's landmark *Abraxas* album in 1970. Eric Clapton brought over his band, Derek and the Dominoes, to the studio to check out Santana. At night, with the lights dim and the band blowing off steam after the pressure of recording, they jammed on the blues even later into the night. Young guitar whiz Neal Schon was there, too; he'd often go into another room and play on his own while the band recorded, but when Clapton and crew showed up, he jumped right in with them. A couple of days later, Clapton invited Schon to join the group. A phenomenal opportunity, for sure, but he didn't really want to move to London. Luckily, he didn't have to. Carlos Santana invited him into his group's fold the next day.

Catero recorded Santana's rock, jazz, salsa, and blues concoction the way he usually does: with everyone in the same room and with very little use of gobos and/or isolation booths. As was typical of the '70s musician timetable, sometimes the band would show up an hour late. As was typical of the '70s recording studio, sometimes the heat didn't work. It was cold, which dragged down the session. Despite their virtuosity, not every session went smoothly, especially on cold days. Bassist David Brown might end up playing the same part over and over, hour after hour. No wonder they wanted to blow off steam at the end of the session.

For Catero, one of the most memorable and hilarious moments involving *Abraxas* happened after the album's release. He tells this story often, he says, and rightfully so. On a break from recording and touring, Jose "Chepito" Areas decided to fly home to his native Nicaragua. "He was going to bring money and a copy of the album for his family and money for the people in his village because he came from a poor village," says Catero. "So he boards the plane, and he's clutching this package with maybe a dozen LPs, wrapped in brown paper with tape around it, on his lap. The plane's getting ready to take off and the stewardess says, 'May I have your package?' He picks it up and holds it to his chest and says, 'Oh no, it's alright it's alright. I carry it, I carry it.' And she says, 'Well. I'm sorry sir, you'll have to either store it under the seat or on the overhead compartment.' 'Oh no it's alright. I'll hold it.' So she says, 'Well what's so important?' 'Oh…its dynamite!' She went away.

The plane turned around, went back to the hangar, the FBI came on board, and they hauled him off the plane with his little package! And when they opened the package they saw that it was just the records. He didn't speak English very well, he couldn't understand what the hassle was about! Bill Graham had to go down and explain to the FBI, 'Look, it's just a term we use…'"

The vibe shifted a bit down the hall in Studio D, as Cal Tjader and band set themselves up to record an LP for Fantasy Records. On one particular day, as reported in the November 8, 1970 *California Living* magazine, a supplement to the *San Francisco Examiner* and *Chronicle,* Tjader handed out sheet music for a particular song and let each musician know what he did and didn't want. "Baka-baka-baka-cheese," he chanted to drummer Dick Berk, explaining the kind of rhythm he wants. Burk nailed it, and Tjader moved to bassist Jim McCabe and conga drummer Michael Smithe, easing into a smooth sashay across the studio floor to describe the Latin feel he's going for. Engineer Russ Gary set up mics around the room while Fantasy producer Ed Bogus listened to Tjader's arrangements. Gary placed 10 mics around the drummer, the percussionists, and Tjader, while bass and electric guitar went direct. Once the band started playing, all written arrangements were ignored as Tjader moved into an improvised groove on the vibraphone. The band picked up on the melody, eased in behind Tjader, and together they performed a near-perfect first take. They ran through the track a few more times, and after Gary threaded a new reel of one-inch tape on the 8-track machine, Tjader and band launch into the track for real this time. They finished three or four tunes in four hours, on their first day, while Santana down the hall was still trying to get that bass part figured out.

After Tjader's swift exit, two landmark albums from late 1970 and early 1971, *American Beauty* by The Grateful Dead and David Crosby's *If I Could Only Remember My Name,* overlapped in Studio C, an arrangement that supported "cross pollination" between sessions.

Despite its high profile, the local music community remained small and close-knit. Schmitt witnessed this camaraderie during the recording of *Volunteers;* Bill Halverson and Stephen Barncard saw it during *Déjà Vu,* when all sorts of folks dropped by to hang out and help out in the studio. The ever-present Jerry Garcia even played steel, electric, and banjo on Kantner's 1970 epic *Blows Against the Empire,* which was recorded at Heider's with David Crosby adding guitars and vocals, Graham Nash adding percussion and vocals, and David Freiberg of Quicksilver Messenger Service singing backup. Kantner and Crosby later played with a spontaneous assemblage of Northern California rockers later called Planet Earth Rock and Roll Orchestra (PERRO), also the name of a widely circulated bootleg featuring rough mixes of their playing, many culled from the Crosby sessions.

But when it came time for the Dead to record *American Beauty,* their follow-up to *Workingman's Dead,* they hunkered down in Heider's Studio A with a veritable skeleton crew—the band, lyricist Robert Hunter, a roadie, and Barncard. Most of their extended family, including regular engineers Bob Matthews, Betty Cantor, and Dan Healy, were traveling across the U.S. on the Medicine Ball Caravan, a tie-dyed carnival of hippies and musicians who played free live concerts with a different act in each city—B.B. King, Joni Mitchell, and The Youngbloods among them. French filmmaker François Reinchenbeck directed the documentary about the tour, and Tom Wolfe wrote the book. The Grateful Dead had signed up as the house band, but the night before the entire entourage, including their sound company, Alembic, hit the road, they backtracked. They had a bunch of songs written and rehearsed, and they apparently decided they should get them down on tape while the inspiration was still high. This arrangement worked well for Barncard, who engineered and mixed the album, because he could work without interference from their watchful family.

The Dead, however, probably felt more stress than bliss at this time. They had just lost at least $150,000 to Lenny Hart, Mickey's father and the band's money manager, who skipped town with the cash. As a result, Mickey Hart left the band. Despite the loss of a lot of money and their drummer, *American Beauty* came together, well, beautifully. Call it a miracle, a burst of brilliance from principal songwriter Robert Hunter, a result of months of rehearsals, or a combination of all three, but when the band walked into Heider's Studio C, they had their act *together.* "It was unbelievable! They were like CSN," says Barncard, who had to prove himself to get the gig. "They came in completely because Heider's was the world-class room in 1970, and they were looking for a better bass sound. They said if I won over Phil [Lesh], I got the project." Lesh must have liked what he heard, because Barncard got the gig, and mixed the album back in Studio C on the DeMedio. He thinks that Garcia recommended him to David Crosby when it came time for him to record his solo debut in September 1970.

Though Crosby's painful memories of his late girlfriend Christine still haunted him (he would later dedicate the album to her), a more peaceful Crosby walked into the studio alone to record that album. During his first few sessions, Crosby sat in a chair, acoustic guitar perched on his lap, playing a batch of songs written during his most intense period of grief. Barncard and assistant Ellen Burke kept the tape rolling constantly. By this time, Barncard knew any little bit of offhand noodling could lead to something interesting.

"David made it easy for me by not working late," says Barncard, who worked from 10 a.m. to 6 p.m. mixing *American Beauty,* and from 7 p.m. until around 11:30 p.m. with Crosby, having a little dinner on the hot plate in between. "Sometimes it was just him, sometimes he'd bring a girlfriend, sometimes Nash would come by...It was so much more leisurely than *Déjà Vu* had been, which was a real pressure-cooker." The guest list grew during the recording process to include Garcia, Phil Lesh, Mickey Hart, and Bill Kreutzmann from the Dead; Grace Slick, Paul Kantner, Jorma Kaukonen, and Jack Casady from Jefferson Airplane; Gregg Rolie and Michael Shrieve from Santana; Frieberg from Quicksilver; Neil Young; and, up from L.A., former paramour Joni Mitchell. The album's beautifully recorded standout track "Laughing" features Crosby with Garcia, Lesh and Kreutzmann, and Mitchell in a brief cameo. "It was probably the most perfect record and recording situation that I've done," says Barncard.

With the 3M 16-track capturing every nuance, Barncard took a few risks on the record, like printing echo from the Heider chamber not only on Garcia's pedal steel but also on the guitars and other instruments. While many tracks happened quickly, which was

Crosby's preferred way of working, "Laughing" required a few run-throughs. "It wasn't one of those spontaneous tunes; it's one they had to work on to get it right because it has a few tricky changes in it. Garcia played very little on the basic track—just tiny little riffs because it called for that."

Stephen Barncard

A typical live setup for David Crosby when he played with San Francisco buddies Jerry Garcia, Phil Lesh, and Bill Kreutzmann.

Crosby's gorgeous vocals tumbled forth many times over. "He has such a great ear and he would just go in and sing a part, double it, maybe triple it, then do the next part and the next one," Barncard says. He kept each vocal stack on a separate track, which worked for most songs. Although on "Laughing," by the time Mitchell came in to sing on the bridge, Barncard had run out of free tracks, so "I punched in Joni's double of 'In the sun...' on one of Phil's two bass tracks for the duration of her part and compensated the level during the mix."

This ease of recording went on for months, until Crosby felt it was complete. "At that point we just pulled in all the rough mixes—some we used and some I redid—but he wouldn't let me spend much time on the mixes. 'That's good, that's good...we got it,' he'd say." Barncard mixed to a 3M ¼-inch 2-track at 30 ips and gave Crosby cassette mixes to listen to on the boat he stayed on in Sausalito. The ease that everyone felt in the studio translated to a classic for Crosby and a crowning achievement for Barncard. "Because [Crosby] had the freedom to record whatever he wanted," explains Barncard, "and because these songs wouldn't have had a place anywhere else but on this record."

Stephen Barncard mixing a David Crosby session, 1970.

Ellen Burke (Photo courtesy of Stephen Barncard)

After Crosby wrapped up this masterpiece, the New Riders of the Purple Sage recorded their self-titled debut, the first of three records they made at the studio, with Barncard. In 1972, Jerry Garcia holed up in Studio D to record *Garcia* with Bob Matthews and Betty Cantor. The solo album was a fringe benefit of The Grateful Dead's renegotiation with Warner Bros. (When they re-signed to a three-album deal, the label gave band members the opportunity to release solo albums.) Garcia played most of the instruments (acoustic guitar, electric guitar, pedal steel guitar, bass, piano, organ, samples, vocals), only bringing in bandmate Billy Kreutzmann for percussion enhancements and using Robert Hunter's lyrics. They wrote, recorded, and mixed the album all in Studio D in only three weeks. Like with CSN, the record light stayed on at all times during the *Garcia* sessions, which allowed Matthews and Cantor to grab some one-of-a-kind jams, especially on "The Wheel," which features some of Garcia's finest pedal steel work. "They were just groovin' on stuff, 20 minutes into it they were into this groove and Garcia turns around and says 'Okay Matthews, did you record that?' Of course. You always record. He came in, listened to it, and made some changes. During playback Hunter was there, and he was writing the words in his notebook on the wall because there wasn't enough room for him to sit down."

To ensure privacy, they hung a sign outside the Studio D door that read: "Closed Session: Anita Bryant." "And you know what?" Matthews says, "People really weren't that interested in finding out what an Anita Bryant session was like!" That sign probably played a big role in providing the creative space for Garcia to create an album from scratch in three weeks.

Jerry Garcia in Studio C, getting ready to record steel with New Riders, 1971.

Stephen Barncard

Other members of the Dead, both separately and together, continued to populate the studio. Weir's *Ace* album and the Dead's *Europe 72* followed, not to mention Crosby and Nash's first duo album, and the Doobie Brothers' hit album *Toulouse Street*, engineered by Barncard and Marty Cohn. Country-folk duo Brewer and Shipley came to record the follow-up to their smash *Tarkio Road* album, *Shake Off the Demon*.

Stephen Barncard

New Riders of the Purple Sage, posing for a publicity shot for CBS Records in Heider's Studio C. From L to R: John Dawson, David Nelson, David Torbert, Spencer Dryden, and Buddy Cage.

This just scratches the surface of the volume of projects that flowed through Wally Heider Recording in 1972, one of the studio's busiest time periods. Between major album projects, which dominated most of the time, myriad indie projects, one-offs, and demo deals of all genres—from belly-dancing music to ragtime to jazz—squeezed themselves into any block of time available.

At a time when what would later be called "classic rock" seemed to dominate Heider's smoky lair, Tower of Power's presence was a welcome change, especially for engineer Jim Gaines, a.k.a. "Memphis Slim." Gaines already knew these 10 blazingly talented Oakland boys from their time in Memphis, where he worked on their original demos. After signing with Warner Bros., the group recorded their debut, *Bump City,* in Memphis at producer Steve Cropper's studio... the one Gaines had just left less than a year before.

Engineer Ryan Capone did a fine job recording and mixing the large horn-driven group's first album, but the vocals on "You're Still a Young Man" needed a little bit more...*something.* Cropper called up Gaines at Heider's to remix the track out West, which he did, and the band loved the results. So when it came time to record their self-titled follow-up, they thought "Why should we all go all the way to Memphis to record when we've got Memphis sitting right here?"

If they wanted a taste of Memphis soul on their album, they could visit Memphis Slim just on the other side of the Bay Bridge. They could team with an engineer who had worked on some of the greatest songs to come out of Stax Records while they were still in raw form—an engineer who had a strong sense of R&B and the blues, and who would have the patience to go through two separate run-throughs, with two different bands, to record *Tower of Power*.

The original Tower of Power lineup rehearsed five days a week at a shared rehearsal hall in Berkeley, not far from their gritty Oakland home base. Bandleader/tenor sax man Emilio Castillo took special care with arrangements for this record, since it was his first album as producer. "When we rehearsed, everybody was there. We'd just start hammering at it. I was coming up with chords on guitar and finding ways to sing to the groove," said Castillo in a November, 2004 *Mix* magazine interview. "The horns were sitting around and somebody would come up with a lick; it was pretty much a group effort." Trumpeter and arranger Greg Adams played a key role in the arrangements, especially the voicing. The horn section and rhythm section merged on songs such as "What is Hip?" with machine gun–like trumpets hitting the up notes in unison with bassist Rocco Prestia, which gave their '70s funk and soul a more aggressive edge.

When the well-rehearsed ensemble showed up at Wally Heider Recording, Gaines had a hard time squeezing them in. With the studio still booked nearly round the clock, he often worked three sessions a day. Sometimes, Tower of Power couldn't even start until midnight or 1 a.m.—the earliest Gaines could get there.

Tower of Power embodies the tight, dry sound that became fashionable in the '70s. "In those days, we were making R&B records, which were either dry-sounding or had the Motown sound, which was all reverb—two totally opposite sounds," said Gaines in a November 2004 interview with *Mix* magazine. "On this record, we had reverb on the voice, but hardly any on anything else."

With the band on point and Gaines at the board, the recording proceeded smoothly...until about halfway through, when Warner

Bros. fired lead singer Rick Stevens, guitarist Willie Fulton, and saxophonist Skip Mesquite. They missed some gigs, which obviously didn't sit well with the label. Meanwhile, Gaines had a record that was almost done, but it had Stevens and the others all over it. What to do? To protect from possibly getting sued by an ousted musician, the label said to start over.

They brought in Lenny Pickett, who would later lead the *Saturday Night Live* house band, to play lead sax, Bruce Conte on guitar, and Lenny Williams on lead vocals. Chester "C.T." Thompson, who would become Carlos Santana's keyboardist/bandleader in the mid-'80s, also came in during the second round. "We started out with one killer band and went to another level with a second killer band," said Gaines. "But it took almost a year, because we recorded it twice."

Gaines mixed the album in Studio C, by hand, as automated consoles hadn't been invented yet. Not only did Gaines have his hands on the board, but the whole band had a chance to move a fader. "So you've got five guys at the console pushing faders up and down, with their little marks," Gaines said earlier, referring to a common dilemma that engineer Fred Catero calls "the great horse race." "By the time you get to the end of the mix, all the faders are wide open because everybody wants to hear more of their parts, and you've got to start all over. In those days, it was community mixing, and the more community got involved, the worse the mix got."

The community didn't do too much damage, because after two different lineups and a year in the studio, *Tower of Power,* released in 1973, became one of the best of their catalog. Another almost-finished master with the original lineup sits oxidizing in a tape vault.

Wally Heider Recording cruised into 1973 maintaining its active pace. By this time, the facility had expanded to four studios and a post-production room. More projects from Jefferson Airplane/Starship, Hot Tuna, and Pure Prairie League filled Studios A and D, while Commander Cody and other projects occupied Studio C upstairs.

Cross-pollination also continued at Heider's, and not only between the CSNY parties and the Dead. As was common in multi-room facilities, a musician from Studio A might strike up a conversation with a musician from Studio C during a smoke break, which might lead to an unplanned guest appearance or two later. For musician/producer Pete Sears, this sort of collaboration led to joining a whole new band.

In 1974, Sears co-produced Kathi McDonald's debut album, *Insane Asylum*, with David Briggs. "We were up in Studio D," he recalls, "and Herbie Hancock was down the hall, and Jorma Kaukonen was downstairs doing a solo album. When they needed a hand, all they had to do was put the word out around the building. There was this long section on the title track where we needed a male singer; they'd come out right at the chorus and Kathi would sing an answer. One vocalist we tried couldn't come out at the right spot, because there were no cues. Sly Stone was downstairs recording, and he came up and did it in one take! The Pointer Sisters sang backup, the Tower of Power horns played, and David got Nils Lofgren to come up and play on the album. There was definitely a good atmosphere at Heider's."

In the midst of all this activity, Grace Slick and some of the Jefferson Airplane parties worked on Slick's solo album, *Manhole*. "They asked me to sit down and play some piano," says Sears. "So I went into the studio and played some blues piano, and Grace wrote words on the spot." That led to the song "Better Lying Down." Not long after, Sears received a phone call from Slick and Kantner, who asked if he would join their new group Jefferson Starship. He signed on in 1974 and stayed with the group for 13 years.

David Schwartz joined the Heider staff as an engineer in '73. A few years later, he would put together a little music 'zine, a resource for musicians with listings of recording studios and articles about recording called *The Mix*, which would grow to become *Mix* magazine.

The engineering staff worked as fast as they could that year to turn out as many as 15 albums at the same time, while David Rubinson and Fred Catero took up residence in Studio A after officially saying so long to Pacific Recording. In rotation were Herbie Hancock's groundbreaking *Head Hunters,* the Pointer Sisters' first album, Lydia Pense and Cold Blood, the Hoodoo Rhythm Devils, and an album by Latin rock group Malo, led by Santana's brother Jorge.

The Rubinson-Graham-Rohan partnership had dissolved in November 1971 after a tumultuous two-year run. This led to the dissolution of The Fillmore Corporation and its two labels, Fillmore and San Francisco Records. During the labels' existence, Graham had his hands full with concert promotion and his other already established ventures, including management and booking, thus he had little time to devote to the venture. But Rubinson poured himself into the label: He set it up from scratch, bought the desks, hired the staff, and signed the talent. He ran the show, but Graham erroneously thought he could run Rubinson. Big mistake. The laws of physics clearly show that it's *opposites* that attract and that forces of similar ilk, like the north poles of two magnets or two Type-A personalities, will always resist each other.

"Bill Graham wasn't somebody who had partners. He had slaves or he had enemies," says Rubinson. "And I'm not a slave and I'm a very bad enemy. When we weren't in business together we got along great, but he was difficult to deal with as a peer." The breaking point came when Graham wrote Rubinson a salary check for zero because he disagreed with some minor studio expenses. "I had two children by that time. My daughter had just been born and he was fucking with me, and I wasn't going to let that happen."

The year before The Fillmore Corporation dissolved, Rubinson signed the Pointer Sisters. He bought their contract from Graham and took over the publishing company in exchange for his company stock and reimbursement of funds that he had invested in the company to keep it going. He moved downstairs from Graham into his own office at 1550 Market Street and formed David Rubinson and Friends in January 1972. Not long after, Malo's self-titled debut reached Number 14 on the Pop charts launched by the hit single, "Suavecito."

The Pointer Sisters' Rubinson-produced 1973 debut climbed to the top of the R&B charts, fueled by their Allen Toussaint cover "Yes We Can Can." Rubinson's career soared from this point forward, and the Pointer Sisters came along for the ride for six good albums.

The Pointer Sisters' vocals were the lead instrument of the group. They drove the band; they formed the orchestra. With this in mind, Rubinson and Catero recorded "Yes We Can Can" sparsely: bass, drums, and guitar behind their classic four-part vocal harmonies. Anita recorded her lead vocals first, "terrific, as always," says Rubinson. "She was relaxed and related to the mic beautifully."

They recorded complete takes live with the band, doing small fixes later if necessary. "The flow was more crucial than any note-by-note perfection," he says. "Toward the end, I brought in Willie Fulton from Tower of Power to put his signature guitar on the track. It was an obvious hit. As always, when it's right, it's easy."

Things weren't always so easy for the Pointer Sisters. Ruth, Anita, June, and Bonnie, who grew up in Oakland in a strict household and learned how to sing in the Baptist church, first encountered Rubinson in 1970. They called him in the middle of the night from Houston, where they had been left stranded by an unscrupulous promoter/boyfriend. They asked Rubinson for enough cash to get back to the Bay Area. Rubinson only knew them from his recording work with them as background vocalists but sent them the needed funds anyway. He then promptly signed them up with AFTRA (American Federation of Television and Radio Artists), the union for backup singers. Not long after, the sisters launched a promising career beginning with Sylvester and then backing everyone from Elvin Bishop to Cold Blood.

In 1971, they signed their management deal with Rubinson's and Graham's Fillmore Corporation and recorded a couple of lack-luster R&B singles for Atlantic. Once re-situated with Rubinson's own company, they signed with the Blue Thumb label and recorded their 1973 self-titled debut, beginning in Pacific Recording in San Mateo and finishing in Heider's Studio A. "These were very talented and unique people," says Rubinson. "They were not brainwashed by ghetto radio. They were very free people, so the concept was to take this freedom in a totally different direction [than Atlantic had]. To help them find their voice was really something challenging and wonderful."

That same year, Herbie Hancock would revolutionize music and music recording with the jazz fusion finery on *Head Hunters*, the biggest selling jazz album of all time in '73, recorded mostly in Heider's Studio A. Rubinson first worked with Hancock in 1970, when Warner Bros. hired the young producer to bring forth a "commercial" album for Hancock, who had just joined the roster a year before. The label knew Rubinson mainly through his Columbia successes and thought Rubinson would deliver some Hancock hits. What they got was a three-song album of experimental brilliance called *Mwandishi*, recorded in Heider's Studio C. The album contained the 13-plus minute "Ostinato (Suite for Julia)," with a funky bass line and 15/4 rhythm, and "You'll Know When You Get There"—both Hancock compositions—and the 21-plus-minute "Wandering Spirit Song," written by trombonist Julian Priester. "It was a very noncommercial record but very exciting," says Rubinson. "It broke totally new ground and had two drummers—a jazz drummer and a funk drummer—Ronnie Montrose on guitar, and [Santana percussionist] Chepito all playing on the record. Really great stuff. But when Warner heard it they were really upset! They expected me to turn in a commercial record. They didn't know that I would help Herbie do whatever he wanted to."

Rubinson knew that for Hancock to realize his full potential, he needed the freedom to improvise with his band in the studio. "Most of the time he would spend a couple of hours just noodling," says Catero, who has worked on many Hancock's albums, including *Mwandishi*. "When he finally got it all together, the band would come in, and he'd lay out the structure of the song and the chord changes and they'd just jam. His philosophy for doing material was 'Just roll the tape and I'll edit it down to tune-length later.' So many times he'd start playing and say to me, 'Tell me when we're running out of tape. Give me a sign and then we'll put a tag on it so we'll have an end. But we won't play the song the way it's going to be on the album, we'll just play.'" Sometimes he would play tracks, but without a melody. Sometimes a melody would surface, but no form. Sometimes Herbie would play first, other times the band would get going first. "What you didn't want to do with Herbie was limit," says Rubinson. "Just go. We'll figure it out later." Hancock worked in this Zen fashion on most of his albums, while Catero got it all on tape.

Rubinson and Hancock would spend hours giving structure to a piece of music, listening to tracks, copying some sections, reinserting others. As one would expect, *Head Hunters* happened in a completely different manner. "*Head Hunters* was very much a live recording," says Rubinson. "We had set up a group of live shows in L.A. and S.F., and the music coalesced there, then we recorded it in the studio with everyone playing live."

Hancock's heavy involvement in the editing and mixing process began when he teamed with Rubinson in 1970 (he only rarely attended mixes before that), a time when most artists did not have, or were not permitted to have, any involvement in post-production. Especially in jazz circles, artists would spend a day or two recording their parts and leave, never knowing how the finished product would sound. The glass walls between the artist, producer, and engineer was coming down, though, and Hancock's proactive nature spearheaded this new level of collaboration in the industry. "Herbie was such a genius, both technically and creatively," says Rubinson. "He got it right away. He realized that the mix is when you knit it all together." With *Head Hunters,* jazz and rock combined in a way that the public hadn't heard before, which subsequently led to a new level of production in jazz. "A lot of the rock musicians—the white musicians—had the ability to control their recording, and the black guys didn't," says Rubinson. "They'd still come in and record with the white engineer and the white producer and [after a session] they'd say, 'See you later.' With Herbie's recordings, everybody was in it. He wanted the best technical equipment. He didn't want to be stuck in the back of the bus. And he was really involved in the mixing and everything else, which changed his music and changed the way music was made."

They combined traditional recording equipment (considered "vintage" now) and new technology on *Head Hunters*. Catero used Heider's echo plates and tube gear, while Hancock brought in one of the first drum machines and synthesizers. He liked to record them in the control room, which was another first. (See "Sources and Recommended Reading" for a book on this groundbreaking album.)

As 1973 came to a close, the buzz on Wally Heider Recording began to dim a bit. Jim Gaines was burned out after working 24/7 for three years in S.F. He moved to Seattle to work for Kaye Smith Studios, owned by actor Danny Kaye and Lester Smith, who also owned Concerts West Promotions, one of the largest concert promoters in the world. He would return to the city a few years later, but his days as a Wally Heider staffer were over for now. Likable studio manager Mel Tanner left the same year, replaced by Ginger Mews, while Nina Bombardier (then Nina Urban), who would go on to manage The Plant and Fantasy Studios, came on as receptionist. The oil crisis, the recession, and rising unemployment in 1973 and 1974 affected every industry in America, including the music industry, which subsequently tightened its recording budgets. In addition, new arrivals such as The Record Plant in Sausalito posed very real competition for Wally Heider Recording for the first time. The days of solid, 'round the clock recording at Turk and Hyde had passed, and in order to stay in the game, they had to revise their strategy.

By 1974, Wally Heider's San Francisco studio desperately needed an upgrade. Studio B upstairs had sound leakage problems, and served as not much more than a game room and lounge. The other three studios, as well as the newly created Studio E media room, maintained business as usual; Santana recorded their *Amigos* album in Studio A, and Rubinson continued to use the room whenever he could get time.

The Record Plant was in full swing over in Sausalito, much to Heider's chagrin, as he came so close to opening his own Marin County studio. The Record Plant, with their nice furniture, hot tubs, and 24-track tape machines, stole a lot of Wally Heider Recording's thunder. The San Francisco bands that still had record deals had many more options if they wanted to record in their hometown. Pat and Patty Gleason's Different Fur offered a homey urban retreat; Fantasy Records had its own studio since 1971, so all of its business stayed in-house. The Grateful Dead, who had spent seemingly all of their off-road time at Heider's either recording, mixing, or collaborating with friends, had their own project studios to work in, including the impressive Marin County home studios of Mickey Hart and Bob Weir. Beginning in 1977, the Dead had their own warehouse studio in San Rafael, Le Club Front (it was on Front Street in the Canal District), equipped with a Neve 8058, a Studer 16-track, and scads of outboard gear.

Heider's L.A. facility continued to run strong, and the man himself still had a reputation for running technically top-notch studios, but problems arose when he went to the parent company, Filmways Pictures, for more money. By the mid-'70s, 24-track recorders had become a requirement for the larger studios, and facilities without them faced either lost business or rising machine rental expenses. When he asked Filmways for the funds to upgrade his San Francisco studios from 16- to 24-track, they refused. "It was just the great, classic case of a corporation taking over just to gain something, but not to put anything back," reported former staff engineer Jeffrey Norman. Maintenance engineer Harry Sitam added, "The [Filmways] manager would not allow me to buy parts to maintain the equipment even up to basic NAB specifications." But Heider didn't work that way. This was the man who loaned Al Schmitt his car when he was in town to record Jefferson Starship. This was also the man who infamously told Ginger Mews that if a client came into the studio and said, "Lie down, Ginger, so I can walk on you," then she had better lie down! Sure, he had quirks—he stuttered when he got nervous; he had an unpredictable temper and would often fire and re-hire people the same day; he intimidated his green assistant engineers—but he always put the client first and because of that and because of his talented staff, his studios had a warm, festive, adventurous atmosphere. In terms of technical standards, he raised the bar in San Francisco when he opened in 1969. So Filmways' refusal of a necessary technical upgrade didn't go over very well. This understandably bothered Heider, so he reportedly maneuvered his way into getting fired by Filmways. He even bought a full-page ad in *Hollywood Reporter* that stated "I Was Fired!" in big bold letters.

He then threw a giant going-away party for himself, flying a handful of his San Francisco crew—the ones still around—to Los Angeles for a huge dinner and celebration. Soon after, he moved to his native Oregon to live a quiet life away from the recording business. While Filmways didn't share Wally Heider's passion for the San Francisco studio, great music continued to happen from within those isolated walls.

Jefferson Starship officially formed in 1974, retaining remnants of Jefferson Airplane—Paul Kantner on rhythm guitar and vocals, Grace Slick on lead vocals, David Freiberg on vocals and keys, Papa John Creach on electric violin, and John Barbata on drums—with some newer additions. They brought in Craig Chaquico, who had played on a Slick-Kantner duo album, on lead guitar and Jorma's brother Peter Kaukonen on bass. Kaukonen didn't work out, so they invited Pete Sears, with whom they had worked on Slick's *Manhole* album. Together, this newly formed combo entered Wally Heider Recording's Studio A to record *Dragonfly* with producer/engineer Larry Cox.

Sears recalls that most of the band members contributed material to the album. He and Slick wrote "Hyperdrive" together. He remembers the mood: "We had the lights down, and Paul would have his little table with tablecloth and candles burning. Everybody had their thing, their studio routine." Unlike some of the Airplane sessions, they cut most of the tracks together, getting as much as they could on tape during the initial two weeks of tracking, then spending their overdub time mainly on vocals.

Rubinson and Catero continued to hold court in Studio A. In 1975, the Pointer Sisters returned for *Steppin'*, recording a fine mix of danceable funk and R&B with a stellar team of guest players, including Herbie Hancock, Stevie Wonder, Taj Mahal, guitarist Wah Wah Watson, and some of Hancock's touring band.

"It shows everything these talented artists could do," says Rubinson of the album, which reached Number 3 on the R&B charts. Just as the album featured an amalgam of funk, jazz, R&B, and blues, it also benefited from a variety of production and studio techniques.

"At Heider's, we laid down a very simple track for 'How Long (Betcha Got a Chick on the Side)': drums, bass, maybe rhythm guitar, very spare," Rubinson says. "The Sisters sang *live* in the studio with the band. I always did this on vocal records, and even with jazz records. The synergy was the most crucial element. We laid simple tracks to give them as much room as possible to create, plus to make sure we had tons of space for interactive background vocal parts and room for leads and background parts to expand and synergize. Anita sang the lead, the others sang backgrounds, and we had a blast with it. The recorded version went on for maybe 10 to 15 minutes! We never did repeated takes. We'd rehearse, get comfortable, and go. It was free and open. Then I would edit the track for the best creative parts, and then we'd go back in and re-do the lead and background vocals where needed. After that we would think about adding things, if at all."

"Sleeping Alone" would not have happened in such a special way if it weren't for some very efficient people in Rubinson's office. He was down in L.A. with Hancock when he received a message from his San Francisco office that Stevie Wonder had called. When he returned his call, Wonder said that he wanted to come up to S.F. to record some songs he had written for the Pointer Sisters. "When?" Rubinson asked. Wonder replied, "How about three o'clock?"

"You mean *today*?"
"Yeah."

"I grabbed Herbie," Rubinson recalls, "and we flew up to S.F. My office people got the studio and the other musicians and the Sisters together, and we had tape rolling by five p.m. What a session! We had Stevie and Herbie on keyboards *together!* Standing in the studio in the middle of this was one of my most memorable moments."

After all of that rushing around to accommodate Wonder, he didn't actually have *complete* songs written when he showed up; just a hodge-podge of riffs, ideas, and a few bass lines and chords. "He would start playing a groove, or a melody or a riff, Herbie would check it out, and something would start happening," says Rubinson. "But for some reason, Stevie's 'phones went out. This was common then. So he yells out, 'Hey, I can't hear my piano in my 'phones!' I couldn't hear him, and the engineers in the booth didn't, either. So he says louder, 'Hey, I can't hear my piano in my 'phones!' Again, we couldn't hear him. So then he says, 'Well, I'll just *pretend that I can.*' Such a profound statement, really. It says, 'The hell with letting the technical shit become crutches instead of tools. We run the technology.' And, most crucially, 'I know what the hell I'm playing, and I can hear it in my head anyway.' We cut three tracks, but they had no titles, no lyrics, no real form, they were just tracks of music. So, we had to get a basic concept for the title and create a song form from the fragments and pieces we had. That meant we had to experiment with rough stereo mixes of all the music and with different forms. Then we spliced it for hours into a few plausible song forms. The Sisters wrote a song that fit the track, called 'Sleeping Alone.' So then I had to splice the 2-inch multi-track tape to re-create the song form we used on the multi. Then we could record vocals. Every splice was tedious, but we got it done, finally. And the synergy is still terrific. Not precisely simultaneous, but palpable."

The Pointer Sisters continued with Rubinson through *Having a Party,* recorded in L.A. in 1975 and released in 1977. At that point, the group's new attorney, Jim Walsh, fired Rubinson. The next Pointer Sisters album, *Energy,* out in 1978 and produced by Richard Perry, gave them another Top Ten album and the Number Two hit "Fire," which finally put them over the edge into pop's mainstream.

Back on the operations side of Wally Heider Recording, a light bulb went off in the Filmways brain. With the departure of Mel Tanner and now Heider himself, they realized the studio probably needed someone to oversee the business. Their choice, an L.A. cat named Gary Blum, didn't gel with the others on staff. As engineer Susie Foot recalled in an earlier interview, "He dripped L.A., and this guy heading up a bunch of San Francisco hippie engineers was just ludicrous."

In response, the S.F. Filmways/Heider staff joined forces to try to send Blum back to L.A. and presented a petition to the Filmways execs signed by both studio employees and clients, including engineer Pat Ieraci and producers David Rubinson and Skip Drinkwater, among others. Blum didn't budge. When staffers

Sitam, Michael MacKenzie, and Gray Odell threatened to quit en masse, Filmways finally rectified their blunder and fired the short-lived studio manager.

Apparently, they had no trouble firing an employee but they still wouldn't spend money to upgrade the studio. David Rubinson and Fred Catero had asked for a few simple modifications to the control room, none of which ever happened. Rubinson even offered to do the upgrades himself, including putting in a new console and machines, for a long-term lease on Studio C. They still refused. This ultimately suited Rubinson fine. By 1975, he had realized he needed his own studio anyway, and promptly found it—on the opposite side of Market Street—at CBS/Columbia Studios. We covered its early years in Chapter 10, and we continue its story in the next chapter.

CHAPTER 15

The Automatt: The Next Cycle

When the Columbia Recording studio complex in San Francisco ceased operation in late 1977, Columbia Records shut the door on both The Automatt and Rubinson's ability to produce. It didn't matter that they had a long relationship. He and Roy Segal, who ran the studio, had worked together off and on since before 1966; Rubinson had produced several hit albums for Columbia and leased a year's worth of studio time. Columbia's studio operations had serious problems, and the hot producer operating his own studio in the back was of less importance than the urgency to close the studio and cut their losses.

During their six-year stay in San Francisco, the studio never did break even, despite the label's efforts to boost business by funneling in Columbia acts from New York and L.A. There were many reasons for Columbia's inability to thrive in San Francisco. For one, the union shop had about 20 people on payroll, which sent their expenses through the roof. (Most high-end facilities at that time had about half that many employees, if not fewer.) Increasing competition from independent studios also contributed to their decision to forsake the S.F. studio business. They had studios all over the U.S. and essentially wanted to be out from under the uncompetitive union contracts. As these contracts lapsed, they closed the satellite studios one by one.

New York, Nashville, Los Angeles, Chicago, and San Francisco were all shuttered in a matter of years, though L.A. and New York would open and close a couple more times. The Automatt wasn't part of the union, so Rubinson asked Segal if they could stay. Nope. Columbia closed, leaving most of the equipment inside, all part of the lease they held with the godfather of audio himself, Bill Putnam. Columbia's San Francisco engineers were locked out of the studio; naturally, they protested and picket lines ensued. Columbia artists could not record anywhere in San Francisco until the issue was solved.

Backed into a corner, Rubinson consulted with Putnam, who still held the lease on the building's office space and Columbia Studios' recording spaces and equipment, for advice on how to proceed with The Automatt. "These corporate [*$%**] are screwing us both. What do we do?" Rubinson said. Putnam, ever the wise businessman, and one who didn't want to lose money either, responded, "We're going to stay open. I'm going to leave everything right there. And you're going to pay me a monthly amount and we're going to operate. There's no way we're going to let these guys do this."

But Rubinson didn't really want a multi-room facility. He wasn't interested in the business of running a studio; he just wanted a nice place to create. Rubinson, one of the top independent record producers in Northern California mulled over the idea. He could hire some second engineers and rent out the other studios. Plus, inhabiting the entire large, multilevel building would give him more synergy between his management, publishing, and other business ventures and the creative side. He took the place lock, stock, and barrel.

The Automatt opened in full-blown fashion in 1978, replacing a corporate, union-regulated atmosphere with a grown-up playground, a creative environment for all types of music, from the fledgling grassroots labels to top-of-the-line talent, and it operated at a level that San Francisco proper had yet to experience. Just as Rubinson had a gift for spotting raw musical talent, he spotted similar potential in his engineers and staff. Aside from having Catero, one of the industry's best engineers, as his lead man, he assembled a solid team of second engineers who would go on to achieve amazing success in their field. Leslie Ann Jones came first, followed by

Ken Kessie, Chris Minto, Maureen Droney, and later David Fraser, John Nowland, and Michael Rosen.

Mike Larner, who had worked at both Golden State Recorders and Columbia Studios, acted as chief engineer initially, and Mike Fusaro served as maintenance engineer. After Larner's departure, Fusaro became chief engineer, and stayed for most of The Automatt's history. Vince Caspar assumed the maintenance engineer role. Rubinson brought back Phil Brown and Paul Stubblebine to work in the mastering department; both of them had mastered dozens of Rubinson productions on Columbia's payroll. Brown soon took a job at Warner Bros. in L.A., but Stubblebine stayed for the entire Automatt lifespan. Rubinson's long-time secretary Gail Brodkey managed The Automatt for its first few years, followed by Michelle Meisner for a brief stint, then Michelle Zarin, who came to The Automatt from The Record Plant in 1981.

The Automatt's original Studio C remained essentially the same, with its automated Harrison console. Studio A, a fine-sounding Bill Putnam–designed room previously held close to CBS's chest, was upgraded with a Trident TSM console (40-in, 32-out, 32-monitor) equipped with the Allison 65K Automation system. Its recording area, at 1,500 square feet, was the largest in town. The smallest studio, Studio B, originally contained a custom Columbia console, but in 1980, Rubinson replaced it with an MCI.

Though technically advanced, the studio felt more intimate than clinical, with décor that reflected Rubinson's tastes and personality. His extensive collection of colorful vintage Wurlitzer jukeboxes lined the facility; they had been provided by his antique jukebox company Judith's Jukes, named after his daughter. He owned every model of antique Wurlitzer ever made and filled them with cool vintage 78s. The vending machines sold cigarettes, candy, and sodas at cost, much to the delight of the neighboring businesspeople, especially Studio Instrument Rentals (S.I.R.) across the street. The smell of freshly popped popcorn wafted through in the afternoon, and in the evenings, clients such as Con Funk Shun would often bring in their friends and family for huge feasts provided by a staff chef.

The Automatt's Studios B (above) and C. Note Studio C's Allison 65K Automation System, interfaced with a Zilog Z-80 computer system.

Photos courtesy Kaz Tsuruta Photography

The headquarters for Rubinson's other businesses, which included management, publishing, and production companies under the umbrella name David Rubinson and Friends, occupied the much of the second and third floors. Francis Ford Coppola's American Zoetrope had moved to Columbus Tower when Rubinson took over the Automatt building; Coppola's large office became Rubinson's large office. There was even room up there for a spacious rehearsal studio where Coppola's screening room had been. Rubinson's baseball uniform collection was up there and loads of Brooklyn Dodgers' memorabilia: autographed baseballs from the '50s, Dodger yearbooks, and a classic pennant. Worn Persian carpets rested next to a floor mat that read, "Feets Don't Fail Me Now." Crayon drawings from his two children hung on the wall next to Gold and Platinum albums from Herbie Hancock,

Santana, the Pointer Sisters, The Chambers Brothers, and many others. A wine connoisseur and season-ticket holder to the San Francisco Symphony and Opera, Rubinson would uncork a bottle from his personal collection after 5 p.m. on Fridays.

David Rubinson with two of his vintage Wurlitzers.

Yes, The Automatt was Rubinson's playground, but he had no problem sharing his toys. The Meters, Santana, Journey, Patti Labelle, Huey Lewis and The News, Wynton Marsalis, Jaco Pastorius, Wayne Shorter, and Herbie Hancock all paid their respects in the early years, as did folks such as New York producer Sandy Pearlman (Blue Oyster Cult, The Dictators, and Dream Syndicate), who brought in The Clash in August 1978 to finish their second album, *Give 'Em Enough Rope*. That the band had teamed with a "hard rock" producer caused a minor uproar in the punk community. They started the album in London, but Pearlman felt there were too many interruptions, including the band's constant fighting with their manager, Bernard Rhodes, and the filming for drama/documentary/concert film *Rude Boy* in which the band starred. For about a month, the film crew would show up in the studio with their cameras and bright lights, subsequently cooking guitar strings and ruining most of the work done that day. Needing to get out of England and get some proper work done, guitarists/vocalists Joe Strummer and Mick Jones and Pearlman finished the record during a three-week overdub session at The Automatt.

"I recorded part in San Francisco because it was very cheap and The Automatt is the best-sounding studio that I knew of in the U.S. I felt it was the best studio to do the guitar overdubs," said Pearlman in an earlier commentary. He got particularly good results on "Guns on the Roof." "Joe Strummer broke a blood vessel in his mouth because he sang with so much passion. At the end of one of the takes, he said, 'I got blood in me mouth,' and so I kept that and used it on the final mix of the song. At first he didn't think it was a good idea. I don't know why; I thought it was amazing. Given the revolutionary rhetoric that is the content of the song, I thought it was pretty cool to bust a blood vessel singing! The point is he worked so hard, taking things to the extreme, that there was a lot of extreme raw material to utilize." The Automatt itself even spawned some ideas during the band's three-week stay. One of the jukeboxes had the Bobby Fuller Four's "I Fought the Law." The band liked the song so much, they made it one of their own.

The band also played pranks, such as demanding that Muff Winwood, then head of A&R for CBS in the U.K., send them a copy of the film *Battle of Britain*. If he didn't, they would come after him. They got the film and played it on the studio wall while they worked. "There were just things that never ever, even in some dream state, were going to happen again because they and the Sex Pistols kind of ruled Western Europe for, like, 18 months, and they could pretty much do whatever they wanted and say whatever they wanted," Pearlman stated. "This was a time when artists actually had an ideology."

In 1979, folk songstress Joni Mitchell joined Herbie Hancock for a rehearsal session in Studio C, as Ken Kessie, assigned to record the performance, recalls. "Joni was at the peak of her career then, and I was nervous as hell," he says. "She showed up late, razor thin, all cheekbones and nerves. She was as shaky as I was, not used to Herbie or jazz or compromise. She chain-smoked, turning the studio blue with her smoke and sad refrains. By night's end she and Herbie had arrived at some delicate and touching arrangements. I heard the concert [a benefit for the Bread & Roses foundation held at the Greek Theater in Berkeley] was smash."

The Automatt also became headquarters for one of the most renowned, time- and content-intensive music projects to come through San Francisco and arguably one of the most important pieces of modern filmmaking and scoring: Francis Ford Coppola's *Apocalypse Now.*

Former 829 Folsom occupant Coppola brought Rubinson into the fold in 1979 to produce the music for the project, after rejecting most of the music made by composer David Shire and L.A.–based electronic music and production company Sound Arts. The company had started the project in 1977 with costs totaling approximately $100,000. Composing, scoring, recording, and mixing consumed the last seven months of the film production. Rubinson used three studios simultaneously—The Automatt, Different Fur, and Richard Beggs' Zoetrope—as well as hiring four synthesists, a pianist, plus subscore percussion composers Mickey Hart and Airto Moreira (who worked from The Grateful Dead's Front Street studio), guitarist Randy Hansen, and various other associates.

Francis asked his father, Carmine Coppola, who had won an Oscar for his score for *The Godfather* and had composed music for some of the original cues, to compose the entire score. He chose Carmine not just because of the family bond, but because of his pedigree as a Julliard grad and flutist for the New York Philharmonic for 18 years. The Coppolas also shared a devotion to composers, many of them opera composers, who formed the key creative inspiration for the music. Most importantly, Francis Ford Coppola had an atypical vision for this film and needed to align with others who could see it, too. He and Carmine conceived of an overall "sound design" with brilliant innovator Walter Murch. They heard all aural aspects of the film integrating with one another; helicopter rotors transformed into a subsonic basso continuo, machine gun sounds as rapid-fire percussion, the whine of the bullets playing a secondary melody, and acid-crazed rock and roll from an old FM radio jamming with a savage light show of bombs and rockets. In order for the music itself to fuse Western symphonic and operatic traditions with cutting-edge electronics—classical melodic ideas with avant-garde New Music concepts—the only solution was to perform the entire score totally on electronic music synthesizers. A psychedelic guitar score (Hansen) and an intricate percussion score (Hart and Moreira), both improvised, as well as source music ranging from Wagner to The Doors, would supplement the all-synth score.

Rubinson's mission was to create a synthesized score that would blend with the already existing sound effects, dialog, and narration and fit it all together like a tapestry. "It was low-tech back then," Rubinson says. "We had no SMPTE." In a 1980 interview with *Modern Recording,* Rubinson noted that the sound effects alone involved thousands of loops. For premixes, they used 68 channels, each with at least 75 different events on them. Track sheets were 20 feet long and taped onto the floor of the studio. Somehow, the music had to interact with all of that. Rubinson and Coppola pegged synthesizers as the best tool for the job.

"They are the only instruments that can make the transition from total musicality, all the way to machine gun and bullet sounds, without any loss of musicality," Rubinson told *Modern Recording.* "Francis's concept was that the whole movie had to be organized like a big band, and everybody got his solo. Sometimes it's a solo for an actor, sometimes a synthesized trumpet."

To tackle the project, Rubinson assembled a new team of synthesists and musicians, including the now well-known film composer Shirley Walker. He also brought in Bernie Krause, already an experienced film synthesist and one of Mills College's Tape Music Center's most successful exports. Krause was also part of the Sound Arts assemblage. Rubinson then brought in Don Preston, who had an extensive jazz background including tenure with Frank Zappa's band for about eight years; Nyle Steiner, a classically trained trumpeter, as well as instrument designer and manufacturer of the Steiner Wind Synthesizer; and master synthesist Pat Gleeson, co-owner of Different Fur, solo artist, former member of Herbie Hancock's Mwandishi band, and a contributor to two Hancock albums.

Each artist possessed unique skill sets that complemented the others. Alone in Different Fur, Gleeson produced abstract music on his E-mu keyboard; Steiner and Preston, who often worked together, came up with more organic sounds. Krause excelled at combining real and machine instrument sounds. The group began working in February 1979 with an initial and impossible eight-week deadline, which was later extended when the film got pushed back three months. Music was recorded onto 24-track analog, a montage of sounds, remixes, submixes, and layers of overdubs. Rubinson's secondary mission was to mix these tracks on to a group of tracks on a new 24-track tape so that tone colors were grouped together in a logical way and tracks were properly balanced. "If I didn't have a Harrison automated console, we'd still be mixing the picture," Rubinson told the late Bob Moog in a 1980 *Contemporary Keyboard* interview. "We had two 24-track tape machines rolling in sync with the music on them, and we'd have to mix it to six separate tracks of another 24-track machine. It was a killer. It was the hardest thing I'd ever had to do."

The Grammy-nominated original soundtrack was a two-record set that combined the music, dialog, and sound effects to re-create the film experience. Richard Beggs, who later produced the all-music, single-LP soundtrack for the film, and sound-design genius Murch, completed the final overall mixing process for the film, combining music, dialog, and effects, at American Zoetrope's studio. Paul Stubblebine mastered the two-LP project in-house. "It was a challenge for everyone involved," he says of the project. "It was certainly a challenge to master." In the end, sources estimate that the score cost more than half a million dollars. Well worth the price of admission.

Fresh off his successes for Steve Miller Band, Jim Gaines moved back to San Francisco in 1977. Wally Heider Recording had asked him to come back and work for them, which he did, for close to a year. He also did some early work at The Automatt and spent a good portion of 1978 cutting demos for Huey Lewis and the News, Tommy Tutone, and Pablo Cruise. All three got record deals, but none of them called Gaines back. Initially, anyway. Fed up with the music business, Gaines walked away. "I packed up my family and moved to Oregon and got out of the business," he says, although he did help Steve Miller. Miller had purchased a working ranch with more than 400 head of cattle in Grants Pass, Oregon, and Gaines helped him build a studio in the barn, though it never completely happened. "I bought some other businesses up there and said, 'I'm never coming back. It's too political now.' So for two years I didn't do any music. And then Huey Lewis calls me and says, 'You *have* to come and do our record.' That was *Picture This*."

Gaines knew the band's manager, Bob Brown, which made Chrysalis Records' decision to use Bill Schnee in L.A. for their 1980 self-titled debut even more frustrating. Brown also managed Pablo Cruise, who, among other things, used to open for Steve Miller Band. Brown grew up on R&B and earned a living in rock and roll, much like Gaines. "Bob Brown is an old R&B guy like me," says Gaines. So when the time came to record *Picture This* in 1982, Lewis knew who to call. Gaines not only had a background that fit with the band, he knew that their music didn't need much polishing. "At the time, Huey Lewis was known as a 'New Age' band, which now would be called Alternative," Gaines says. "They wore T-shirts and black jeans and did this music that was a little funky—a mix of rock, R&B, and blues."

They recorded at The Automatt with Maureen Droney lending a hand as assistant, then they handed over the tracks to Bob Clearmountain to mix at the Power Station in New York. Producing the album themselves this time, *Picture This* gave the band their first Top Ten single, ("Do You Believe in Love") and paved the way for their next album, *Sports,* to sell upwards of 8 million.

The day Gaines finished *Picture This*, he got a call from axe-slinger Ronnie Montrose. He had recorded some tracks for the third and final album with his prog-rock band Gamma but didn't like them. "Man, can you please stay and work on my record?" he asked. Gaines was supposed to be in Oregon, away from the music business, but he agreed, finished the record at The Automatt, and *Gamma 3* inched its way to Number 72 on the *Billboard* album charts in 1982. He was almost on his way back to Oregon, but Carlos Santana stopped him. Santana had plans to go back into the studio for their next album but wanted to record away from the CBS executives. They chose The Automatt and wanted to "try out" a couple of new engineers—Gaines and Phil Kaffel. After their first day together, Santana asks Gaines, "Well, what are you doing the next six months?" Not going back to Oregon, that's for sure. Instead, he spent half a year at The Automatt with producer Bill

Szymczyk and others recording *Shango*, which would yield some of the group's highest charting material until the multi-Platinum *Supernatural* some 23 years later. Szymczyk's Eagles-seasoned production moves, combined with Gaines's try-anything approach, served as a solid sonic platform for the full studio sessions. Gregg Rolie, original keyboardist for the group and later member of Journey, made a welcome appearance. During this time, Gaines lived in a hotel in Corte Madera, but he still had a home in Oregon and kept saying he wasn't in the business. But here he was, back in the business. When Huey Lewis called back and asked him to engineer *Sports,* he had to accept the fact that yes, he really was back in the business. He permanently re-relocated to San Francisco. Again.

Kaz Tsuruta Photography

From L to R: Greg Rolie, Carlos Santana, engineer Jim Gaines, David Rubinson, and Paul Kantner hang out during the opening of The Automatt's new Studio A, 1980.

From the time they opened as a multi-room studio, The Automatt rocked. Rubinson created a sanctuary for musicians of wide-ranging genres, from young upstarts working on their first demo to established acts aiming to outsell their last multi-Platinum hit. He also donated studio time to promising but often insolvent artists. He didn't always have the newest gear, but he knew how to make the most of what he had: He surrounded himself with brilliant technicians and talented, hard-working staff. That said, The Automatt still felt the heat from its competitors, especially newer facilities that *did* have top-of-the-line gear. "The Automatt was a profit-making studio and people loved to record there, but when

Fantasy opened, they had unlimited funds, and [the recording industry] became very different. It was tough," says Rubinson. Another major stressor (and a primary contributor to a near-fatal health condition that would soon manifest) arrived in 1981, when the California State Board of Equalization, in its efforts to collect back-taxes on studio time and royalties earned from producing master tapes, sent Rubinson a bill for $1,900,000!

Rubinson had opened The Automatt as his "laboratory," a place where he could excel as a producer and have his creative family around him. He owned a multi-room facility because he had no other choice in 1977, not because he wanted to make big money in the studio business. "I couldn't afford to *lose* money, but it wasn't my main source of income," says Rubinson.

On the other hand, Roy Segal, the man who locked the door on Rubinson when Columbia Studios closed, did very well in the business of running a studio, and as the new head of Fantasy Studios, he aggressively pursued some of The Automatt's clients. That sort of competition disheartened Rubinson. He was becoming increasingly disenchanted with the studio business as a business. The seven-figure tax bill didn't help, either. Then, around 1982, Bill Putnam's master lease on the Folsom Street building ended, but Putnam had given his former partner, Rubinson, first refusal rights to buy the building from its owners, the Vitlin family. "At that time, stupidly, I didn't buy it," says Rubinson. "Bill and I had always had good relations with the original owner, the Vitlin family. When the son Victor, a lawyer, took it over, everything changed. Victor didn't care about the music, he didn't care about anything but the money. He was pure accounting."

At this time, Rubinson usually worked 12- to 16-hour days and survived on coffee and adrenalin. In between recording sessions, deal-making, business running, and ego-soothing, plus fighting the California State bureaucracy, Rubinson would squeeze in time with his two kids. Then on Wednesday, February 10, 1982, after an evening out with his wife at the Magic Theater, he returned to the studio feeling terrible. Stomach pains had nagged him for the past few days, and this time they came on with a vengeance. He ignored it at first, and he went back to the studio and got called in to do an odd vocal overdub on a Ronnie Montrose session. By 11:30 that night, he lay down on a sofa in the lounge. The pain hadn't gone away. He went to Maureen Droney and said, "Maureen I'm not feeling well. You've got to drive me to the hospital." When they got to his car, he got in the driver's seat! "David, you're sick!" Droney said, hoping he would change his mind and rest in the passenger's seat like a good sick person. Nope. He drove the car to Kaiser. "Just park the car; I'll be right back."

He didn't come right back. He was 39 years old, and he had just had a heart attack. "In the cardiac care unit, I realized it was important for me to live," he said in a 1982 interview with the *San Francisco Examiner & Chronicle*. "I loved everything I was doing. It wasn't a matter of making a choice. The choice to me was to live." He had quadruple-bypass surgery in May that year, and as doctors wheeled him into the operating room, he remembers looking at the ceiling from the gurney, thinking, "I'm not going to do this again." Rubinson had to make some changes, not only to his business, but to himself.

He stopped producing, and he toned down his Type-A, my-way-or-the-highway behavior. He started eating better. He took behavior-modification classes. He gradually evolved from the guy people called "intense," "Triple-A," and at worst "egomaniac" into someone more soft-spoken, aware, and over time even fairly humble. For that reason alone, Rubinson considers his coronary "the greatest gift, because I would be dead if I hadn't had a heart attack. And I'd still be treating people—and myself—the way I treated them then." Which wasn't always good.

At the same time, Rubinson had to restructure the studio, mainly because he would no longer be there as its main client. He still had a playground; he just had to stay off the jungle gym. Faced with the threat of an empty studio, he had to start looking at it like a commercial enterprise—the thing he didn't ever really want to do. He delegated portions of his publishing and management duties to others in his operation, branched out into commercial real estate, and brought in Michelle Zarin from The Record Plant to manage the studio. "She was a gift," says Rubinson. "She took over the studio and treated it like it was her own. Everybody loved her; she was phenomenal."

She walked into The Automatt on her first day having never been in the building before. A self-described "Mill Valley snob," Zarin had spent the last few years at The Record Plant, only to find, as we'll see in Chapter 16, that it had essentially become unmanageable. Her world there centered on catering to the musical elite in a swanky studio, but The Automatt was more diverse, catering to a mix of established acts and local upstarts. "I got to see a whole other aspect of the record business in the Bay Area," says Zarin. "I met people from a crowd that I didn't even know existed. If I had to pick one word, it was about *creativity*."

Though Rubinson says The Automatt struggled to make the monthly nut, he continued to attract quality projects. Sandy Pearlman returned in 1983 to work with Blue Oyster Cult (whom he managed), Dream Syndicate, and disco mixer François Kavorkian. The Automatt became Ground Zero for Narada Michael Walden, whom Rubinson managed and who had evolved from monster drummer to monster drummer/songwriter/producer. He debuted as a producer in 1982 with Stacy Lattishaw's *Let Me Be Your Angel,* followed by hit albums for Angela Bofill, Patti Austin, Phyllis Hyman, Margie Joseph, and Sister Sledge. Whitney Houston put him over the top in 1985 with her self-titled release and its mega-hit "How Will I Know" recorded at The Automatt. This recording happened just after Aretha Franklin's *Who's Zoomin' Who,* with its huge hit, "Freeway of Love." He worked with a stellar group of players that included at various times, Randy Jackson (now of *American Idol* fame) on bass, himself on drums, Preston Glass, Frank Martin and/or Walter Afanasieff on keys, and Corrado Rustici on guitar. "Live band tracking with Narada Michael Walden was always exciting," says Ken Kessie who assisted on a few Narada sessions, including one of Narada's solo albums, *Confidence.* "His crack band could knock out a chart-busting arrangement in 10 minutes and nail it on take one. Narada really knew how to keep the energy up on a session. He was a great drummer, a severe taskmaster, and he worked *fast.* They were so fast, that by the time I tail-leadered a keeper take, Narada would be out there yelling to get [the machine] into record for the next song. I really got up to speed working with those guys."

That one-take band worked well with Aretha Franklin, also known to nail a vocal in one pass. When Arista Records brought together Aretha and Narada, her career was on hiatus. It was her first time back in the studio after her father had passed away a few years earlier, so she was just getting back into a full workload. She needed a hit, and Narada, who was on fire at the time, delivered. One of the first songs he wrote for her was "Who's Zoomin' Who," penned with Preston Glass. Franklin recorded that song and "Until You Say You Love Me" at United Sound in Detroit, but by the time "Freeway of Love" came around, the sessions had moved to The Automatt. Walden wrote "Freeway of Love" with lyricist Jeffrey Cohen, a Rubinson staff writer and longtime pal, for one of his own albums, so it was originally written for a male singer. As Cohen recalls, Franklin really liked the line, "Knew you'd be a vision in white/How'd you get that skirt so tight." They reworked the lyrics to suit a female, including changing "skirt" to "pants," and off to the studio they went.

"It was my first Platinum, Aretha's first million seller, and my first Grammy. It was such a beautiful time," says Walden. He also learned how to get the best out of her vocals. "She can do all these incredible flips and imaginative things," he says. "But if you want her to do it again, more to the melody, the only way you can get her to do that is to say that you want a 'straight reading.' And then she would do a version for you singing a song more to the melody. Not entirely, now, but enough. Without knowing that word, I wouldn't know how to get it out of her because she'd be like, 'No, that's how I hear it.' And she would be right. And if I thought something was a little bit off, she'd say, 'No, that's just how I feel it.' And I would live with it for a few days and she would be right. The Queen is always right."

Con Funk Shun featured two killer frontmen: Felton Pilate (later a hit producer) and Michael Cooper (who would go on to a brief but successful solo career). In the early to mid '80s, they brought their Bay Area party funk sound to The Automatt for several albums, with Leslie Ann Jones, Ken Kessie, and Fred Catero lending a hand at various times to engineer and/or mix. Catero describes a typical scene in front of the Harrison. "This is one of those mixing sessions where everybody's got a comment; there is no one producer," says Catero. "You start a session with the faders halfway up, and then it's a horse race to see which fader can end up at the top. And usually the drummer wants to hear more snare, the bass wants more bottom, the guitar player isn't happy with his sound…it's always like that. After a while they're almost even again, but higher. So then they start all over again, until you reach the top, but that's no good because you're overloading."

One time, Catero put his foot down. "Whenever I work with people I always try to explain what I'm doing. So here we are mixing, and they're doing this thing with the faders going up and up and finally I stop the tape and say, 'All I've been hearing is that you want to hear more bass, more guitar, more piano, more organ. Is there anything you want to hear less of?' And one of the guys says, 'Yeah! Your mouth!' I got up and gave him a high five right there because I thought it was so clever! I've never heard such a good comeback in my life."

Rubinson readily offered the studio at deeply discounted rates or pro bono to independent artists and/or record labels. He nurtured acts such as activist/singer/songwriter Holly Near, saxophonist/composer Oliver Lake, the Gay Men's Chorus, and labels such as new wave trailblazers 415 Records and Megatone Records. The latter was founded by Marty Blecman, a producer/keyboardist who had worked at Fantasy Records, and keyboard/synth player Patrick Cowley. "David was very instrumental in helping small record companies with creative, sharp people get off the ground and survive," says Michelle Zarin.

Both 415 Records and producer David Kahne, who became the label's principal producer in 1980, flourished in part because of Rubinson's belief in them in the early stages of their careers. Founded in 1978 by rock journalist Howie Klein, Aquarius Records co-owner Chris Knab, and silent partner Butch Bridges (also partner in Aquarius), 415 Records started off releasing singles or EPs from The Nuns, The Mutants, The Imposters, SVT, and Jo Allen and the Shapes, among others. Klein and Knab were some of the first to support San Francisco's new wave and punk scenes, with the team playing new wave singles on their late-night "Outcaste" show on KSAN with DJ Norman Davis. Klein also played a key role in bringing these acts to the legendary Mabuhay Gardens, along with bands such as Devo, Blondie, and The Ramones.

The buzzed-about label's first compilation, *415 Music,* featuring cuts from 11 Bay Area bands, came out in 1980. Paul Stubblebine, also a supporter of local music, executive produced and mastered the album. The success of Romeo Void in 1980 led the label to a distribution deal with CBS, which allowed them to bring Kahne into the fold and begin taking acts into the studio. Previously, 415 only offered licensing deals. Still working on a bare-bones budget but needing a studio to work from, they approached Rubinson. "So here I am with the means to help me get my record made and he's saying, 'I want to support you. The details will work themselves out.' That floored me," said Klein in a 1983 interview with *BAM* magazine. "He was telling me to go in and record the album, and the details did work themselves out. He has made it possible for our company to exist. I think of him as one of the godfathers of 415."

Megatone Records brought their first recordings to The Automatt's Studio C. "David told Marty [Blecman], 'Have your artists play for my artists and I'll give you time to start your company,'" Zarin recalls. That win-win situation led to the *Megatron Man* and *Mindwarp* albums in 1982 from Patrick Cowley, who, through his work with Sylvester, was instrumental in bring the synthesizer to dance music.

"Pat was the most creative musician I ever worked with," says engineer Ken Kessie, who recorded and mixed most of Cowley's productions. Maureen Droney took an active role in *Mind Warp*. "He wrote incredible songs, and laid killer grooves and synths over them. After Pat finished fine-tuning the sounds, it would take three days to record them and one day to mix. Twenty five years later, they are still stealing his synth licks and not doing them half as well."

AIDS took its toll on the Megatone scene. Cowley died from the disease 1982, not long after *Mind Warp*'s release. Sylvester died suddenly in 1988; Blecman, in 1991. Kessie recalls one of his last encounters with Cowley: "I'll never forget hearing Pat's last record played in a packed disco. The placed was jammed and moving in unison to his songs. He listened happily in a wheelchair, just days away from his death. Even sick with AIDS, Pat was more cheerful and together than most healthy musicians. An incredible talent!"

Occasionally, Rubinson gave studio time to the completely DIY artist. On one particular day, Rubinson gave studio time "on spec" to jazz singer Mary Stallings so that she could mix her newly written symphony. At first, Zarin, the rate-conscious studio manager, questioned her boss. As Zarin recalls, he replied, "Look. She's African American, she's a woman, and she wrote a symphony. She found someone to record it, but how's she going to mix it? We've got to help her." "Most people don't know that about David," says Zarin. "He's a very artistic person, involved in all kinds of culture, and really a strong creative force in the Bay Area on a grass-roots level."

As the '80s wore on, the studio continued to stay out of the red, but a few wrenches got thrown in the mix that made running the business more challenging. First, Victor Vitlin, the building owner's son and heir, informed Rubinson, "The lease is coming up, and the building's worth a lot more than when you first rented it, so I think four times what you're paying now is fair." "Four times what I'm paying now?" Rubinson answered. "I'm barely making it on what I'm paying now! You want to look at my books; no problem. You want a percentage of the profits, fine, but I can't pay you four times. And I'm going to leave you with a building that can only be a studio. I mean, what are you going to do? Rip everything out and spend $1,000,000 turning it into apartments? What are you going to do with this space? Give me a break."

Vitlin wouldn't budge, so in retaliation, Rubinson stopped paying rent. He put the rent money into an escrow account instead. In the meantime, the studio business remained as competitive as ever. One of his regular clients, Santana, who had worked with Rubinson for more than 15 years at this point, had blocked out three months in Studio A to record a new album. One afternoon, a week before the Santana booking, Rubinson got a call from Zarin. "David, you're not going to like this, but Santana just cancelled."

"They cancelled three months?" he answered, blood pressure starting to rise.

"Yeah, they're going to Fantasy."

"Oh, I see. We've been working together since 1968. I had a heart attack and an operation. They had three months booked and they're going to *Fantasy*? Okay." Rubinson thought about things a minute and said to himself, "I'm outta here. I'm not going to do this anymore."

He saw no real good reason to keep The Automatt open. To remain competitive in the industry, which was rapidly changing technically, he would have to invest hundreds of thousands in a major upgrade, which he didn't really want to do. And the lease renegotiations continued to cause trouble. With all of this in mind, in 1984, he closed.

Narada Michael Walden moved into his own studio, Tarpan Studios, in San Rafael. Janice Lee, who had worked in The Automatt's office, went with him, along with most of his regular crew of musicians and engineers.

There's a sad group photo floating around of the day Rubinson broke the news to his staff. "Leave it to David to have the locksmith and the photographer both there," says Droney.

As Zarin walked through the building for the last time, she found in the tape vault an empty tape box from a Paul Simon session, a holdover from the CBS/Columbia years. On her way out of the building, she tossed the empty tape box onto the middle of the floor in Studio A, letting it serve as a reminder to whomever came in later that building held a history more valuable than the price of the real estate.

But no one really had that chance. The building had cracks running from the roof to the ground. To fix it properly would have been very expensive, so Vitlin tried to sell the vacant building, but was unsuccessful. Vitlin then sued American Zoetrope, Francis Coppola, Bill Putnam, and Coast Recorders, plus Rubinson and

The Automatt, claiming that they had made structural changes to the building without his permission. Vitlin won a settlement from the insurance companies who covered the larger defendants, and Rubinson paid him his back rent, at the *old* rental rates.

In the meantime, vagrants broke in and began using the space as a flophouse. Then, when the Loma-Prieta earthquake of 1989 hit, The Automatt building fell to the ground. People used to joke that the studio space would make more money as a parking lot, and a parking lot is what it became. Some nice new luxury condos then went up at that address, part of the revitalization of the South-of-Market (SOMA) neighborhood.

CHAPTER 16

The Record Plant: New Roots

After his partner and friend Gary Kellgren passed away in 1977, Chris Stone continued to run The Record Plant, the Marin County party studio they created together, but he gradually lost interest. When Kellgren died, much of the freewheelin' spirit that made the studio so special died too. Stone began searching for the right buyer.

A year later, in 1978, a teenager named Laurie Necochea received $7.6 million in a malpractice suit, claiming paralysis from over-radiation during a stay at Mt. Zion Medical Center in San Francisco. She was a huge music fan, especially of Rick James. And now this nice, naive girl—who was stuck in a wheelchair and had a whole lot of money and not too many years left to spend it—decided to buy The Record Plant so she could live out her dreams and hang out with the stars.

Stone, a sensible businessman and, more importantly, one with integrity, was obviously hesitant at first. "I investigated the situation thoroughly before we completed the sale," he says. "We talked to her lawyers, her doctors, and had long conversations with her as to what her motivations were. She had two to three years to live and she wanted to live them in this fashion, and she had the money to do so." He sold her the studio in 1980, but under certain conditions.

First, Stone kept the name "The Record Plant," reserving that longstanding title for the original L.A. and New York facilities. He did let Necochea later rename the studio "The Plant," which had become the studio's unofficial nickname anyway. Second, he insisted that he stay for at least two years as a consultant "because all the vultures were hanging around waiting to take advantage of her," he says. "There were a number of vultures I was able to get rid of." For the requisite two years, he made regular visits to the studio, kept an eye on the books, and when those two years came to a close, he walked away. Left to grow on its own, The Plant entered a new saga of dramatic twists and turns, while continuing the tradition of great records.

During the ownership transition, Tom Flye brought in Rick James to record *Fire It Up* in 1979. As Sly Stone eased his way out of The Plant and The Pit, Rick James, who seemed to copy Sly's moves, including stealing Stone's wife, Kathleen Silva, inched his way in. Like Sly, he even moved in for a while, turning the former waterbed/conference room into his office and then his bedroom. But unlike Stone's overdub style of recording, James liked to record live, even though the final tracks would all come from James. "Quite often Rick would end up playing one of the instruments because no one could play it like he could," says Flye. "He was always playing something. And singing along."

James had three other albums to his credit before hitting his peak in 1981 with *Street Songs*, recorded mostly at The Plant with Tom "Super" Flye at the board. By this time, James had a drum machine, and with it, he developed a new method for working in the studio. "First, he'd make a demo of the song. He and I would sit there, and he'd play all the parts and sing them the way he wanted them," says Flye. "It would often be the same verse over and over because he hadn't written all the lyrics, but the song was there. Then he'd give it to me and the band, we'd set everything up, and the band would learn the song and get it all sounding good and then we'd record it." *Street Songs* included James's two most recognizable hits, "Super Freak" and "Give It To Me Baby." He assembled an esteemed collection of players to record the album, including Narada Michael Walden on drums, The Temptations singing backup, Gerald Albright on sax, and Stevie Wonder on harmonica. Not bad.

Despite changes behind the scenes, The Plant still attracted top talent. Prince, who opened for James on his first national U.S. tour, recorded parts of *For You* at the studio in '78. Bob Weir and Van Morrison, both of whom recorded there in the early days, came back in the late '70s and early '80s. Now under the guidance of producer Ron Nevison, Jefferson Starship moved to The Plant, recording *Freedom at Point Zero* in 1979. Grace Slick and Marty Balin had left the group, replaced by Mickey Thomas. Though the album went Gold, critics unfavorably compared their glossy new sound to AOR staples Foreigner. "Our sound started to get more sterile; everything had to sound the same live as on the record," says bassist/keyboardist Pete Sears. "We started using click tracks for perfect time, there were less echo chambers, more plates and gradually more digital equipment used." This trend continued all the way to *Knee Deep in the Hoopla*, the first album recorded as simply Starship, which would materialize in 1985.

In the midst of all of this activity, Necochea's trust fund administrators and other so-called "advisors" attempted to upgrade the facility. Studio A received some acoustical changes (they turned the speakers in the control room upside down and re-aimed them), and they made some minor cosmetic changes to the facility, giving the illusion that they were upgrading, assuming a new coat of paint would make the studio seem prepared for the future.

They also replaced the custom API consoles with Trident TSM boards, which, in their minds, seemed like an improvement. However, in the minds of the engineers, who realized the API manufactured some of the best-sounding consoles ever, it was the biggest mistake they made.

Tom Flye left the facility to work as an independent engineer shortly after a Trident TSM found its way into Studio B. He had stayed with the company through the ownership change mainly because he knew he had a great room (Studio B) that worked well, and it had a console he liked. He and Necochea even laid out plans to expand Studio B, but her lawyers nixed them. Between the equipment changes, the unstable atmosphere, and watching lawyers make odd decisions, he realized it was time to move on. When Tom Flye left, he didn't come back for a long, long time.

Even worse, the vultures had returned, but now they were on payroll. Service with a smile and a knife in the back. Salaries and expenditures grew for no logical reason. New hires on the administrative side were known to give major record labels days of free studio time in exchange for promo CDs, because that's all they knew or cared about: free concert tickets and free CDs. Huge bouquets of flowers would show up for Necochea, with a card signed "From your loving staff." She thought she had the best team in the world; meanwhile, they billed these gifts to the company account. Whether she didn't realize her staff's negligence or she just didn't care, it's hard to say. Those who knew her believe that it didn't matter to her much that she was losing money; she knew her time would be up soon, and the money wouldn't come with her.

Michelle Zarin had returned to The Plant in 1980 after a stint at The Record Plant L.A. to find the studio a disorganized mess. She did her best to maintain some order and knock some sense into the staff, but it wasn't an easy task. She managed the place as best she could, but when David Rubinson called about a year later and asked if she would consider moving to The Automatt, she immediately said yes, without ever having set foot in his San Francisco facility.

Necochea's trust administrators soon began putting pressure on her to sell the studio—her dream—because they thought she was mishandling the money. She fought them, but ultimately they won. "Her lawyers started fighting her and made her sell it. It broke her heart," says Flye. "Shortly after that, she died."

In early 1984, local entrepreneur Stanley Jacox bought The Plant from Necochea and hired Jim Gaines as his GM. Gaines worked regularly at The Plant as a client at that point; by becoming its GM, he could maintain some sort of control over the staff and working conditions, which was sorely needed at the time.

Under Jacox's short tenure, The Plant underwent more renovations. He rebuilt the kitchen, installed new carpeting in the studios, and purchased the area's first Kurzweil 250 synthesizer. He also remodeled Studio C (formerly The Pit), which had morphed into a rehearsal room, and returned it to a small but functional recording room for independent projects. John Fogerty broke in Studio C in 1985 with his comeback album, *Centerfield*. "He played all the instruments himself so he didn't need a big setup," Gaines said in a 1990 interview with *Mix*. "He'd do one thing at a time, so that little room worked exactly the way he wanted."

The Plant gradually rebuilt itself after the neglectful Necochea period. Studio manager Paul Broucek booked clients such as Ted Nugent, Rick Springfield, Romeo Void, and Border Patrol, a new band featuring ex-Doobie Tom Johnston. Old-timers, such as Heart and Jefferson Starship, experienced a comeback with albums recorded at The Plant.

To record their first album as Starship, a reduced and reconfigured version of the group came in 1985 to work on *Knee Deep in the Hoopla*. By this album, Kantner and Nevison were out; keyboardist Peter Wolf and Jeremy Smith were in. Wolf had a Synclavier, which was a new toy for the band and a source of conflict between some of the members. "He did a lot of the drums and bass on the Synclav," says Sears. "Some of us were fighting this tide, others just wanted a hit record. But ultimately it became more about keeping up with the times instead of keeping with who they are." The hit-seekers got their wish. The album yielded two Number Ones (something neither Jefferson Airplane nor Jefferson Starship had ever achieved): "We Built This City" and "Sara," which generated a new fan base for the group. Starship's light would gradually dim as more members dropped off (Sears left in 1986, Slick in 1988), ultimately leaving only Wolf and Thomas until manager Bill Thompson declared the group inactive six years later.

Journey hadn't recorded an album in two years when they entered The Plant to begin *Raised on Radio* with associate producer/engineer Jim Gaines. Drummer Steve Smith had been playing jazz with his own group, Vital Information, during breaks from Journey, and bassist Ross Valory had been in and out of rehab. Also during the break, vocalist Steve Perry recorded the successful *Street Talk* and debated whether or not to continue his solo career or go back to Journey. He chose Journey, under conditions that gave him more control of the group. Early in the tracking sessions, he replaced Valory with Bob Glaub, leaving Neal Schon as the only original member. Tracking resumed for about a month, but on the last day, Perry said that he couldn't sing over the drum tracks, claiming they were too busy, no doubt a byproduct of Smith's extensive jazz training. The decision was made to send Smith home, and the group had to start the record all over again; this time with Randy Jackson on bass and Larry Londin on drums.

Aside from conflicts within the group, personal issues took their toll on Perry. He had recently split with his girlfriend, Sherrie Swafford, for whom he had written "Oh, Sherrie," and he was devastated. Also, his mother had become ill, and he frequently traveled from San Francisco to San Joaquin to spend time with her, which meant more downtime between sessions and a lot of recording with an absent vocalist.

But the band pressed on, and keyboardist Jonathan Cain's skilled chord progressions, Neal Schon's virtuosic guitar work, and Perry's soulful singing came together, despite tensions, to create a Gold record. "We did a lot of layering," says Gaines, which was not unusual at the time. "We spent a lot of time working on lead vocals; not because he can't sing—he can sing his butt off—but he got to a point where he would overanalyze everything. It's really difficult to have two really giant hit records in a row—in their case three in a row—so I think we were overthinking the record and trying to make it too good instead of going for the gut feeling."

As if the band didn't have enough drama going on in their lives, their entire session came to a halt at The Plant in 1985 when Gaines drove to the studio one morning to find 25 federal DEA officers and the Sausalito and Marin County sheriffs standing guard in front of the building. The Feds had just indicted Jacox on charges of tax evasion and drug trafficking and tossed him in jail. Apparently, Jacox's entrepreneurial activities extended to running a methamphetamine factory out of his house in Auburn, a few hours north of San Francisco. The government seized all of his property, studio included.

"They came in the morning before any of the bands came in," Gaines said in the '90 *Mix* interview. "We just called the artists and said don't even come down. We had to get the tapes out of the building, and fortunately the marshals knew that they had no right to hold those tapes because they didn't belong to the studio. Once things had calmed down after the first few hours, we called the bands and told them to come in and get their gear."

Gaines moved the Journey sessions to Fantasy Studios in Berkeley, with additional overdubs taking place at Cain's home studio. After more than a year of work, an understandably "fried" Gaines turned the project over to "the best mixer he could find," Bob Clearmountain, who had mixed Huey Lewis and the News's *Sports* and *Fore!* albums. After the 1987 Raised on Radio tour, Journey disbanded, and Perry, also fried, took a long break from the industry.

After U.S. government seized control of The Plant, they initially intended to liquidate the studio's gear at auction. When an appraiser informed them that the building and its assets were worth more as a unit than in pieces, they decided to hang on and continue running it temporarily, albeit with a skeleton crew to help them.

"They were looking for a drug factory or big stashes of money in the walls," Gaines said earlier. "Well, they didn't even find a joint. And once they realized that we were just people here working that happened to be caught up in this because of the owner, then everybody backed off. After a while we were busy again and the guards disappeared and the marshals just showed up once every two weeks to go over the books." When the Feds took over, Gaines resigned his post as GM, but continued to work there as one of the studio's main clients.

In May, 1986, the government put The Plant up on the auction block. A small group was present on the date of sale, which included Gaines, who teamed with a few others in an attempt to take over ownership. Another interested bidder was Bob Skye, a Bay Area native with credits as a producer, acoustical designer, and radio DJ. Skye also ran a successful remote recording business,

Skyelabs, out of Dover, Delaware, and wanted to expand his operations. Also present for the auction was Arne Frager, who at the time owned Hollywood Central Studios in L.A. and had previously established Spectrum Studios in Venice, California. He planned to move to the Bay Area to raise his family and continue his career in the studio business. When the gavel crashed for the last time, Skye was the highest bidder. He became the proud new owner of The Plant effective January 1, 1987.

By this time, most of The Plant's regular clients had left for less regimented territory, and any new business was likely intimidated by its previous owners. Who wants to make rock and roll with the U.S. government around? And considering the Feds didn't have the musical passion required of a loving studio caretaker, they made no improvements during their time there.

Meanwhile, Frager sold his L.A. studio and, as planned, relocated to the Bay Area. He continued to engineer in L.A., did consulting work for various pro audio companies in the Bay Area, and on occasion paid visits to Skye at The Plant, often bringing sessions there. He noticed that the building still sorely needed renovation, and it didn't seem that Skye had acquired the funding to do so. On top of that, business was still slow even though the government was out of the picture. Every now and again, Frager would offer suggestions to Skye on how to improve the situation. After several months of this, Skye offered Frager a partnership, but at such a low ratio, he turned it down. The offer slowly increased incrementally until finally, in September 1988, Skye said, "Okay, how about 50/50?" Frager accepted.

Frager drew on just about all of the skills he had acquired during his professional years: his MBA from UCLA, his sales and marketing skills in the technology industry, his past experience as a studio owner and engineer, and the record label contacts he developed during that time. He started by writing a business plan, raising funds, and making plans for the most immediate renovations, although the building, renovating, and upgrading to The Plant has really never stopped.

He ripped up Studio A for the first time in 1989, redesigning the control room and installing an SSL 4064 G Series console with a 64-input mainframe and G Series computer. They redid the monitoring system, and Skye and Carl Yanchar of Lakeside Associates redesigned and rebuilt the room, replacing Hidley's original designs.

Studio B remained essentially unchanged. "That room has such a famous history of classic records," says Frager. "It still has the Hidley compression ceiling with the outboard over your head that everybody looks and marvels at, because it's from the '70s." The last of the Kellgren/Hidley rooms from The Record Plant era, Studio B also retains the swirls along the walls, the fabric clouds covering the ceiling—the hippie stuff. This was Tom Flye's room for about a decade and home to albums from New Riders of the Purple Sage, Sly Stone, Tower of Power, and Fleetwood Mac. This is the room where Gaines worked with Pablo Cruise, Journey, and Huey Lewis. Frager mentions that they rebuilt the Trident patch bay early on. "[In] the process of putting the jacks in and out over the last ten years, they've actually worn out. I'd like to walk in there and be dazzled by the glare coming off the console, even though it's ten years old, and have four new tube EMTs, and a few new toys," he said in a 1990 *Mix* interview. "We don't have to turn it into a museum. It's just that, in a way, it's a museum of recording history."

Studio C, their "budget room," was rebuilt as an all-digital room in '89 and renamed Studio 01. The room was centered on a large Synclavier and a 16-track Direct-to-Disk system provided by Synclavierist/composer Greg Shaw. The system offered additional MIDI or sequenced tracks, acting as a tapeless recorder. Frager also essentially reversed the studio, turning the studio area into the control room, and the former control room into a vocal booth.

They also created a fourth studio out of an empty storage space/echo chamber in the back of the building for Mark Keller and Jeff Cohen's successful jingle company, aptly named Mark and Jeff's Jingle Company. They soon changed their name to Keller & Cohen. Cohen was the co-writer of many Automatt sessions, including Aretha Franklin's "Freeway of Love" and other cuts for Herbie Hancock, Narada Michael Walden, Santana, and Patti Austin, among others. Walter Afanasieff, who played keys on many of Keller's and Cohen's projects, promptly christened the studio Boomtown. Skye designed their 18×28–foot control room, which featured a DDA AMR-24 console, a Studer A80 MkIII 24-track, and Sony APR-5003 2-track.

Keller and Cohen had already landed the California Raisins account, which would later earn a Clio Award, as well as the majority of the Levi's 501 Blues campaign, which would win them an *Ad Age* award. Their first project at their new facility was a California Raisins TV spot featuring Michael Jackson as "Michael Raisin." Within a short time, Boomtown became too boomin' for the smallish studio. By 1990, they had moved out, taking a larger warehouse space in Sausalito. Cohen essentially sold his share of the business to Keller around 2001. Boomtown continues to crank out a steady stream of music and commercial productions.

When Frager assumed full ownership of The Plant, clients previously turned off by the federal contingent returned. Acts including The Doobie Brothers, Santana, Tower of Power, and John Lee Hooker booked sessions. Several new visitors came in, as well: Tracy Chapman, The Breeders (for the mix of the alt-rock fave, *Last Splash*), Chris Isaak (for the *Forever Blue* mix), Primus, Kenny G, Michael Bolton, even Marky Mark and the Funky Bunch. Just like the early '70s when Gary Kellgren and Chris Stone hosted a steady stream of out-of-town clients in addition to locally based acts, The Plant continued that trend of bringing a taste of Los Angeles glitz to San Francisco; only now, there was no sister studio to draw from—only Frager's fat Rolodex. Even through the 1990s, engineers and producers still had the wherewithal (and budget) to get out of L.A. to mix. A lot of them came to The Plant for essentially the same reasons as always: They like the laid-back feel (the on-site limo service and waterbed room were gone, but the hot tub and access to lodging remained), augmented by the redwood walls, another holdover from The Record Plant days.

CHAPTER 17

Recording in and out of the City

Golden State Diversifies

Golden State Recorders had as tough a time as any staying afloat in the '70s. Despite its distinction as one of the original San Francisco studios and the first one with a room large enough to fit an orchestra, business gravitated toward the new kids in town, attracted by fancy equipment, a famous client roster, or word of mouth.

Owner Leo De Gar Kulka forged on and continued to bring in a healthy amount of mastering work, a smattering of local acts, and string and/or orchestral dates. All of these took advantage of the studio's inherent qualities and its owner's engineering talents.

"Golden State was really the only studio in S.F. history—you could argue about the Automatt Studio A *maybe*—that had this sound that...you just would die for," says Dan Alexander, who would move into the facility some two decades later. "I've been in hundreds of studios around the world, and you come to recognize that there's a couple of handfuls of these rooms out there that are magic. Where things happen to your ears in a way that just sounds incredible. And it's mostly in these very old, very large, classically built recording studios. Leo built that place on a shoestring and fixed it up a lot from when he opened it, but never changed the ambience of that room."

To keep the lights on in that big building, Kulka did what so many studio owners do to survive, even today: he diversified. In 1974, he founded the College for Recording Arts, one of the area's first dedicated recording schools. It was wildly successful. Vance Frost, who returned to Golden State as engineer/studio manager in 1971 after a stint at Wally Heider Recording, helped Kulka run the school. It soon became so big that Kulka hired another person to manage the school, while Frost headed the engineering department. "We moved from being a real viable recording studio into being…a school, really. That changed the way the business operated. We weren't trying to attract bands so much, because we had a full clientele of students."

Also in 1974, Kulka helped form the Recording Academy's (a.k.a. NARAS) San Francisco chapter, which set up its first office in the Harrison Street space. Its existence would give the city its own identity as a music industry market, apart from the nearby Los Angeles headquarters.

He never gave up engineering and producing albums, and he launched several independent record labels to support that habit. His Sonic Arts releases, which included everything from classical, swing, and big band to polka, recorded as what Kulka described as a "Simul-SQ-encoded" LP. This meant, in less technical terms than Kulka writes in the liner notes, expressly recorded and mixed to create the effect of being at the original performance when processed through an SQ decoder.

Kulka also engineered many direct-to-disc recordings and experimented with the binaural "dummy" head on several stereo recordings, in addition to fielding projects produced by his students. He welcomed local audiophile label Reference Recordings, founded in the Bay Area in 1976 by Keith Johnson, Tam Henderson, and Marcia Martin, and known for producing classical releases of the highest quality, including dozens of high-end/half-speed mastered LPs and high-definition CDs (DDD).

On the lighter side, Kulka produced several albums of space-age pop for Brad Miller's Mystic Moods Orchestra, including *Nighttide*,

More Than Music, *Mexican Trip*, and *Mystic Moods of Love*. The last known recording session with Flamin' Groovies Cyril Jordan and Chris Wilson took place at Golden State in August 1981.

Kulka kept Golden State running for the rest of his career; later on, most would come to see him for his mastering services. No matter how hard it became to make ends meet, he never gave up and retained ownership of the studio until his retirement in 1994. After 30 years as Golden State Recorders, the studio changed hands and became the new home of another pioneering studio. We'll revisit this Harrison Street space in Chapter 22.

His Master's Wheels

In early 1974, Elliot Mazer stopped by Alembic, the sound and musical instrument company kept busy by the Dead, among others, to look at a bass guitar. He checked out a few instruments, found one he liked, and the salesperson asked if he wanted to hear it in a big room. They took him back to their studio, the former Pacific High space, so he could plug in and play. He not only bought the bass but also negotiated for the studio. "I had gotten used to owning my own studio in Nashville," says Mazer, who co-owned Quadrafonic Studios with musicians David Briggs and Norbert Putnam. "Later on I built a remote truck with Sy Rosen, my business manager. After being on the road for a while, I decided it would be nice to plant it at a studio." The 60 Brady Street space met his criteria. "I could not believe how good the room sounded, how tight and how open it was," says Mazer of the trapezoidal-shaped room, still as large as in the PHR days—about 40×50 feet.

Sale complete, Mazer named the studio His Master's Wheels and moved in his equipment: a Neve 8016 with Neve Melbourne sidecar, two Ampex MM1000 tape machines, and a variety of outboard gear and mics. He made no modifications to Alembic Studios, and the company kept its workshop on a second floor. "I made no changes in the acoustics of the studio at all. Zero," he says. "We rolled our stuff in there, set up our mics, and we were off. It was a beautifully laid out studio, with skylights in the ceiling, so you could see daylight." We installed a 4-channel earphone system that was an upgrade of the 3-channel system we had at Quadrafonic in Nashville.

His Master's control room.

Elliot Mazer

"His Master's Wheels had a great ambience about it that always peaked on the full moon," he said in a 1979 interview with *BAM* magazine. "Some of the really great recordings that were done there were done either on the full moon or right before it. It got to the point where over the years we used to try to schedule stuff that required that extra bit of energy..."

Besides attracting acts such as Barclay James Harvest, The Dingoes, Jerry Garcia, the Dead, and Frankie Miller to His Master's Wheels, Mazer headed a highly successful remote recording operation. In fact, he was the chief engineer on The Band's star-studded Winterland farewell concert on Thanksgiving night in 1976, *The Last Waltz*, which was recorded and filmed for the Marin Scorsese concert movie of the same name.

Mazer mixed parts of Neil Young's *Homegrown* album at His Master's Wheels, one of many Young albums that Mazer produced and/or engineered; The Tubes did a lot of recording at the studio as well. "I later recorded them at the famous Cowboy's-49ers game [NFC championship, 1981] at Candlestick Park, which became the foundation of their single 'Sports Fans,'" says Mazer. "And any album with Nicky Hopkins on it was special. There were a lot of wonderful times with Nicky Hopkins in our studio. There was a magic that Nicky brought into that studio that always blew me away. We did some overdubs and mixes on a yet-to be-released CSNY record. Crosby and Nash recorded parts of their 'whale song' ['To the Last Whale'] until very low frequency noise from the BART train threw them."

In 1977, Journey came in with producer Roy Thomas Baker to record *Infinity*. This was their first album with vocalist Steve Perry, and consequently, their first huge hit. During the recording process, a drunken Baker apparently wanted to blow off steam and proceeded to spray everyone in the control room with a fire extinguisher. As the haze cleared from the chemicals, the soaked observers watched as Mazer's precious Neve bubbled over in a heated mess. Mazer was called in, choice words exchanged, and Baker and band finished the album elsewhere, and Baker never entered His Master's Wheels again.

Mazer maintained the studio until 1978, when he "got tired of the business of owning a recording studio." He worked as an independent producer for a while; doing projects at The Automatt, then moved his offices into the Fantasy Studios complex in the early '80s. We visit them in Chapter 19.

When Mazer left, the 60 Brady Street building ceased to exist as a studio. It recently housed the Brady Street Dance Center and is now the address of an architecture and lighting firm. Sign of hope: There's a music rehearsal space next door.

Elliot Mazer

Anyone who's heard Neil Young's landmark *Harvest* album has heard producer/engineer Elliot Mazer's work. But his 40-plus year career in the recording business encompasses so much more, including record promotion, producing, and pioneering work in audio.

The native New Yorker began his music career on the business side, as an A&R man for Prestige Records in the early '60s. He had met the head of the label while working in a New Jersey record store; the label owner promised he'd be making records within a year. A few months into his label job, he was given the opportunity to produce a bossa nova album featuring Dave Pike, after which the company promoted Mazer to staff producer. Columbia sent Mazer to Nashville to work on an album of Hank Williams songs (in Spanish) for Mexican group El Trio Los Panchos. During this visit, he became enamored with the city's recording studios and session players, which would partially prompt his return a few years later. "The studios were great for rhythm sections, the sound was fantastic and the musicians were amazing," he said in a 2003 interview with *Sound on Sound*. "Nashville studios were built to get solid tight rhythm sounds and isolated vocals. They had good earphone systems and good-sounding echo."

Toward the end of the '60s, he moved to Music City and built and co-owned Quadrafonic Studios with Nashville musician David Briggs and Norbert Putnam. By this time, he had worked in New York with engineering greats such as Rudy Van Gelder, Bob Fine, Fred Catero, Frank Laico, and Joe Tarsia as an independent producer, and he wanted to use some of the ideas he had learned to make records in Nashville. He did just that at Quadrafonic, working on its Quad 8 console, Ampex MM1000 16-track, Altec monitors, and the first multi-channel earphone system, as well as other items.

In 1971, he produced the majority of Neil Young's *Harvest* album at Quad. The two met when Young was in town to record a performance for Johnny Cash's TV show. Mazer invited Young, Linda Ronstadt, James Taylor, and Peter Asher to dinner. Coincidentally, Young had some new material he wanted to record. Young came to the studio the next day and recorded those songs backed by top Nashville session cats drummer Kenny Buttrey, pedal steel guitarist Ben Keith, bassist Tim Drummond (the three of them comprised the Stray Gators and backed Young for many more albums), pianist John Harris, and guitarist Teddy Irwin.

Mazer first came to San Francisco in 1968, while still living in New York, to work with Janis Joplin and Michael Bloomfield. He also did some of Linda Ronstadt's *Silk Purse* album and worked on three *Harvest* tracks in San Francisco before moving there in the early '70s. In 1974, he opened His Master's Wheels, which he held for four years. In addition to several albums for Young, he has also produced or otherwise contributed to albums from Ian & Sylvia, Bob Dylan, Frankie Miller, Gordon Lightfoot, Juice Newton, The Durocs, and Leonard Bernstein.

In 1974 Mazer became involved with Stanford University's CCRMA (Center for Computer Research in Music and Acoustics) research team, helping to pioneer their work with digital audio. "I visited the lab and saw some amazing stuff in the mid-'70s," he said. "They had digital recorders, big digital synths, and amazing processing. I showed them how we made records in the analog world and I learned to use computers."

The Sonic Solutions digital recording and editing system came out of this work, as did John Chowning's developments in FM synthesis, technology later adopted by Yamaha. In the mid-'80s, Mazer served as a consultant for Apple Computer, where he helped define an acoustical standard for the Macintosh that it is still in use today.

Despite his early involvement in the digital medium, until recently, he's been less than impressed with the way it sounded. With sample rates now exceeding 24-bit/192kHz, he has warmed up to the medium enough to produce a DVD-audio version of *Harvest* in honor of its 30th anniversary. He's also mixed several projects in surround, including the *Harvest* anniversary DVD, Big Brother & the Holding Company's *Cheap Thrills,* four Frank Sinatra albums, Santana's *Shaman* and *Supernatural*, and Switchfoot's *The Beautiful Letdown*, as well as helped Pete Townshend with the 5.1 mix of *Tommy.*

When he's not working on a session or designing and building studios, Mazer has devoted time to AirCheck, a system he helped develop with Dr. John Grey that monitors and logs radio and TV broadcasts to identify all of the music that is broadcast. He sold the company to RCS (Radio Computing Services) in 1989.

In 1993, Mazer returned to his native New York, where he lives and works today. This year, Mazer will finish producing a new album with Neil Young's wife, vocalist Pegi Young. He is currently Chairman of the New Entertainment Technologies Working Group CEA, an adviser to Evolution Partners, and is doing business development work for fuzzartists.com, eTreppid, and MusicGiants.

Bear West

One large city block from The Automatt, a team consisting of Chuck Vincent, Tom Sharples, Ross Winetsky, and Mark Needham opened Bear West Studios in 1976. Needham and Vance Frost, whom we first met in Chapter 4, served as the studio's main engineers, with Doyle Williams, Warren Harris, and Jim Renney on board as second engineers. A mid-size "budget" studio, Bear West worked in tandem with Blue Bear School of Music, which opened in 1971 to offer music lessons and engineering classes.

Studio A offered a custom 25-input console and a large 25×50–foot studio area. The smaller Studio B had a 25×14–foot recording room (about the same size as Studio A's control room) and a TEAC Model 5s board. Both rooms contained ample outboard equipment and JBL monitors, and they had access to 16- and 24-track tape machines and an adequate mic closet. They also claimed one of the largest E-mu polyphonic synthesizers on the West Coast.

Kicking Mule Records brought Bear West some of its first business, with Needham citing Taj Mahal as his first "paying big name" client. Sons of Champlin did a bit of work there while they were on the Ariola label, and because of the studio's close proximity to The Automatt, David Rubinson would bring clients such as Herbie Hancock and Wah Wah Watson over when his own studio was full.

The studio was only a blip on the radar in terms of Bay Area recording, but it did serve as sort of a launching pad for Needham, who would go on to engineer dozens of popular albums during his San Francisco tenure, including everyone from American Music Club and AMC frontman Mark Eitzel's solo work, to Red House Painters, Cake, Chris Isaak, Flipper (whom he also managed), and Robert Cray. He moved to L.A. in 2001, but continues to work with Isaak and his most recent success, The Killers.

The Music Annex

In the mid '70s, Russell Bond and Harn Soper had a small project studio in Palo Alto, California, about 30 miles south of San Francisco. They recorded educational programs and spots for various advertising agencies. A little farther south in San Jose, Dave

Porter and Roger Wiersema had a single-room studio called the Music Annex, which they grew from a garage operation to a 16-track facility over the course of three years.

Both pairs knew each other, and all wanted a larger space to record music. In 1976, they decided to join forces and create that larger facility in Menlo Park and secured a 12,000 square-foot building not far from Soper's original Palo Alto spot. Keeping Porter's Music Annex marquee, the partners opened Studio A first, which offered a 34×28–foot recording room with a 10×8–foot iso booth and a 28×25–foot control room containing an Amek 2824, a pair of JBL 4333A speakers with BGW 750/250 amps, and a pair of Auratones. Additional equipment included EMT 140 and 240 plate reverbs, MXR digital delay, and an assortment of Neumann, AKG, Shure, and Sony microphones. Clients could record to either 24- or 16-track MCI tape recorders and mix to either an Ampex or MCI 2-track. The Porter-Soper confab also offered a Yamaha grand piano, one of the finest on the West Coast, they claim, along with Moog and Buchla synthesizers, used often for their mix of music, commercial, and film clients. "Dave was a musician in his own right, and good at marketing, so he'd bring in a lot of [illegible] projects, mostly local bands," says Bond of the studio's be[illegible] "Harn and I would bring in ad agencies and 'industri[illegible] or communication work."

Studios B, C, and D came not long after [illegible] catering to overdub and mixing clients wit[illegible] designed control room with a second Ame[illegible] 22×18–foot studio area. Studio C handled [illegible] work and rehearsals, offering a Tascam Model 10 mi[illegible] 14×12–foot studio area. Studio D originally opened for media production, but was soon upgraded to a mastering suite.

San Jose's Los Tigres Del Norte recorded some of their earliest norteña music at Music Annex, and would continue to bring their work to the studio for nearly 40 albums over the next 30 years. In 1979, The Tubes used the Music Annex to record *Remote Control,* their first full album for A&M and their first with Todd Rundgren as producer. In 1983, the partners upgraded Studio C to offer 24-track recording and began construction on a new 3,000 square-foot video soundstage. By this time, they had also upgraded Studio A to include a Neve 8036 console, and had equipped all studios with SMPTE-based automation. Clients around this time included Ronnie Montrose (recording an EP with Mitchell Froom), local band The Kids, Windham Hill guitarist Alex DeGrassi, various radio specials, and Windham Hill acts.

In fact, the Music Annex began a long and fortuitous relationship with Windham Hill in the early '80s that extended far beyond DeGrassi's work. Founder Will Ackerman, a friend of Soper, brought many projects from his Palo Alto–based label to the studio at a time when the label's acoustic Americana sound was just being defined by a number of artists including Michael Hedges, George Winston, Scott Cossu, and Ackerman's own work. "We recorded basically the first real season or two of Windham Hill," says Bond. "The first 11 or 12 albums that really put them on the map." The relationship also put Music Annex on the map. "With Ackerman, we developed a tight, close-miking technique that became the 'Windham Hill sound,'" says Bond. "I spent many hours with Ackerman, fine-tuning mic placements until we got the right sound for this new kind of guitar music."

Stevan Pasero, head of SUGO Music, a South Bay company that creates mood music and custom compilations for such companies as Sharper Image, Crabtree & Evelyn, and Macy's, reportedly developed his production success at Music Annex, as well. "We always just sort of went for it," says Bond. "We weren't afraid to say, 'Bring it on!' Roger always found ways to integrate technology into our existing wiring schemes."

Since its inception, the studio was known as a prime spot for analog recording. As the '80s dawned, it became one of the first facilities to incorporate digital technology, partly due to the convenient location between Silicon Valley and San Francisco. It was, as Bond colorfully describes, on the "bleeding edge."

1750 Arch Studios

Tom Buckner walked into Pacific High Recording with about 18 other musicians in 1970 to record the improvisational Ghost Opera ensemble. Phill Sawyer engineered the project, and though he'd recorded plenty of rock bands at San Francisco's hippie studio, this one tested his abilities of mic placement, improv recording, and proper mixing techniques.

He must have made a good impression, because two years later, Sawyer got a call from Buckner. He owned a large home up in the Berkeley hills, and asked Sawyer if he could build a multitrack recording facility in it for a new record label that he had formed with a diverse catalog of early music, classical, jazz, avant-garde, and new music. He also had space for a concert hall in the same house. Obviously, this wasn't your average East Bay bungalow. At the time of its construction, the North Berkeley home with the beautiful gardens was one of the most earthquake-proof buildings in the area; its walls were so solidly soundproofed that its hearing-impaired owner could play an instrument at maxed-out volume without disturbing the next-door neighbors. Perfect for a studio and concert hall.

Sawyer, intrigued by the offer, told Bucker that while he didn't have the skills to build the studio himself, he had the contacts to plan and organize it. He hired Scott Putnam, son of the great Bill Putnam, to handle the acoustical construction of the control room and studio. He also brought in Bob Shumaker, his colleague from PHR, to handle the wiring and installation of the equipment.

Shumaker put in the MCI console; Sawyer had most of the mics from PHR brought over, and bought a pair of 3M 8-tracks with gold connections from Wally Heider Recording. The control room connected to a recording room, as well as the 49-seat concert hall on a separate floor. Video cameras and monitors in the control room aided communication between the rooms. The studio would also link directly with KPFA, the local radio station that signed on to broadcast the 1750 Arch concerts live.

Online a week and a half early and, amazingly, under budget, Sawyer fulfilled his mission and resumed his business as an independent engineer, while Shumaker stayed on as the chief engineer, working in the studio and running the club sound.

Every Friday night beginning in 1972 and continuing for at least 12 years, KPFA broadcast live from the studio. In the early 1970s, the venue became the place in Northern California to hear classical music of all periods, particularly contemporary. The Berkeley club space became "quite the scene," says Shumaker, due to its commitment to showcasing innovative music of all genres. "We made it a point, particularly with the radio broadcasts, to book anything that was appropriate to play in a concert hall of 50 people, of any kind of ethnicity, any kind of music."

The record label released product from San Francisco Tape Music Center co-founder Pauline Oliveros and keyboard inventor/musician Don Buchla, as well as, Denny Zeitlin, John Dowland, Roscoe Mitchell, John Adams, Conlon Nancarrow, Big Black, Art Lande, Lou Harrison, George Marsh, John Cage, Charles Amirkhanian, Jon English, Candace Natvig, Laurie Anderson, Tom Buckner, Randy Weston, Mel Graves, Don Buchla, Guillame Machaut, and many others.

Three years later, Sawyer returned to serve as 1750 Arch Street's executive director and began building the 1750 Arch Records catalog. He stayed until 1984, when the operation folded and Buckner dispersed the recordings to other labels, including New Albion Records and Other Minds, both based in San Francisco.

The original 1750 Arch remained virtually untouched the entire time. The 1750 Arch building now belongs to University of California, which operates its Center for New Music and Audio Technologies (CNMAT), a music research, composition, teaching, recording, and performance facility, out of the large space. They hold regular electronic and improvised music performances in the same space as 1750 Arch did during its decade-plus history.

Bay Records

A few years after 1750 Arch folded, Shumaker moved to Bay Records, which is now located in the old Sierra Sound Labs building. But Bay Records' beginnings date back to 1972, when owner Mike Cogan started running a small record label out of his East Bay home, intending to help California bluegrass and folk artists reach a wider audience. He released nearly 20 LPs out of his home-based operation, recording many of them in a makeshift studio he built in his garage.

In 1975, he took the leap of faith: He quit his day job (previous careers include design engineer for Ampex and KQED and co-founder of video production house One Pass Video) to pursue the record label and coinciding studio full-time. He heard that a space had become available on the third floor of the *Alameda Times Star* building. The space had housed an FM radio station in the late '40s and early '50s, with two studios and an office. Perfect. The old radio studio changed occupants many times through the years, and when the last one retired, Cogan took over the lease.

Gradually, as activity with the Bay Records label diminished, the Bay Records studio became more popular, especially in jazz, bluegrass, and Central American folk circles. "Grupo Raiz, a Chilean group, recorded several albums at Bay Records," says Cogan. "This was during the start of the whole South American and Central American folk music scene in the Bay Area, which was centered around La Pena Cultural Center. Then I started recording traditional jazz, which most people know as Dixieland. Somebody decided I was an expert in it so I had to learn it really quickly. I ended up doing most of [trombonist] Turk Murphy's recordings and various other bands from the Bay Area's [traditional jazz] scene." Murphy had been a member of the esteemed Lu Watters Yerba Buena Jazz Band in the '30s and '40s and opened the popular Earthquake McGoons' Jazz Club in San Francisco.

In the Alameda building, Cogan worked on a Tascam Model 10 board, which he modified, with a Sony 4-track ¼-inch (which he still has) as his first recorder. Not long after, he bought a half-finished 8-track one-inch machine from a friend at Ampex; the friend had started building the machine and Cogan finished the job. He later purchased a 3M 16-track machine, but that's as many tracks as the Alameda studio would have, even at a time when other professional studio clamored over the new 24-tracks.

In 1986, Cogan realized he would have to move Bay Records out of the historic Alameda building. A new owner had purchased the *Times Star* building and subsequently quadrupled the rent. Unsure of where to settle next, Cogan found out that Bob DeSousa, owner of Sierra Sound Labs in Berkeley, was shutting down his studio to retire and had his building for sale. Bay Records bought the building, commenced renovation, and moved in 1987.

The new Bay Records locale would require more work than first assumed, given that it had been a studio before. To ready the building for sale, DeSousa began tearing down a few walls, thinking the building would sell faster as office space than as a studio. Cogan went to work rebuilding the place, improving the acoustics in the process. Randy Sparks of RLS Acoustics handled the design of the room. By this time, Cogan had ceased all record label activity and focused solely on recording. He thought about changing the business name to something more studio-sounding but by this time, everyone knew the facility as Bay Records anyway, so the name stuck.

Bob Shumaker arrived around this time and became one of the studio's primary engineers, often working alongside Cogan. "When I decided to move here from Alameda, I knew I needed another engineer and Bob was the first person to come to mind," says Cogan. "Then I heard that 1750 Arch had folded. Just as I was thinking, 'Well I better give him a call,' the phone rang—he called me! We're sort of the odd couple in many ways. He has the ears, and I'm more on the technical end. We have a lot of fun together recording, trying new techniques and bouncing things off of each other."

Aside from equipment upgrades, the studio hasn't changed much in the last 20 years. The main Studio A measures 1,200 square feet and includes a large iso booth and Yamaha C7D grand piano. The control room offered a Bimix 2016 and a small Mackie CR-1604 16-channel mixer in its early years, later upgraded to 40-input Otari Series 54 with Diskmix 3 Moving Fader Automation. Once in the former Sierra Sound Labs location on Alcatraz Avenue, they did get that 24-track machine—an Otari MX-80. They had a modest-sized but high-quality microphone collection, offering more than 15 Neumann condenser mics, RCA and Coles ribbon mics, and a large selection of dynamic microphones.

Studio B, the studio's transfer, mastering, and editing suite, now contains a Pro Tools 001 system, several CD burners, and a wide assortment of plug-ins for mastering and restoring. They keep their analog tape machine collection in the B room for those who need to transfer tracks from analog tape to hard drive. In terms of digital audio, the studio recently acquired a Pro Tools HD2 Accel system, with 24 channels of Apogee converters.

Their clientele has remained a steady stream of jazz, folk, and acoustic music, with a smattering of classical, bluegrass, and film work. John Santos has recorded several albums there, Afro-Cuban groups visit often, and even Turk Murphy continued to record at Bay Records until his passing in 1987. Really, any type of music that requires a large recording area does well with Bay Records. "It's a big room, and that's hard to come by these days," says Cogan. "Its acoustically right and it's got a grand piano. So if you're doing something like combo jazz, where you can't just sample it or do it in your bedroom, you really need a good acoustic space."

Cogan calls Bay Records a "workaday" studio. His clients don't have enormous budgets to work with, but they work efficiently when they're there and end up getting more than their money's worth. His regular flow of traditional music from various genres and cultures requires a live-to-tape style of recording. In that regard, unless jazz music disappears, Cogan feels that his studio is "future-proof" because so much of the work can't be done at home.

The Church

When Sons of Champlin broke up for the first time in 1970, their engineers, Bruce Walford and Paul Stubblebine, had a decision to make: Find another band to record or focus on studio recording. They chose the latter, and in 1970, teamed with business partner Alan Rockefeller to open The Church, a "homegrown" studio located in, you guessed it, a renovated church in the Marin County town of San Anselmo.

Be it good timing or good fortune, Walford, originally a guitar player and a Sonoma County native, had his eye on 1405 San Anselmo Avenue for a long time. He knew the woman who held the lease and had asked her to keep him in mind if she ever planned on moving. Around the time he and Stubblebine decided to delve deeper into the studio business, he bumped into that woman, who just happened to be moving out. They seized the opportunity.

The space they acquired consisted of three separate buildings. The original church, built at the turn of the century, had space in its sanctuary for about 50 people. When the congregation outgrew the little space in the 1950s, the original building was converted to living quarters and a new, larger sanctuary was built beside it. A small, two-bedroom house stood out back.

The largest building became the studio, after some renovations made by a team of self-described "enthusiastic amateurs." Partner Alan Rockefeller, who later oversaw the business details of the studio, moved his family into the old church building. "We were young and naive," says Stubblebine, "We made acoustic treatments out of insulation and burlap, and we called in a lot of friends with construction experience to help us build it. Phil Brown was one of those." Brown worked mainly as a road manager for locals such as Michael Bloomfield and Electric Flag, but he apparently knew how to wield a hammer, too, as did a few of their other musician friends. Many donated manual labor in exchange for studio time.

They remodeled and expanded the choir loft into a sizable 20×12–foot control room, which looked down on to the sanctuary, now a 34×22–foot live room. The area underneath the control room became the shop and storage space. They opened in 1970 as a 2-track studio—way behind the times, yes—and started recording their friends' bands. "We were doing the same stuff we had been doing in the practice halls, but we decided to have them come to us instead," says Stubblebine. They used a process called two-to-two: The engineer would record a stereo mix of the band on one 2-track machine, then play that back through the mixer, send it out to the headphones, and the vocalist would sing over that. Then, they combined the music bed and vocal onto the other 2-track. Walford recorded the demos that got The Sons their deal with Capitol in just this way in the band rehearsal space. That's also how he recorded most sessions at The Church. But when The Sons reformed in 1970 to record *Follow Your Heart* for Capitol, they asked their friends to bump things up a notch.

Working with a borrowed 3M 8-track, Trident board, and a couple of reverbs from the Quicksilver Messenger Service camp, Walford recorded the band, minus saxophonist/horn arranger Tim Caines, though the entire group rarely assembled at one time. Bill Champlin and bassist/keyboardist/saxophonist Geoff Palmer played a lot of the bass and drum parts, leaving drummer Bill Bowen and bassist Al Strong off of some tracks entirely. "I remember banging my head on a 2×4 going up the stairs [to the control room]," recalls Champlin. "It wasn't the most comfortable setup, but it got the job done." The album fulfilled their three-record deal with Capitol. In 1971, after only a few West Coast gigs to support the new release, the band broke up again, so it never really had much chance to sell.

Realizing they were long overdue for an upgrade, The Church acquired Pacific High Recording's Scully 284 8-track when that studio shut down. "It still had the 12-track heads, which we also owned, but never used," says Stubblebine.

In 1973, the three partners sold The Church to David Kessner and Bill Steele of Prune Music. Stubblebine joined Brown at Columbia Studios, and Walford took an engineering job at Fantasy Records. By this time, the room had an MCI 16-track machine to go with the Scully and an Audiotronics console. Outboard gear had expanded to include a Fairchild reverb, UREI LA3A, and instruments included a Yamaha grand piano, Hammond B3, Fender Rhodes, Hohner Clavinet, and a set of drums and percussion. During their four-year tenure at The Church, Van Morrison also stopped in to record a portion of *The Philosopher's Stone*, and Boz Scaggs did some work there. Still, the majority of their business came from demos, indie records, and some commercial work. In 1977, Marty Balin took over the facility and began using it as his rehearsal space.

"The Church was sort of this homegrown funky thing that we were trying to turn into a professional studio, and the guys that took it over continued that," says Stubblebine. "It never had that great collection of Neumanns and ribbon mics, but it was a good place to make music."

Bill Champlin

As a founding member of Sons of Champlin, guitarist/keyboardist/singer/songwriter Bill Champlin became known as one of the Bay Area's most accomplished and innovative musicians.

Encouraged by his mother, a songwriter and piano player, Champlin first took up the piano at age three. He stuck with the instrument through his teens, but learned other instruments as well because he had his eye on a Master's degree in music. When the rock-and-roll craze hit, he picked up the guitar and put together a James Brown–influenced rock/R&B band called the Opposite Six, which later morphed into Sons of Champlin while Bill studied music at College of Marin. Upon the advice of an instructor who suggested he would make better music in his band than he ever would in school, Champlin dropped out.

Sons of Champlin struck a deal with Verve to issue their first singles (see Chapter 3) and went on to release six albums between 1968 and 1977 for various labels, including their own. Their recorded efforts lacked nothing in musicianship, but the group's live performances—most notably at The Fillmore and Avalon Ballroom in the late '60s—became simply mind-blowing experiences. R&B–style horn sections meshed with funky Hammond B3 parts and extended guitar riffs to create a sound quite unlike any of the psychedelic rock bands to follow, although their skills influenced many. At their most eclectic, the group played acid jazz before it even had a name.

The group endured breakups and lineup changes, but toward the end of the '70s, Champlin let it go. "The Sons never could get over that one hump," he says. "We didn't have enough money to go on the road to push the record, but to make more money we had to go on the road. We weren't on the same page musically, and we'd been together too long with too little success."

As Champlin gravitated toward a heavier R&B sound, he also became more involved in the L.A. studio scene. He had become friends with songwriters/producers David Foster and Keith Olsen, both of whom began hiring him frequently for session work. In August 1977 he moved there and after six months "made as much in a week as I had in a year in Marin County," he says. As a songwriter, he co-wrote "After The Love Has Gone," which was a hit for Earth, Wind & Fire and Grammy R&B Song of the Year. He would win a second R&B Song of the Year Grammy for co-writing the George Benson hit "Turn Your Love Around."

In 1981, Champlin joined Chicago, a natural fit due to their mix of pop, rock, and R&B horns. Their first album with Champlin, the David Foster–produced *Chicago 16*, gave them a Top Ten album, a Number 1 hit worldwide with "Hard to Say I'm Sorry," and marked a resurgence of the group's popularity. He's been with the band ever since.

In between recording and touring with Chicago, Champlin scored his own hits "Tonight Tonight" and "Sara." He sang "The Last Unbroken Heart" with Patti Labelle for the TV series *Miami Vice* in 1987 and sang the theme for another television show, "In the Heat of the Night."

After a 20-year hiatus, Sons of Champlin reunited for a few reunion gigs, then went to Ex'pression Center for New Media in Emeryville, California, to record *Hip Li'l Dreams*, released through Dig Music. Champlin and family currently live in Nashville.

Tewksbury Sound

In the early 1970s, Dan Alexander, John Cuniberti, Eddie Money, Chris Solberg, and John Nelson had a group called The Rockets, a rock band that produced zero hits but propelled each member into varying careers in music. Tom Lubin, an assistant engineer at CBS/Columbia Studios at the time, heard the band and promptly secured them free studio time at a facility in Ojai, California. While in the studio, Alexander turned to Lubin and said, "One day I'm going to own a recording studio." Little did he know he would go on to own not just one but four, beginning with Tewksbury Sound (named after the Tewksbury Heights neighborhood) in the hills of Richmond, California, just across the San Francisco Bay from Marin.

In 1976, Alexander rented a vacant 3,000 square-foot mom-and-pop grocery store. With guidance from Lubin, he teamed with Cuniberti, Solberg, and a small team of other musicians and set about building Tewksbury Sound. "It was built by a bunch of hippie bums," says Alexander. "We had a carpenter friend come in and frame the 31×22–foot studio and control room, which took about two days, and then we spent four or five months finishing it. It never had air conditioning—it had some primitive exhaust system that never functioned—so there were a lot of sessions with guys wearing shorts and not much else."

Dan Alexander (top) and John Cuniberti take a break from hammering together Tewksbury Sound, 1977.

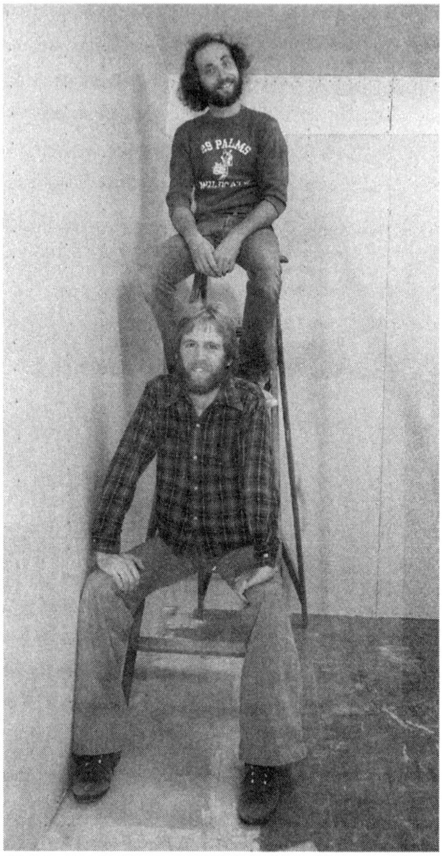

John Cuniberti

Lubin advised them on basic studio design issues, such as erecting nonparallel walls and how to install the control room window, and he left them with a copy of Howard Tremaine's classic reference book, *The Audio Cyclopedia*. "It's about four inches thick," says Cuniberti. "It includes the basic math and design concepts and drawings for recording studios. We called it 'The Bible' and used it exclusively to build our studio."

Alexander again, probably wondering what the heck he got himself into.

They built the whole place from used materials. "We'd pile all of this building material from the Berkeley dump on the roof of Dan's car and fill the back seat and the trunk with Fiberglas, stuff we had pulled out of a wall, then we'd drive up there and unload it all," says Cuniberti. "We made 10 to 20 trips until we got enough crap to build a studio."

Alexander, who had built a successful business dealing in vintage guitars and had just started dabbling in audio equipment, drove to L.A. and purchased an 8-in, 4-out Opamp Labs console that they named "The Podium." On the same trip, he picked up some Spectrasonics 610 limiters from Allen Sides, who was also just getting going in the studio business. They opened with an Amepx 8-track, Altec and JBL speakers, RCA tube limiters, Bill Putnam's UREI LA-3A limiters, and a few reverb and EQ units. But as Alexander's business as an audio dealer ramped up, Tewksbury's setup changed—early and often. "We always had a nice selection of microphones," he says. "I bought my first Telefunken 251 from Skinner Audio in San Francisco in 1977. We had an EMT [plate reverb] and an acoustic echo chamber that we built ourselves. It didn't sound like a classic chamber, which has a fairly long decay time. It was a little funky and had a rather short, sharp decay time but worked great."

Cuniberti began his engineering career at Tewksbury, working on sessions for Richmond Records, founded by Alexander. His projects included 7-inch singles for Psychotic Pineapple, The Blitz, and Little Roger and the Goosebumps, among others. The studio also brought in The Readymades, SVT (a seminal punk band featuring Jack Casady from Jefferson Airplane), The Squares (featuring Joe Satriani), and Soul Syndicate, the first record Cuniberti worked on from top to bottom. Tons of demos came out of Tewksbury, including Earth Quake, The Rubinoos, Tommy Tutone, and one for former bandmate Eddie Money, who came in to record a primitive version of "Two Tickets to Paradise" with Alexander.

Alexander's vehicle (pictured, right), used to haul lumber and Fiberglas, sits outside of Tewksbury Sound.

John Cuniberti

Once Alexander bumped up the studio to 16 and later 24 tracks, he brought in a string of tape machines that were, he confides, "technical disasters." After the original Opamp Labs board, the consoles produced problems as well. The modified Podium, which fared pretty well, was succeeded by a "pumpkin orange" Spectrasonics console from a studio in Cincinnati. "It…wasn't great. Then I bought Helios console Number One, which came from Studio 2 at Olympic in London. It was a complete piece of broken crap," explains Alexander. "So there it sat while we worked on it, and in the meantime, we installed a Midas monitor mixer, which sounded okay, but was a royal pain in the neck because it had no proper patch bay, but we made good recordings with it."

Technical difficulties aside, Tewksbury became a reasonably successful budget studio, especially toward the later half of its short, four-year life span. It became a center for several punk rock records and various reggae releases for percussionist Warren Smith's Epiphany Records label.

In 1980, many of those clients, as well as the Tewksbury staff and the sad Helios console, traveled to San Francisco when Alexander closed Tewksbury and moved into Wally Heider Recording, the lease of which he and partners Michael Ward and Tom Sharples took over that same year. We'll pay them a visit in Chapter 18.

Tres Virgos Studios

In the late 1970s, Allen Rice, Rob Yeager, and Mike Stevens opened Tres Virgos in Mill Valley. The modest 8-track facility catered to commercial radio jingles, with an in-house production company that wrote, performed, recorded, and produced spots on site. In 1982, Tres Virgos moved up to 16-track and moved in to a spacious new building in San Rafael. The first-week openers were Randy Thornton and Hot Feet, who were in recording with Gordon Mogden. Studio manager Yeager engineered a session for California Zephyr, who recorded four songs for Nashville's Foglesong Records.

With co-owner Gerald Jacobs brought into the fold, the facility put a serious eye on the music scene, and it became a popular spot for both major and independent projects (partly due to their reduced "indie band" rate). Takers included Merl Saunders, Physical Ed (with an album produced by Ronnie Montrose), Question Men, and Mingo Lewis. In 1983, Police drummer Stewart Copeland used the studio to produce parts of the *Rumblefish* soundtrack, and Van Morrison came in to work on two separate albums: *Philosopher's Stone* and *Inarticulate Speech of the Heart.*

In the new space, artists had a 25×35–foot studio and 9×8–foot drum booth to work out of, with a 1935 Baldwin Salon grand piano in the corner. Engineers, including a mix of independents, chief engineer Robert Missbach, Gordon Lyon, and Yeager, worked on a custom MCI console, along with an assortment of UREI, Teletronix, Lexicon and Eventide gear, an Echoplate, and UREI monitors.

The Chips Davis–designed room was one of the first to adopt the Live End Dead End (LEDE) acoustics, meaning the area around the monitors is deadened, or made acoustically absorbent. The remainder of the control room (behind the listener) is made "live," or reflective. The design staggers the arrival of reflections at the console so, ideally, the reflections don't interfere with monitoring. With its pecan paneling, oak trim, and parquet flooring, the studio had certainly taken a step up from the small Mill Valley spot, but it maintained a comfortable atmosphere.

It wasn't long before charmed producer/songwriter/drummer Narada Michael Walden would walk into Tres Virgos, fall for its roomy, nicely appointed recording room, and deem it Tarpan Studios, his private recording facility and home to many Number One hits. We'll visit this hit factory in Chapter 20.

Sonoma Recording

While engineer Paul Stubblebine continued to master dozens of albums at The Automatt, in the late 1970s he became a partner in Sonoma Recording, a mid-size studio in Cotati, California, built by former CBS engineer David Brown. Jim Coe, Jefferson Starship's soundman, equalized the 18×30–foot studio and 10×11–foot control room. The 16-track facility offered a Neve 16×16 console, used to record musicians Pete Sears, Nicky Hopkins, John Cippolina, Nick Gravenites, Chico David, and others from around the Bay Area.

Not long after Stubblebine came aboard, he and co-owner Nancy Evans moved the facility from its rustic setting to scenic Sausalito, taking over the Scott Putnam–built White Rabbit studio.

Now named Harbor Sound, the studio contained an automated MCI board, an MCI 24-track tape machine, and ample outboard gear, and served the growing independent engineer/artist community. Stubblebine, Evans, acoustician Bob Hodas, and others engineered and/or mastered at the studio, as did a handful of freelancers. Demos and label-issued products came out of the studio, including work for Con Funk Shun, Marty Balin, Gina Schlock of the Go Go's, and David Crosby. The studio closed in 1986.

SECTION FOUR

The Eighties: Excess Goes High Tech

The time between the close of the 1970s and the rise of the 1980s was a period of transition on many levels. Despite CBS/Columbia's departure in 1977, which many took as a disappointing sign for local music, the recording community in San Francisco stayed healthy. In fact, the music scene became more exciting. Punk rock and new-wave acts filled local clubs such as the famed Mabuhay Gardens. The funk that ruled the '70s gave way to an exciting R&B and hip-hop scene in the East Bay. Both percolated in the early '80s, then blew up toward the middle of the decade. Too Short led the way in the rap community, groups such as Tony Toni Toné brought Bay Area R&B widespread appeal, and later, hip-hop artists such as Digital Underground created a nice buzz in and out of the Bay Area. As the '80s closed and hair gel gave way to Aquanet, Bay Area metal bands such as Metallica and Exodus, and their more progressive counterparts Faith No More and Primus, all moved into a larger spotlight.

The industry also received a couple of nasty blows between the late '70s and early '80s, the first of which came from the government. The problems gestated back in the late '60s and early '70s, when two California-based record companies, Capitol Records and Warner Bros., decided to re-categorize their master tapes as "tangible personal property" and thus take tax deductions for depreciation on these assets.

Almost immediately, the California State Board of Equalization (CSBE) decided to reinterpret the existing California State Tax Regulation 1527 regarding sales and use tax on sound recordings, which mandated a 6 percent sales tax on "recording media," including master tapes. They proceeded to tax not just the sale price of a blank reel of tape, but expanded the tax to include studio time, engineering fees, artist and producers' royalties, and other costs involved with turning the blank tape into fully recorded master tapes. They did this retroactively, going back seven years into the sixties, and added interest and penalties, which often doubled or tripled the amount supposedly due.

As a result, studios, independent engineers, artists, and producers began to receive unexpected bills from the CSBE, followed quickly by aggressive pursuit from the CSBE collection department. By the late seventies, many of these people had their personal and business property attached and in some cases confiscated, forcing industry-wide hardship, bankruptcies, and insolvencies. Among the better-known victims, The Beach Boys and Joni Mitchell received high six figure bills and attempted to fight the SBE.

In 1981, a group of recording-industry leaders including David Rubinson, Tom and Diane Vicari, Chris Stone, and George Massenburg formed The California Entertainment Organization (CEO) to collectively fight the CSBE on behalf of the California recording industry. The group ultimately gained the support of then-governor Jerry Brown, then–assembly speaker Willie Brown, and a majority of the California Legislature. In 1985, Amendment Regulation 1527 passed, which clarified that sales and use tax were only applicable to the actual recording media (i.e., blank tape). Unfortunately, the legislature could not make this amendment retroactive past 1976, and though it saved many recording industry people many millions of dollars, many more were still forced to pay large tax bills going back to the late sixties.

Another hit came with the ongoing advancement of home-recording technology. Thanks to the arrival of MIDI, ADATs, and other digital pro and semi-pro equipment, setting up a decent home studio became feasible for more people, even though most were not necessarily high-quality—think TEAC PortaStudio. A professional-sounding recording still generally required a professional studio. But the die was cast.

MTV introduced the element of video to music in 1981, causing another explosion of interest in music and broadening the appeal of rock and pop music. The arrival of the music video also changed the way listeners think about music. When I hear Huey Lewis' "I Want a New Drug," for example, not only do I hear the song, I see the video in my head, too.

With record labels concentrating their money on the hit single and its hot music video with mass appeal, affordable recording became more of a necessity for the eclectic, album-oriented artist—such as alternative rock acts—who fell out of favor with the majors. Thus, a number of independent labels sprang up to support these and other new acts, and considering the Bay Area's historically independent mindset, some of the most successful indies sprang up in and around San Francisco. English reggae/new wave label Rough Trade had an outpost here; Nuns guitarist Mike Varney founded Shrapnel Records; women's music, such as Holly Near and Cris Williamson, found homes at the Olivia and Redwood labels; Ralph Records existed for The Residents; Subterranean had Flipper and their rock single, "Sex Bomb" ; and 415 Records, which we covered in Chapter 15, hit their stride in the 1980s.

The cassette started to give way to the compact disc in 1983, which seemed to signify the industry's acceptance of digital recording equipment, and simultaneously kicked off the ongoing digital-versus analog debate. In the studios, producers and engineers began requesting digital reverbs, processors, and recorders, as well as 48 tracks of analog. Studios began considering purchasing two 24-track tape machines and a Q-Lock so they could lock them together for their track-greedy clients. Of course, chief techs would often spend a whole day locking these machines together. Then again, artists still spent about that much time in the studio getting drum sounds, but now they could combine them with MIDI tracks and sampled snares, potentially spending even more time in the studio. The Golden Age continues.

CHAPTER 18

From Heider to Hyde Street

Filmways/Wally Heider Recording pressed on through the late '70s, weathering a slight slowdown in the mid '70s, with things picking back up toward the end of the decade. Jim Gaines moved back to San Francisco from Seattle in 1977, and after six months working as an independent engineer, resumed his senior engineering gig at Heider's. He immediately went to work on Norton Buffalo's Capitol debut, *Lovin' in the Valley of the Moon*, the first session of a steadily booked spring. Internal issues reared their head again, leading to a succession of ownership changes.

In 1980, Filmways sold Wally Heider's San Francisco studio, along with most of its gear. When Dan Alexander heard the studio had closed, he called colleagues Michael Ward, who operated the 16-track Rancho Rivera studio in San Francisco, and Tom Sharples, his partner in Rancho Rivera and a design engineer for Otari, both of whom had helped build Tewksbury Sound. They agreed to take over the Heider complex and formed a 50/25/25 business partnership, with Alexander holding the 50-percent share. On August 15, 1980, the facility reopened as Hyde Street Studios.

The basic studio setup stayed the same, with Studios A, C, and D fully operational, but they had to make a lot of improvements as well as move in some equipment to get there. Aesthetically, the place was "a disaster," as Alexander recalls. "It was indescribably horrible. Studio D was carpeted with this speckled commercial carpet. The floors were orange and the walls were marine blue. It was really ugly." Alexander stated earlier in a 1980 *Billboard* interview that he believed the studio was "a victim of the Filmways bureaucracy, and they never had the funding to do the obvious things necessary to improve the place."

To bring the studio to a visually acceptable level, the three partners, Tewksbury alum John Cuniberti, and a handful of others pitched in to put up rock and mahogany on the walls (which are now tell-tale signs of an "old school" studio) and to handle painting, wiring, and other maintenance issues. The orange carpet went away, and Ward went to great lengths to construct nice wooden desks for the consoles. Some consider the enclosures more reliable than the equipment.

When it closed, the Heider operation left very little behind: lights, air conditioning, wiring, a few speaker systems, and not much else. Alexander moved in equipment from Tewksbury, which he had closed to launch Hyde Street. He installed the Helios console and moved Ampex 16- and 24-track recorders into Studio C, and he set up his pro audio dealership on the building's first floor. Despite its famous track record (Rolling Stones' *Beggars Banquet*, Queen's *A Night at the Opera*, Led Zeppelin's *Led Zeppelin II*), the Helios was a problematic board, difficult and expensive to maintain. And besides, "it was a terrible sounding console," says Alexander. "We ended up selling it to the Moonies."

John Cuniberti

The difficult Helios in Studio C, 1981.

Sharples and Ward brought over a cantankerous 24-input Electrodyne console and additional Ampex multitracks for Studio A. The group also purchased an Otari MTR-90 24-track and a 40-input Trident for Studio D. Studio E, which was used for commercial spots in the Heider days, would remain as such, but was left unfinished for the first several months.

The new equipment package would have worked fine for a facility at the more "budget" level of Tewksbury, but it certainly didn't compare to the Neves of the Heider days. Plus, they had a hard time adequately filling three, and soon to be four, studios. In hindsight, the trio bit off more than they could chew.

With the exception of assistant tech Dennis Rice and Cuniberti, who initially became one of their house engineers, Alexander was unable to retain the Heider staff and still bring over the Tewksbury employees, so the Heider crew was let go. Most of the regular Heider clients left, too, in favor of the nicely appointed Fantasy Studios, The Plant, The Automatt, or their own home studios. "We just couldn't provide that level of service," Alexander admits. Live and learn, as they say, but these sorts of shakeups happen in most businesses when there's a changing of the guard. By the early '80s, The Plant had gone through similar problems three times.

Hyde Street Studios gradually built their equipment inventory. Alexander, who also owned a retail studio equipment store in L.A. that specialized in microphones and vintage Neve equipment, played a major role in this department. The studio also built up its client base and again became one of the city's popular multi-room studios. The Tewksbury regulars migrated from the Richmond hills to the Tenderloin district to record, and the facility brought in new business as well. The first two official Hyde Street sessions were New York synthesizer duo Our Daughter's Wedding, engineered by Richard van Dorn, and local new-wave group The Imposters.

Hyde Street also hosted commercial and jingle work and a heavy concentration of Bay Area bands, including the Dead Kennedys, who first came in 1982 to record parts of *Plastic Surgery Disasters*. Oliver DiCicco, who engineered their full-length debut *Fresh Fruit for Rotting Vegetables*, worked on other portions of the album at his studio, Mobius Music. "Thom Wilson [The Adolescents, TSOL] started producing the record, but left halfway though," Cuniberti recalls of *Plastic Surgery Disasters*. The band produced from there on out. "They were really outstanding," he continues. "They really stood out from the pack of punk bands happening at the time."

By this time, Cuniberti had been appointed Hyde Street's studio manager, which meant keeping the three studios booked and somewhat clean and organized by day, then engineering sessions at night. He worked in this fashion through two more Dead Kennedys albums: *Frankenchrist*, which he engineered and mixed with Dead Kennedys frontman Jello Biafra supervising, and *Bedtime for Democracy*, which he engineered. "The way those DK records were recorded and mixed created an ambience that was atypical of other punk bands at the time," he says. "Most of their records were recorded very dry, but they wanted to manipulate the recording environment to produce a sound that no one else had. *Frankenchrist* is like no other punk record ever made, and no other has been made like it since. There was a sound to that record that was very uniquely Dead Kennedys. Jello knew what he wanted and was very well prepared when he came into the studio. The band recorded very straight; almost like a live performance. Later, they became enamored with reverbs and delays—anything to make them *not* sound like the Sex Pistols."

East Bay Ray of Dead Kennedys in Studio C.

John Cuniberti

While Cuniberti maintained his dual roles in the studio, relationships between the three partners became more and more strained. The stress from maintaining a business with an extremely high overhead in a competitive market took its toll. "By the mid '80s independent studios were springing up all over town and driving the hourly studio rate down," says Cuniberti. "The owners were forced to buy more and more equipment to stay competitive, putting even more pressure on bookings to pay for it all."

Dead Kennedys in Studio C.

John Cuniberti

In 1985, Sharples bowed out to focus on his new position as head of research and development for Otari. Alexander and Ward decided to continue on as partners. They lasted two weeks. "It was a disaster for all of us," Alexander says. As many have learned through the years, friends don't always make good business partners. "Michael, this just isn't going to work out," he told Ward. "Why don't I just take one studio and you can have the rest of the building." For the first time in years, they agreed.

Alexander took over Hyde Street's Studio C, renamed it City Sound, and kept an office for Dan Alexander Audio and a "cave" for a tech shop. Ward assumed control of the rest of the building, including Studios A and D and all of the large building's various alcoves, offices, lounges, and the remaining two echo chambers, as well as the Hyde Street Studios name.

Alexander, Cuniberti (who now managed only Alexander's portion of Hyde Street), and Matthias Mederer, with the help of Paul Wolfe from API and a few others, spent a year rebuilding Studio C. They installed a 40-input API console and a monitor system copied from Allen Sides' units. Meanwhile, Ward replaced the Trident B-range in Studio D with an AMEK 2500.

Jello Biafra in Studio C. Don't mess with his mix.

John Cuniberti

Less than a year later, Alexander leased Studio C to producer Sandy Pearlman, who moved his Alpha and Omega studio into the space. With Pearlman in the building, acts such as Blue Oyster Cult and Ronnie Montrose came in, as well as World Entertainment War, a band signed to his MCA-distributed Popular Metaphysics label. (Popular Metaphysics became the new name for 415 Records, which Pearlman purchased in 1989.) Pearlman also rented Alpha and Omega to outside clients, including engineer Mark Needham, who worked in just about every San Francisco studio from the late '70s through the '90s, including his own.

Around 1986, a young guitarist by the name of Joe Satriani came to Hyde Street to record his debut album, *Not of This Earth,* with Cuniberti at the board. The two first worked together in the late '70s when Satriani led power pop trio The Squares. They recorded three albums worth of material together, much of it at Tewksbury, but none of it got released and the band eventually folded. "So when Joe came in and said, 'Hey, I want to make a solo record, we already had three albums under our belt," says Cuniberti. "So we were already ahead."

Satriani's wild guitar licks caused a huge stir in the guitar community. His phenomenal talent, studio experience, and Cuniberti's sharpened skills as an engineer/producer culminated in the follow-up, *Surfing With the Alien*, also recorded in Pearlman's Alpha and Omega, propelling the master guitar player, and his engineer, to a new level of success.

Jeff Campitelli

John Cuniberti, during a late night of mixing Surfing With the Alien.

By 1988, Dan Alexander Audio was running "swimmingly," and he had recouped most of the money he had lost in the studio business. Then, he got a phone call from Allen Sides. A well-known studio, just a matter of blocks away, was seeking a buyer. We'll pick up that tale in Chapter 22.

CHAPTER 19

A Public Fantasy

Through the 1970s, Fantasy Studios operated as a private facility for artists recording under the umbrella of Fantasy Records and its many subsidiaries, as well as a place to produce their high volume of reissues. In 1980, when the two-story building grew to seven, Fantasy Studios likewise expanded from three rooms to four rooms and opened to outside clients for recording, mastering, and film scoring. The recording community, both in and out of the Bay Area, responded with much enthusiasm.

Many factors contributed to Fantasy's success. Right off the bat, they hired Roy Segal, who had been working as an independent engineer since Columbia's S.F. Studios closed in 1977, to manage the studio. Segal immediately advised that the three existing studios receive new equipment and an acoustical upgrade.

The original Studios A and B contained DeMedio consoles; Studio C had an API. To bring the facilities up to modern standards, Segal had Neve 8108s installed in Studios A and C and put a Trident Series 80 in Studio B. They purchased Mitsubishi X-80 digital 2-track recorders in 1981 for various mixing projects and acquired the popular X-880 32-track digital recorders a few years later.

In terms of recording space, Studio A sprawled to 28×48 feet, with two isolation booths and its own private lounge. The mid-sized Studio B offered one iso booth, which doubled as a lounge, making for an affordable overdub option. Studio C, another large space, featured a 24×37–foot main room, private lounge, bathroom, and kitchenette. It was also the site of a film soundstage and Foley pits, which could also be used as music recording spaces. The building also had three live echo chambers to complement the spacious studios.

The new Studio D, designed by Tom Hidley and constructed by Sierra Audio, offered an automated Neve 8108, along with Hidley monitors and an assortment of Ampex 16- and 24-track recorders, a Studer 24-track, outboard gear, and a closet of more than 164 microphones. "We don't have to hunt for that weird esoteric microphone, because it's sitting there in the locker already," technician Steve Toby told *BAM* magazine in 1981.

Just as important as the equipment, if not more so, Fantasy hired a top-notch staff. In addition to Segal, who sold many on the studio based on his credentials alone, Fantasy brought in George Horn, another Columbia Studios alum, to run the mastering department. He had moved to Los Angeles in the late '70s to help open Criteria West, which never did get off the ground, then returned to the Bay Area in 1980 when Fantasy gave him a call. He's been there ever since. Engineers included Richie Corsello, Eddie Harris (a Fantasy alum since 1970), Danny Kopelson, Mike Herbick, and Phil Kaffel.

In 1982, the owners asked Segal also to head up the three-year-old Saul Zantz Film Center, which meant he had to delegate some of his studio duties. In September of 1982, after much courting from Segal, Nina Bombardier joined as studio manager. Like Horn, she's been there ever since.

As with Wally Heider Recording more than a decade earlier, the arrival of Fantasy Studios caused a stir in the local recording community. They opened to the public with the best of the best: excellent equipment, a highly trained engineering staff, and support staff who could pamper the clients and take care of oft-overlooked details such as fresh coffee and bagels in the morning and snacks in the afternoon. In Segal, they had an aggressive operations manager who knew how to generate steady business. In the first six months alone, Journey, George Duke, Pablo Cruise, the Greg Kihn Band, Stanley Clarke, and many others crossed the Bay Bridge to work in what had become one of the most modern facilities in the Bay Area.

Meanwhile, the Saul Zaentz Film Center operated out of the same building as Fantasy Studios and, like its musical partner, upgraded with the times, per Segal's recommendations. To accommodate their increasing TV and film ventures, they offered 16-track facilities equipped with Q-Lock, video monitors, and projection to do every form of synchronized sound, mixing, post-production, ADR, Foley, 16/35mm film/video sweetening, and scoring. Segal made several trips to Hollywood, networking with the right people and selling them on the Bay Area studio. Still, most of their work came from Northern California filmmakers and projects actually produced by Zaentz. Within the first two years under Segal's direction, the film center had earned two Best Sound Oscars for *Amadeus* and *The Right Stuff*, and established itself as a premier sound-for-picture site for the next two decades.

While Segal and an expert team of editors and mixers upped the film center's reputation, Fantasy Studios remained steeped in a wide variety of album and single projects. Huey Lewis and the News cut most of the tracks for their peak album *Sports* at Fantasy Studios in 1983, then moved to The Plant for overdubs and vocals and The Automatt for both guitar solos and to recut a couple of tracks.

For this album, the band hung on to Jim Gaines, with whom they had reconnected for *Picture This*. As with their previous album, the band produced themselves while Gaines served as the objective middleman. "He's such a big part of our records," said Lewis in a 1984 interview with *Mix*. "We all sort of yell and scream at each other and hopefully end up with the right answer. He lets us go through our movie, and on issues where we're really split he can add that touch of objectivity that we don't have."

Gaines added just enough studio polish to Huey and the band's live rock and roll energy to make them suitable for Top 40 radio and MTV. "We were trying to capture the energy of the band as much as possible without getting into this slick, pristine L.A. sound," says Gaines. "That wasn't what the band was about. With this band, we could step outside the lines a little bit, so that's what we did. And people loved it, because it was quote-unquote 'fresh.'"

The unassuming engineer thrives on pushing the envelope, as proven with his toy keyboard experiments on Steve Miller Band's *Fly Like An Eagle*. By this time, Huey Lewis and the News had become comfortable enough in the studio to experiment with modern technology, including synthesizer pulses and playing to click tracks. That's a backwards piano you hear on "Heart of Rock & Roll."

"'Walkin' On a Thin Line' was cut with a JP-8 that we ran with a Roland drum machine to [repeat 16th notes]…" Lewis said. "We just let the machine do that, and cut drums, bass, and guitar. Then we redid the keyboards and built it from there…By starting with the click, we learned where we were speeding up and slowing down. Oftentimes we'd play to a click a few times and then get rid of it."

In terms of recording, the band preferred an organic method. They worked fast, getting as much down on tape in the beginning as possible and putting down a guitar part in, say, two hours rather than eight. If after a few takes a song wasn't good enough, they would re-do the song later instead of struggling with it for hours upon hours during the initial tracking process. On *Sports,* for example, "What we did, pretty much, was let somebody fix a little clam here and there—but if it was more, we'd usually do the whole thing over again just to cop a *performance,*" said Lewis.

The album generated five hit singles, and almost every track on the album had that potential. "I Want a New Drug" became a radio hit even though it came out when U.S. Interior Secretary James Watt was coming down hard on drug-related lyrics on the radio. "We were all concerned about, 'Are they even going to release this as a single?'" says Gaines.

They already had two hits, "Do You Believe in Love" (from *Picture This*) and "Heart and Soul" (from *Sports*), so the band had some leverage with radio. As Gaines recalls, "We said, 'Hell, let's put it out there. If there's a controversy, maybe that'll make people want the record even more! So that's what we did, and that's exactly what happened." The band didn't alter their lyrics to please other people, and by the same token, even as music trends shifted away from gritty, guitar-driven rock and roll to clean, keyboard-centered pop, the band remained true to themselves, and developed their career without selling out.

As the decade progressed, Fantasy's client roster diversified, with everything from bluegrass to punk rock coming through the doors. Santana came in for the first of several albums in the '80s. Though they remained a premier facility, they also reached out to the indie community, offering package deals to unsigned bands at discounted rates. Around 1986, it was time for Studio D to receive a makeover, and its Neve console was then replaced with an SSL 4000 E Series desk. The Trident and Neve remained in Studios B and C, respectively (and still do); Studio A would receive its new accessories some years later. Throughout all of the technical changes, they never changed the basic structure of the studios. "The rooms were so big and beautiful to begin with, we never had to change the basic foundation," says Bombardier.

Mark Needham had recorded several versions of "Wicked Game," Chris Isaak's first Top Ten hit and the catalyst for his rise to stardom, before entering Fantasy Studios in 1988. They went to Fantasy to cut basic tracks for that song and a few others for the album *Heart Shaped World* with producer Erik Jacobsen—the same guy who produced Isaak's previous two albums, and had previously worked with the Lovin' Spoonful and The Charlatans, among others.

Isaak, already a Bay Area club favorite, had played the song live with his band, The Silvertones, dozens of times. By the same token, they had recorded the song several times, but had never quite gotten it right. This time, timing and technology worked together to create a winner. While the basic elements for "Wicked Game" and a few others tracks were recorded at Fantasy, the extensive editing process took place at the now-defunct Dave Wellhausen Studios in San Francisco.

Kenney Dale Johnson's drum tracks were sampled into an Akai DD1000 sampler; then they began making endless loops and samples, thus re-creating Johnson's groove. "For 'Wicked Game,' the samples came from various 24-track outtake versions that we were never really happy with," Needham said in a 2002 *Mix* interview. "We'd take six or seven different brush patterns and make loop patterns we could trigger off a MIDI note." He had to come in later to overdub cymbals, of all things.

Isaak played two acoustics: one standard and one in a Nashville-style high-strung tuning he'd picked up from Night Ranger's Jeff Watson. The haunting lead parts came from Silvertone guitarist James Calvin Wilsey—again, meticulously overdubbed, comped, and edited. The album version resulted from numerous tracks overdubbed over a period of a couple of weeks, then comped and refined piece by piece. "Jimmy's Strat had a custom MIDI setup," notes Needham, "and he played the underlying string pad that goes along with the guitar. [Keyboardist] Frank Martin also played a little sustaining part along with it. It's the only keyboard part on the song; you hear it like a little drone."

Isaak sang into a Sanken C-41 mic, recorded through a Massenburg preamp/EQ, and an English EAR (Esoteric Audio Research) compressor. Instead of using headphones, Isaak sang to speakers in the small control room, which resulted in the "big" vocal sound that appears on record. "If you listen really carefully, there's a change in the cymbal sound every time the vocal comes in, because you're hearing the bleed of the cymbals through the monitors into the vocal mic," Needham recalls.

While a lot of the major tracking sessions gravitated to Studios A and D, producers Denzil Foster and Tommy McElroy preferred the smaller Studio B. They liked the Trident Series 80B, and the smaller square footage suited their layered style of recording. Fantasy was *the* place when they brought over En Vogue in 1992 to record *Funky Divas*, the follow-up to the highly praised *Born to Sing*. For the quartet's debut, Foster and McElroy had used their traditional Starlight Studios/Live Oak combo, which served them well through numerous hit albums (Club Nouveaux, Toni Tony Toné, and others), but now they were in the big leagues. They knew they had to top *Born to Sing*, and in the MTV age, competition in the pop and R&B market was tough, and the stakes were high. Throughout their career, Foster and McElroy had kept image and marketing in their peripheral vision, so when planning En Vogue's sophomore release, they factored these elements more prominently. "We had to be a little more studious about what we were doing, have more of a plan with the music," says McElroy. "We knew what we were doing when we did 'Free Your Mind.' That was a rock song—we wanted to get on MTV! And we made sure it sounded good and that the video was looking good. In the beginning we just tried to be innovative. Later we were trying to be innovative, plus try to hit a certain market with the music and appeal to the masses."

It helped that all four women were immensely talented. They could sing well—there was no Auto Tune used on these women—and they were willing to sing until a part was done right. Of the two producers, Foster usually took on most of the vocal recording duties.

"They were workhorses in the studio," Foster recalls. "They were willing to work really hard, and it shows in the final vocal performance on the record. It sounded good all the time." They used samples only on occasion. "We'd use sampling to speed up the process for background vocals, but there was no pitch correction, and some parts you couldn't sample because the parts they were doing only happened once in the song—either one big harmony, or a 16-bar, 3 or 4 part harmony. Like the break on 'My Lovin' (You're Never Gonna Get It),' you can't sample that. They had to do it all the way through and they had to do it right. And they had the skill to do that."

The combination of En Vogue's skill and their producers' musical talent and marketing savvy led to an album that topped the R&B album charts, hit Number Eight on the *Billboard* 200 album charts, and yielded three Top Ten pop hits. Both critically and commercially successful, *Funky Divas* became a definitive album of the '90s, and set the standard for future stars such as Destiny's Child. And it all came from Fantasy's Studio B.

CHAPTER 20

Eighties Outposts

While San Francisco remained the Bay Area recording center, a number of studios continued to set up shop in surrounding areas. Just like the '70s brought us a mix of homegrown havens and high-end entities in and around S.F., the new crop included a wide range of facilities in locations all around the Bay Area. To follow are a few studios of interest from all points on the compass.

To the East

Starlight Studios

In the early 1980s, engineer/musician Peter Brown opened Starlight Studios in Richmond, California. Within a few years, it would become a home base for the happening East Bay R&B scene, as well as a mix of rap, rock, metal, and…silly Christmas songs. Norman Kerner, who would later go on to open Brilliant Studios in S.F., ran Starlight, a bare-bones sort of place affectionately nicknamed "The Bunker" by its clients. Starlight had a moderately sized studio and control room, no lounge, and a shoebox for an office. Despite its size and lack of frills, it brought in an amazing roster of talent.

In 1986, a young Denzil Foster and Tommy McElroy—locals who had met three years prior on Oakland's Laney College basketball court—walked in to use the automated Harrison 4032, MCI 24-track machine, and various digital reverbs and delays. They blocked out some time to record a variety of acts for rapper/producer Jay King's label, King Jay Records. They had about 10 hours of studio time left, so with the encouragement of King, they decided to record a singer named Michael Marshall who had a 4-track song demo called "Rumors," written by bandmate Marcus Thompson, Marshall, and Alex Hill.

Foster and McElroy used their leftover studio time to re-record and mix "Rumors" to 24 tracks, working with engineer Carl Herloffson, who sadly got deported back to his Scandinavian home not long after the project. "The reason it sounded so fat was because of him!" says Foster. "He had all these reverbs and was really experimental. He was able to get this really big drum sound that we liked. Poor Carl, we never saw him again."

The big drum sound originated from a LinnDrum linked to the now-classic Roland TR-808 drum machine. Foster played a Fender Rhodes patch on a Roland JX/XP live. All of the instruments on the record (and there weren't many) were overdubbed or sequenced, and Marshall nailed most of the vocals on the first take.

When Foster and McElroy produced the track, King intended to find another artist to record it, which could land something bigger for the label and a full-blown production deal for Foster and McElroy. They couldn't find anyone who could sing it like Marshall, so King released the single as it was, using 500 leftover 12-inch vinyl lacquers. The single eventually sold three million copies. Foster and McElroy ultimately got the credit they were working toward, and they proceeded to shake up R&B music with their defining style, which married hip-hop beats with strong R&B melodies and featured stripped-down instrumentation but ample hooks.

"'Rumors' came out [with that sound] and [radio] didn't know if they should call it a rap record or an R&B record," says McElroy. "The rap guys didn't want to claim it because the guy was singing, but the R&B people didn't want to claim it because the *way* he was singing sounded more like a rap record. It was one of the first R&B records with just a straight-up stripped-down sound; no guitar, just all synth and hip-hop drums. And this was before sampling was really big. Plus Mike was more of a street singer. He wasn't singing like Luther Vandross. So that song started a whole sound for Denny and I—kind of a stripped down sound with a lot less instruments but an emphasis on drums, melody, and hook."

The newfound production team carried that sound over to Club Nouveau who had a hit with "Lean on Me," from the album *Life, Love & Pain,* recorded between Moon Studios in Sacramento and Starlight Studios in 1986. Samuelle Pratter and Valerie Watson were the voices for the group, but Foster, McElroy, and Jay King were the creative forces, writing and arranging all of the material, playing all of the instruments, and producing each track. They're even credited as members of the group on the album.

With Club Nouveau, Foster and McElroy began experimenting with the Ensoniq Mirage sampling keyboard and E-mu Emulator sampler, using them as a programmer might today. "When we did 'Lean on Me,' the bass sound was actually Denny's voice sampled, with another keyboard sound underneath it," says McElroy. "We were doing that kind of programming before keyboards had really good presets." The tom sound on the song was actually inspired by Tears for Fears' *Songs from the Big Chair* album. They were fans of producer Trevor Horn's work with ABC and Frankie Goes to Hollywood and influenced by the dozens of new-wave bands that were huge at the time. Steve Counter engineered segments of *Life, Love & Pain* and would continue to work with Foster and McElroy for the next three decades. Between Foster/McElroy sessions, he also worked on five Digital Underground albums at Starlight, all for the TNT Records label, through the late '80s.

While Foster and McElroy quietly worked their way toward redefining R&B music with their big beats, heavy hooks, and sparse instrumentation, they experimented within those confines and sought ways to keep their music fresh. McElroy became a stickler for solid rhythms and original samples. "Any sound that we put on a record I didn't want to hear on anyone else's record," he says. Foster made an ideal partner with his intense focus on well-crafted melodies and near-perfect vocals. Even in personality, the two best friends fit together like yin and yang. Foster was the outgoing, charismatic social butterfly, and McElroy the more subdued counterpart.

While they held onto their original stylistic concept through most of their career, Tony Toni Toné, a group that McElroy essentially discovered before his success as a producer, presented a new challenge.

"They were a group that I wanted to play with," admits McElroy. "They were coming up around the Bay Area around the same time [Denny and I] were. They weren't the group Tony Toni Toné yet, but Dwayne and Ray [Raphael] Wiggins and Tim Riley had a group and also played in separate groups, so I would always see them around. I met them all at a studio in Oakland where I was recording Jane Terry, and they became her backup band. We became friends, and I said if I ever had a chance to get them a record deal, I would do something with them. They had their own thing going on; they didn't act like they were from Oakland. At that point they were more on the Minneapolis sound tip. So after Denny and I had success with Club Nouveau, we got a chance to produce some other groups. We got them into a studio and landed them a deal with Wing Records, a subsidiary of Polygram/Mercury."

By this time, Foster and McElroy had met engineer Ken Kessie, who would also continue to work with them for several more years. Kessie mixed Tony Toni Toné's debut, *Who?*, in 1988 at Live Oak in Berkeley and Can Am Studios in Tarzana, California. The album was recorded mostly at Live Oak and Starlight Studios. For the first time, the production team had an equal partner. Tony Toni Toné group members and producers alike wrote lyrics and melodies, whereas on their previous efforts, the producers wrote and arranged all of the tracks and played all of the instruments, with the artist contributing vocals and image. The Wiggins brothers and Wiley knew how to play guitar, bass, and keyboards and write songs, so the Foster/McElroy sound evolved somewhat to include live instruments.

Raphael Wiggins (who later changed his name to Saadiq and enjoyed a successful solo career) came up with the initial idea for their Number One R&B hit "Little Walter," recorded at Starlight. "They were church singers and players before anything else and one of the songs they used to sing was 'Wade in the Water,'" says McElroy. "He started singing that on top of the track. And then Denny says, 'That's nice but we should change it to 'Hey little Walter,' and we can make it into a story about this guy Walter…'" That single, which soared to the top of the R&B chart, distinguished Foster and McElroy yet again. They began working with the Roland Juno 106 and SB12 sampler, which changed their drum sound. Also with this song, Foster and McElroy were two of the first producers to take the basic melody of an older song, change the words, spice it up a bit, and throw it on top of a hip-hop beat. The gospel community didn't like it one bit, but apparently Sean "P. Diddy" Combs, who would adopt the concept some years later, sure did.

By the time Foster and McElroy assembled En Vogue, the girl group they had envisioned since the Club Nouveau days, they had a bona fide "sound" and had established themselves as hit producers. When En Vogue came out with *Born to Sing* in 1990, Denzil Foster and Tommy McElroy rose to become the Bay Area's first, if not only, R&B superproducers. What Jimmy Jam and Terry Lewis started in Minneapolis, Foster and McElroy started in the East Bay.

Like the sparse "rhythm & beats" sound they created with Timex Social Club, they brought new life to the girl-group concept, which by the '80s, had grown stale with soulless singers and drum machines. With En Vogue, they wanted to bring together four equally talented, beautiful singers and dancers, each with distinct personalities. "We wanted to take the best of all the girl groups and put it into one, so you don't leave nothing undone!" says Foster. "Most of the time there's something lacking in a female act—either there's just one good singer and the rest are just background singers, or it was all about the music and the producer, and the girls didn't have any identity." They wondered, "What would happen if you had Patti Labelle, Diana Ross, and Gladys Knight all in a group together?" They kept this grand idea in mind during their year-long search for vocalists, so when they discovered Terry Ellis, Dawn Robinson, Cindy Herron, and Maxine Jones, and brought them together as En Vogue, the women had some pretty high standards to meet.

The four women were not only strong vocalists, but they each portrayed a confident, positive self-image, sophisticated and unafraid to show off their intelligence as well as their sexy dance moves. As their producers, Foster and McElroy crafted equally strong melodies, but with heavier use of loops and samples, and added a rock and roll edge for the MTV crowd.

Like Toni Tony Toné, En Vogue recorded their debut at Live Oak and Starlight. Everyone's career took off with this album: the producers, engineers Steve Counter and Ken Kessie, and the foursome themselves, who scored two pop hits and two more R&B hits with this album. "EV had it all…great songs, great voices, great videos," says Kessie who mixed the album at Can Am Studios in Tarzana. "Tommy and Denny had a real knack for the unusual. It was a total pleasure to work with guys who didn't over-produce, who valued the concept of space and great tones. Every time I had mixing problems, they had the right solutions."

When the time came to record En Vogue's smash follow-up, *Funky Divas,* Foster and McElroy found it hard to get into their little hideaway in Richmond. East Bay rap and hip-hop acts frequented the studio, including Too Short (considered Oakland's first rap star), E-40, Mac Mall, Tupac Shakur (who launched his solo career while living in Oakland and recorded his debut *2Pacalypse Now,* at Starlight with Counter engineering), and Richie Rich. The studio also saw acts like Primus, Faith No More, Jeff Fogerty, and Elvin Bishop. And how could we forget Elmo & Patsy, who recorded "Grandma Got Run Over By a Reindeer" at Starlight Studios in 1989. The studio, now owned by Bill Thompson and Neil Young (not *that* Neil Young), closed in the mid '90s.

Live Oak Studio

In 1984, Jim and Priscilla Gardiner opened Live Oak Studio in a significantly converted basement in their Berkeley home. They wanted a studio they could use both personally and professionally. They certainly got it, and in the process gave the East Bay a mid-level studio with well-maintained equipment and a nice-sounding room at reasonable rates, catering particularly to the independent musician. By the mid '80s, the Bay Area had dozens of studios like Live Oak, but unlike a lot of rooms that shuttered within a few years, Live Oak has remained strong for the last 22 years.

Designed by Sonic Landscapes, Live Oak featured an MCI JH-24 track as its main recorder, with a control room adorned with Bryston and Yamaha monitor amps, JBL Bi-radial 4430 monitor speakers, and loads of outboard equipment and echo, reverb, and delay systems. Jim Gardiner's impressive keyboard collection and a nice view of the San Francisco Bay offered additional selling points, while its wood walls and ceiling (oak, we presume) gave the studio a cozy, non-basement-feeling vibe. The studio marks one of many professional home studios that Randy Sparks' company designed during this time. With Live Oak, Sparks converted the Gardiner basement into a popular overdubbing and demo studio. Through the years, they've attracted an impressive client roster that's heavy on R&B and hip-hop. Producers Denzil Foster and Tommy McElroy used Live Oak during projects for Tony Toni Toné, Club Nouveau, and En Vogue. Acts such as Bobby Brown, Too Short, Spice 1, E-40, Karyn White, and Jody Watley have also used Live Oak at various stages of their career. Other visitors include Eddie Money, David Grisman, and a young Destiny's Child, recording their 1999 smash *The Writing's on the Wall* (Columbia/Grass Roots Entertainment); Tony Toni Toné's Dwane Wiggins was one of the producers.

They've upgraded their studio over the years with improved equipment. In 1997, the studio installed a 64-input Otari Elite, which gave them a boost in bookings. "We've been doing tons of mixing," said Priscilla Gardiner in a 1998 *Mix* magazine interview. "People are raving about the sound and they love the automation." Mix sessions with the new Elite included three albums for AWOL records and a song for E-40. In the new millennium, Live Oak upgraded again to add a Pro Tools HD|3 system.

To the South

The Music Annex Goes Digital

The Music Annex continued to play a key role in the music recording industry down in Menlo Park. As the '80s progressed, the studio began to broaden its clientele in ways unique to its physical location. A studio midway between San Francisco and San Jose seemed out-of-the-way for many bands, but it worked well for the burgeoning Silicon Valley high-tech industry. Nearby companies such as Apple Computer, SUN Microsystems, 3Com, Pacific Data Images, Digidesign, and Opcode brought in their prototypes, early iterations of MIDI interfaces, computer software, and other devices to see how they worked in a studio environment. When Apple was developing the Macintosh computer, chief engineer/owner Russell Bond recalls taking a Mac 512 machine home with him over a weekend and staying up all night playing with MacPaint. The Music Annex produced some of Apple's "guided tour" software programs, which were audiocassette tapes that ran in real time (considered progressive back then). Digidesign brought over one of the earliest versions of Pro Tools, and Music Annex became one of the main installation facilities early on.

In 1986, Dave Porter decided that, based on Music Annex's success in Menlo Park, he wanted to expand into San Francisco and create a post-production house. He found a spot on Green Street, strategically located near a number of advertising agencies, and built another three-room facility called Annex Digital; first he took the top two floors, then later acquired the whole building. Through the years, the facility grew to offer multiple editing suites, voiceover rooms, and mixing suites. The impressive Studio 5 developed into a surround mix room featuring a Euphonix CS3000.

In 2003, Porter opted out of The Annex operation, and Roger Wiersema moved in, teaming with Patrick Fitzgerald to open Polarity Post, which still runs strong today. Bond took over the Menlo Park studio, now named simply The Annex, which still attracts an interesting mix of music clients, high-tech and toy-development companies, game audio, film post work, and more.

OTR Studios

A scenic drive through San Mateo County will lead you—if you know where to look—to OTR Studios, another little-known gem, operated by producer/engineer Cookie Marenco. Founded in the late '80s as the recording home for her label, OTR Records, OTR Studios sits high in the hills of Belmont in a secluded residential building, equipped with pro equipment and recording spaces from top to bottom.

The 17×23–foot control room is actually larger than the studio area and contains a 48-input Soundworkshop console with Moving Fader Automation. The room comes well stocked with the requisite Millenia, Studer, and Neve preamps and EQs, Otari 2-inch and ½-inch analog recorders, and a small but well-chosen mic selection.

The adjoining studio measures 14×23 and includes a Steinway grand piano, originally built in 1885, later rebuilt by Sheldon Smith. Upstairs, there's an 11×11–foot iso booth and a 17×27–foot "Retro Room," decorated with decidedly retro red shag carpet, for rehearsals and jamming.

Though OTR Studios is certainly Marenco's recording home, the studio brings in a mix of in-house and outside clients. She recorded The Chanticleers—12 male voices, a capella—direct to 2-track. They ended up with more than 800 takes. Saxophonist Peter Apfelbaum and the Hieroglyphics Ensemble, a 17-piece jazz ensemble (not to be confused with the Hieroglyphics hip-hop collective), followed suit, recording live to 2-inch. Engineer Kevin Scott, an assistant and lead engineer at OTR Studios since it opened, worked on both of those sessions and many more through the years. Beloved by many in the Bay Area recording community, Scott died from a heart attack in October 2005.

The basics of OTR Studios' recording facilities measure up to most mid-level Bay Area studios. They stand out, however, in the audiophile community for their sonic experimentations and their ongoing work in surround-sound recording and in the SACD and DSD formats.

Marenco, a well-known name among audiophiles, has worked on nearly 100 projects for Windham Hill, including the Gold-selling *Winter's Solstice Vol. 2*. Other album projects include Ladysmith Black Mambazo, Paul McCandless (of the band Oregon), Turtle Island String Quartet, Tony Furtado, and Alex Di Grassi. Her work as an engineer extends to Mary Chapin Carpenter, Praxis, Charlie Haden's Quartet West, and Max Roach.

In 2004, Marenco and engineering partner Jean Claude Reynaud developed the ESE recording technique, which they designed to accommodate surround-sound recordings with a "no compromise of quality" attitude. ESE combines the best of traditional recording techniques (for example, strategic mic placement) with the latest developments in technology. After experimental sessions at The Site, another hidden-away gem up in Western Marin, Marenco and Reynaud consulted with Sony for their DSD and SACD developments and mixed on Sony's Sonoma system. The ESE technique also led Marenco to form Blue Coast Records in 2005, an acoustic music label that allows her to continue to explore the SACD format. Most artists are recorded live in the studio without the use of headphones, overdubs, or digital effects. Check out "Sources and Recommended Reading" for a link to hear the results.

To the North

Prairie Sun

Way up in Cotati, in the lush Sonoma County area, lies Prairie Sun, a three-room studio that has brought residential recording to the independent and budget-conscious artist for more than 30 years.

Prairie Sun rose in 1978, when owner/producer/musician Mark "Mooka" Rennick, looking to create a control room window, bashed a hole in his living room wall. Rennick, a former student of East Indian music, bassist in the local Kay Irvine Band, and performer in a spoken-word ensemble called The Abolitionists, ran the facility out of his own home for three years. Eventually, the neighbors strongly encouraged him to seek a more remote setting.

He did just that. Teaming with art collector and Cotati Accordion Festival co-founder Clifton Buck-Kaufman, Rennick moved to a 12-acre chicken ranch that had been in the Buck-Kaufman family for more than 75 years. There he built a musicians' retreat: a well-equipped turnkey facility with three studios, a mastering house, and two two-bedroom guesthouses. What The Record Plant in Sausalito created for top-tier major-label artists, Rennick created for the independent musician, although several major acts have passed through. Through the years, he's kept the rates low, the quality high, and the atmosphere relaxed at Prairie Sun, named after the Prairie Grass Restoration Project in his native Illinois.

While the facility invites artists to escape city distractions and take in the fresh air and scenic views of Sonoma County, it keeps its clients satisfied with good equipment. Studio A opened with a Trident 80 console in its 600 square-foot control room, which was designed by Manny LaCarruba of Sausalito Audio Works and commissioned by Bruce Millet, a.k.a. "The Desk Doctor." The studio works best for mixing, but its spacious iso booth, with high ceilings, made it suitable for guitar and vocal overdubs. The room also ties (as does each studio) to Prairie Sun's massive 1,000 square-foot live echo chamber, an old hatchery room converted in 1983. This room became one of the studio's prime selling points. Now dubbed The Corn Room, the space produces a cavernous sound that works well for "big" drum sounds or just about any instrument that requires a large ambient room sound.

Most tracking sessions take place in Studio B on its Neve Custom 80 Series desk, now equipped with Flying Faders Automation. The recording area has a Yamaha piano in the corner and measures 23×26 with a 9½×10½–foot iso booth. Both studio and control room were constructed with rich wood for the walls and floors and warm-colored acoustical panels.

Studios A and B share ample outboard gear, heavy on the vintage, as well as a Prophet synthesizer, a drum kit, old Fender Strats and Gibson Les Paul guitars, vintage amps, a Dobro from the 1930s, and other instruments. The assemblage falls in line with Rennick's vision of establishing Prairie Sun as an artist's colony that he is sometimes "forced" to approach as a business, according to a 1999 interview with *Sonoma County Independent.*

In a separate building from Studios A and B and located just off of the live chamber, Studio C provides musicians a cost-effective place to record demos, finish overdubs, or work on an entire project if so desired. There's a Neve 802 with 24 1073 preamp/EQ modules, a Studer A80 tape machine (with 16- and 24-track heads), and ample outboard gear. The live echo chambers expanded from one to two following the arrival of Tom Waits. Waits developed an affinity for recording in an old storage room during the making of *Bone Machine*, the Grammy-winning effort that he and his wife, Kathleen Brennan, produced entirely at Prairie Sun in 1992. Now christened The Waiting Room, the echo chamber has a stone floor, wood panels, and a high ceiling, which gives it an unusual sound that's nearly impossible to re-create digitally.

Prairie Sun has continually expanded both its equipment repertoire and client roster through the years. A snapshot of acts that visited in its early years include Merl Saunders, Van Morrison, Norton Buffalo, Mickey Hart, Kate Wolf, and a slew of under-the-radar locals including One Love, Smoke, Vince Ashton, and Bobby Vitteritti. That mix of new and established acts has continued to include Waits, Primus, Faith No More, The Melvins, surf music phenom Dick Dale, producer/engineer Steve Albini, and Eric Gales. Rennick engineers many sessions at his studio; he shares his audiophile knowledge with his staff and keeps his inventory well maintained.

On the equipment side, they added a mastering facility and later replaced the Trident with an automated SSL 4080 G/E console, acquired Pro Tools HD|3 rigs, and added an extensive amount of old and unusual mics, compressors, and other gear.

As the name implies, the studio's most distinctive quality doesn't come from black and silver boxes. It comes from its acres of farmland and cypress trees, meandering trails, sheep, cows, and horses in the pasture outside, all creating an almost magical setting for this remote Bay Area treasure.

Skywalker Sound

Back in 1975, filmmaker George Lucas and producer Gary Kurtz hired a young USC film school grad named Ben Burtt as their director of sound. They wanted someone who could create and implement the audio equivalent to the cutting-edge visuals they were creating for their film in progress, *Star Wars*. They certainly got it. With Burtt and his outstanding talent on board, they developed Sprocket Systems, a sound studio that shared space in San Rafael with post-production and visual-effects facility Industrial Light & Magic. Within a few short years, it became clear they needed a much bigger space.

In 1985, crews began pouring concrete for what would become the 155,000 square-foot Technical Building at Skywalker Ranch, Lucas' sprawling 2,500-acre working ranch located far up a winding road—coincidentally called Lucas Valley Road—deep in the hills of Marin County. Skywalker Ranch operates as a campus unto itself, containing everything from guesthouses and an overnight inn to an organic garden, a vineyard, a baseball diamond, a fitness center, a firehouse, and its own general store. By 1987, the ranch also contained Skywalker Sound, which was a greatly expanded version of Sprocket Systems operating inside the new Technical Building. Tom Scott, whom we met in Chapter 11 as The Record Plant's chief maintenance engineer, became Skywalker's chief engineer.

Skywalker Sound has evolved through the years to offer six mixing studios, ADR and Foley stages, audio/video transfer suites, and several sound-design and editing suites, all developed "by a filmmaker for a filmmaker."

The impressive scoring stage, which came about a year after Skywalker's Sound's opening, caters to both the filmmaker *and* the music-maker. Measuring 60×80 with a 30-foot ceiling, the main recording area easily accommodates more than 125 musicians. In its original form, the studio offered one iso booth next to the control room and a modest selection of outboard equipment and monitors. Enhancing the equipment inventory with equipment rented from Stephen Jarvis' audio consulting business, Skywalker's Scoring Stage hosted its first session with the San Francisco Ballet Orchestra in 1988.

The San Francisco Ballet Orchestra, in session at the Skywalker Sound scoring stage, 1988.

Photo courtesy of Skywalker Sound

View of the stage from the control room during the same session, 1988.

Photo courtesy of Skywalker Sound

Shortly after that session, the room was remodeled to add three 16×16–foot iso booths at the far end of the stage. "It was a massive undertaking because that part of the building was the support for the back part of the Technical Building," says Leslie Ann Jones, Skywalker Sound's director of music recording and scoring. Jones arrived in the Bay Area in 1978 to work at The Automatt (see Chapter 15), after a three-year engineering stint at ABC Recording Studios. She then returned to her native L.A. in 1987 to work at Capitol Studios and returned to the Bay Area to accept the Skywalker Sound position. She continues, "You can still see the steel crossbeams to the left and right of the iso booths that help support the back of the building." They also incorporated a variable acoustic system that allows the reverb time of the room to be varied from 3 to .6 seconds. Audio, video, SMPTE, and MIDI tie lines connect all recording areas with the 26×23–foot control room.

Scott's former partner at The Record Plant, engineer Tom Flye, recorded at Skywalker not long after the revamp. "We took Mickey [Hart]'s drum set in there and recorded on a Sony PCM-F1, one of the first digital processors," says Flye. Other acts followed en masse, including Linda Ronstadt, Chet Atkins, Bonnie Raitt, Third Eye Blind, Rusted Root, Faith Hill, Vanessa Carlton, Brad Paisley, and a number of classical projects including Issac Stern, Kronos Quartet, New Century Chamber Orchestra, California Symphony, the Eroica Quartet, and the San Francisco Gay Men's Chorus. In addition, film projects that have come through the scoring stage through the years include such films as *Indiana Jones, Terminator 2, Jurassic Park, Fight Club, Contact, Titanic, Finding Nemo, Rent, Cars,* and *Ballets Russes.*

A 72-channel Neve 88R with Encore Automation currently resides in the control room, preceded by a Neve V3 and a Neve VXS. Their equipment list goes on for pages. Recording options include everything from the trusted Studer A827 24-track analog machine up to Pro Tools|HD. They're continually upgrading, acquiring premium mic cables, additional outboard...whatever's necessary to best serve their film and music clients and make the transition time between these two types of projects run as seamlessly as possible.

In 2004, the rest of the facility went through extensive renovations, partly in preparation for *Star Wars Episode III.* Mix stages G and D were rebuilt to include large client lounges and producer areas, with large glass windows opening onto the dub stage. Nine new 6.1 sound design/premix rooms, all tied to the various stages, went online. Also, a Hitachi 9980V central storage server was added, along with Apple Xserve and Xraid, bringing machine room FibreChannel storage to 38 terabytes. A new Skylink service, developed with codec manufacturer APT Technologies, was implemented for remote work. Lucas wanted to streamline his film operation by allowing pre-dubbing to take place solely via digital audio workstations in a 6.1 environment, as well as to give clients the advantage of working with Skywalker's engineers and services remotely.

In terms of Bay Area recording facilities, Skywalker Sound stands in a class by itself. The studio and its staff strive to consistently maintain high standards of excellence in music and film sound; its technical and creative achievements alone warrant a book of its own. Please refer to "Sources and Recommended Reading" for a book that covers this very subject.

Studio D Recording

Producer/engineer/musician Joel Jaffe played on a lot of sessions through the '70s, many of them at The Plant in Sausalito. So in 1983, when he and partner Dan Godfrey leased a building in Sausalito from Keith Mason of Mason Studio Services to build a new studio, they knew just the type of room to build. The initial idea was to work in tandem with Mason, who had plans to build a sound stage for film projects next door. Jaffe and Godfrey built their studio, which took about a year, with the intention of handling much of Mason's post-production work. About a year after the studio opened, Mason relocated to San Francisco. Since Jaffe and Godfrey also intended to host music recordings, the change in plans didn't mean much more than having a vacant building next door.

Located just a stone's throw away from Sausalito's most successful recording studio, The Plant, they carved a niche for themselves by offering an alternative. "At the time, The Plant had three rooms—A, B and C—and they were all pretty dead sounding," recalls Jaffe. "We wanted to build a 'live' sounding room. As a joke, we named our facility Studio D—and it survived."

Studio D features a 30×36×20 recording room, equipped with three iso booths, one of them a large, stone drum room that's one of the best-sounding in the area. Jaffe insisted on installing skylights in the ceiling. He remembered not seeing much daylight as a studio musician and how strange it is to not know whether it's 2 a.m. or p.m. Dr. Richie Moore, who also lent a hand during the construction phase, worked with Jack Crymes and Jaffe to tune the control room (later re-tuned by Bob Hodas), which housed a Trident A Range console and custom Westlake monitors, among other items.

When The Automatt closed in 1986, David Rubinson sold them the Trident TSM from Studio B and sent some of his former clients across the Golden Gate, as well. In due time, Studio D became one of the area's premier tracking rooms. Larry White, who would later produce work for Bobby Brown, came in with Con Funk Shun, while Jaffe engineered. One of the group's co-founders, Michael Cooper, would later record parts of his solo album, *Just What I Like,* at Studio D with White. As a producer, Preston Glass brought in a number of R&B acts to Studio D, including Anita Pointer, The Stylistics, and Earth, Wind & Fire. Jaffe engineered many of these as well.

When Earth, Wind & Fire came into Studio D to record their 1987 comeback album, *Touch the World*, they were missing one really killer track. Lo and behold, when Glass walked to his car one night, he found a crumpled brown paper bag wedged on the front window. Inside, a cassette. On that cassette, a demo for a song called "System of Survival." Intrigued, he played the cassette, dug the song, and used it on the album. The track became one of the biggest hits on the record. And they have Michael Aczon, now a prominent entertainment attorney in the Bay Area, to thank for leaving the mysterious package.

Photo courtesy of Joel Jaffe, Studio D Recording

At Studio D, from L to R: Anita Pointer, Earth, Wind & Fire's Philip Bailey (seated), co-owner Joel Jaffe, producer Preston Glass, and co-owner Dan Godfrey (standing).

Acts such as Huey Lewis, Chris Isaak, and Starship used most of the primary facilities in town, Studio D included. As a studio owner, Jaffe cites Bruce Hornsby's 1986 sessions for *The Way It Is* as one of the more memorable projects to come through his doors in the '80s. Lewis, who had a production role in that album, added harmonica and background vocals, with the ubiquitous Jim Gaines engineering a portion of the tracks. Jaffe also recalls Stan Getz playing on a Lewis project, of which he simply says, "Amazing."

In the early '80s when the recession put a minor dent in recording activity, Studio D sailed through unscathed, benefiting from being a hot topic in town. "We were the new kids on the block, so everybody wanted to hear the new room," says Jaffe. Later, when studio activity picked up across the board, Studio D filled their calendar with lockouts, a concept that had diminished somewhat in the very early '80s.

In 1987, producer/engineers Matt Wallace and Steve Berlin brought a relatively young heavy rock band from San Francisco to Studio D to record tracks for their second full-length and first major label (Slash/Rhino) album. The group was Faith No More, in to record *Introduce Yourself*. The group's rap/rock hybrid sound comes forward with a vengeance on this album, though it's the last with vocalist Chuck Mosley. With new singer Mike Patton on board, the group again used Studio D to record *The Real Thing.* "The guitarist was into ugly metal, the keyboardist liked Sade, the bass player was into art rock…all these very different and disparate influences came together," says Wallace, who worked with the band in their demo days, recording them in a makeshift studio in his parents' garage. "Faith No More was instrumental in doing that kind of thing. They were fearless about playing really heavy, ugly music and then going into a pretty pop song."

The group relied heavily on their creative instincts on *The Real Thing*—they didn't have much more to work with. "The album was made with one drum kit, a keyboard, one Gibson bass, a Peavey head, one Gibson Flying V, and a Marshall half stack. That's all we had," says Wallace. "It was bare bones." They hunkered down with their skeleton setup and completed the album start-to-finish in two months.

Studio D forged through the 1990s with a mix of established and mid-level acts. Right behind Faith No More, Soundgarden recorded parts of *Badmotorfinger* (featuring "Jesus Christ Pose," "Rusty Cage," and "Outshined") at the studio in 1991, just as the Seattle "grunge" scene started to take off. Terry Date produced and engineered that album. Third Eye Blind, who would record all over town in the early '90s, and still more studio dates from Lewis came later. Tower of Power's Lenny Williams did an album, *Chill,* at Studio D in the mid '90s, featuring a stellar local cast that included co-producer/arranger/keyboardist Larry Batiste, co-producer/multi-instrumentalist Preston Glass, Con Funk Shun's Felton Pilate, and many others. Talking Head Jerry Harrison, having relocated to San Francisco in the early '90s, used the studio often (he produced Verve Pipe's *Villains,* recorded at Studio D and The Plant in 1997). Alice in Chains guitarist/songwriter Jerry Cantrell's solo album, *Boggy Depot,* was recorded at Studio D and The Plant with hit producer Toby Wright, the man behind several Alice in Chains albums, at the helm.

In order to stay relevant in the ever-changing recording industry, most studios have to put their rooms through expensive technical upgrades. At best, the studio's regular clients keep coming back, and maybe even a few new ones show up, attracted by a particular new console or some other sonic improvement. It's rare that the studio recoups its expense, but it is a necessary evil in order to stay in business. In 2001, Jaffe put Studio D's control room through an extensive overhaul, most notably replacing the Trident console with a new 48-bus Amek 9098i, a Rupert Neve–designed recording/mixing console that came on the market in 2000. The company promised it as "the last word in analog consoles," for its superior sound and advanced features.

Jaffe reconfigured Studio D's control room for the digital age and surround-sound work and equipped the room with a set of JBL LSR28P with LSR12P subwoofers. Outfitting the room for surround certainly yielded benefits, as Jaffe himself has mixed a number of projects in 5.1 surround sound in the new millennium. The Amek, however, actually hurt business. As far as being a tracking console, "It was the best sounding board I had ever worked on," says Jaffe. Unfortunately, the software that controls the automation apparently didn't work properly, which made it impossible for clients to mix. It became an ongoing nightmare for the studio. Finally, after spending thousands of dollars to try to solve the problem, he returned the console to Amek and installed a Digidesign ProControl (with Edit Pack for surround mixing) and a Pro Tools HD system. He held on to his extensive collection of analog gear, with racks of compressors, EQs, reverbs, and other equipment rack-mounted behind the control surface. "This gives us the best of both worlds," he says. "The room is very efficient and clients have been really happy here." To date, there have been no technical difficulties.

The new setup also keeps Jaffe happy, too, as he continues to mix DVD surround projects, having worked on releases for David Gray, Cake, and the San Francisco Blues Festival. He mixed *Ringo Starr and His All-Starr Band—So Far* best-of DVD in surround, a live concert featuring Carlos Santana and Wayne Shorter from Montreux, and the surround and stereo mixes for the Henry Rollins Shock and Awe tour. He is also excited about a project with blues/R&B vocalist Maria Muldaur.

Tarpan Studios

By 1985, Narada Michael Walden's career had ascended from replacing ace drummer Billy Cobham in Mahavishnu Orchestra in the late '70s to in-demand studio drummer to popular solo artist to hit-making record producer. Acts virtually waited in line to work with him and his set crew of phenomenal session players (see Chapter 15). Walden also had albums of his own to work on and songwriting sessions to embark on. He had a lot going on, and as much as he loved working at various Bay Area studios, it became clear that he could work more efficiently with a room of his own. At the same time, his manager, David Rubinson, had decided to close The Automatt, where Walden did most of his work. Upon Rubinson's suggestion, Walden took a drive up to San Rafael to check out Tres Virgos, a one-room facility that was up for sale (see Chapter 17). The studio was housed inside a nondescript building in an office complex–looking strip—no sign out front, no identifying marks whatsoever. No one would ever guess that some of pop music's biggest stars would be privately working inside.

"It was a big room with high ceilings that I knew we could get great sounds in," says Walden. The MCI console in the control room would have to go, but as far as the room itself, Walden knew it would work great as his new home base. He purchased the facility in 1985 from then-owner Gerald Jacobs and christened it Tarpan Studios, meaning "satisfaction unparalleled." He aspired to this ideal, he's said on many occasions, aiming to give "joy to whomever comes to my door so that they can put that joy on tape."

The studio area had been acoustically treated so that different portions of the room provide different acoustics. Oversize windows provide direct lines of sight between control room, studio, and iso booths. Walden's Yamaha C7 grand piano sits toward the front of the room, near the control room window.

The first Tarpan session was ex-Shalamar background singer and ex-Prince & the New Revolution guitarist Jermaine Stewart, in to record *Frantic Romantic,* with its hit "We Don't Have to Take Our Clothes Off," written by Walden. The song hit the Top Five

Singles charts in *Billboard,* and the album went Platinum. This would be Stewart's most successful album.

After The Automatt closed, Walden bought the Trident TSM from Studio A, replacing the old MCI. Janice Lee, also from The Automatt, came over to manage the studio and would stay with Walden's company until 1998. No sooner was the new equipment turned on than a young jazz instrumentalist named Kenny G came in to record his fourth Arista album, *Duotones.* Though he had albums on the street since 1982, he remained virtually an unknown. Because Walden, who executive produced this one, and his studio were so busy, Kenny G had to come in on the "night shift" and work with Walden's "B staff" of musicians, which in this case was a meaningless term. Studio players included Preston Glass on keys (with additional playing from Walter Afanasieff), *American Idol* celeb Randy Jackson on bass, Kenny McDougald on drums, and a long list of additional players. Gordon Lyon engineered. The album featured an even mix of songs written solely by Kenny G and other tracks written in partnership with Glass, Afanasieff, and/or Walden. The album peaked at Number One on *Billboard*'s Top Contemporary Jazz Album chart and made Kenny G a star for the first time. Two for two at Tarpan Studios.

Through the '80s and most of the '90s, Tarpan Studios brought in the top of the pop daily, with stars such as Clarence Clemons with Jackson Browne, Aretha Franklin, Whitney Houston, and Steve Winwood making their way there. "It was a lovely time," Walden recalls. "People were really excited about the music."

When the '90s came, Walden replaced the Trident with an SSL 4000G with Total Recall. The hits continued. The early part of the decade brought him hits with Cherelle, Taylor Dayne, and *The Bodyguard* soundtrack, which includes Houston's chart-topper "I Will Always Love You." Her album *I'm Every Woman,* out that same year, has his name on the back. Diana Ross, George Benson, Al Green, The Temptations, and Mariah Carey have all generated huge hits with Walden's high-energy presence. The list goes on a long, long way, and when Walden says that Tarpan Studios "has had more Number One hits than any other studio in the Bay Area," believe him. Through the years he has managed to stay "in the mix" in L.A. while maintaining his Bay Area headquarters. He bought a home in L.A. and opened a second studio, Tarpan 2, in L.A. for a short time, but continued to live, work, and record in the Bay Area, usually acquiring business in L.A. and bringing it up to Tarpan. A lot of other producers bailed, but Walden affirms that the Bay Area has always been his home and still is.

After 20 years as a private facility, Tarpan Studios opened to the public in 2005. Walden continues to deliver "satisfaction unparalleled" in his comfortable recording retreat.

CHAPTER 21

San Francisco Hills and Valleys

Russian Hill Recording

In November, 1980, former Funky Features owner Jack Leahy and partner Bob Shotland opened Russian Hill Recording in the tony neighborhood of Russian Hill, at 1520 Pacific Avenue. Wedged between the Marina district near San Francisco Bay, Chinatown, and Nob Hill, the studio was surrounded by exquisitely maintained Victorians, a cable-car line, upscale restaurants, and a gorgeous view of the city. This was a clean, mostly residential neighborhood, far removed from Wally Heider Recording's Tenderloin neighborhood or Funky Features' edgy locale in the Haight.

Studio designer Jeff Cooper and contractor Dennis Stearns made the most of this 2,500 square foot space, giving it two recording rooms with high ceilings, hardwood floors, tunable oak walls, velvet and brass accents, and a graceful ambience on par with its somewhat upscale neighborhood.

Studio A originally offered a 52-input Helios board, Yamaha speakers, and Sony color monitors in its control room, which was attached to a 20×30–foot recording area. The smaller Studio B featured a 28-input Neotek Elite Series III and a 13×22–foot room to record in. Both studios contained grand pianos: Steinway and Yamaha. They offered up to 24-track recording via an MCI machine, an array of outboard equipment, the EMT 140 stereo plate, and a nice complement of mics. Their conference room was equipped with audio and video playback systems to accommodate their expanding clientele.

Neither Leahy nor Shotland were Platinum album producers who could finance the studio with their myriad album projects, nor did they have backing from a record label or a wealthy investor. To plump up their revenue stream, the partners decided to cater not only to album productions but television spots, feature-film scoring, sound design, and post-production. In fact, Russian Hill was considered the first San Francisco facility to handle electronic post-production, beginning with the score to *Never Cry Wolf* with Mark Isham and Todd Boekelheide in 1983. When he wasn't ensconced at Fantasy Studios, director Phil Kaufman used Russian Hill's ADR facilities for scenes from *The Right Stuff*. Music recording for a 1983 *Garfield* TV special took place on the hill, as well.

That same year, Russian Hill opened its film-to-tape transfer room, featuring the first KEM K800 machine in the U.S. The addition of the machine gave the studio 16mm and 35mm transfer capability.

When independent film business slowed in the early to mid '80s, especially in the Bay Area, Leahy and Shotland focused more attention on the nearby advertising community, an important industry in the area for years. To meet the ad industry's needs, they installed Sony BVH-1100A one-inch and DVR-20 D2 video decks. The later of these dominated commercial production at the time. They also acquired an 8-channel 16-track Studer Dyaxis II system to supplement their existing Dyaxis I.

By the early '90s, the studio had expanded to offer three rooms, in addition to its transfer room. Studio A upgraded to an SSL 4048E (modified for film use). Studio B kept the Neotek, and both rooms contained UREI 813 Time Align monitors, pairs of Yamaha NS-10s, and Auratone near-fields. Staying up to speed for their steady film business, both rooms offered Q-Lock 3.10 synchronization, a handy device that allowed engineers to lock together two tape machines. Multi-track options included the Otari MTR 90 and MTR-100A. The newer Studio C housed a 24-input Soundcraft 600 console and two Fostex E-16 ½-inch 16-tracks, with a Kelly Quan/Cypher Shadow synchronizer system.

While Russian Hill became known primarily for film and TV projects, they hosted a fair amount of album work. John Lee Hooker recorded three albums at Russian Hill, and Linda Ronstadt with Aaron Neville, Dave Brubeck, John Hammond, and Charlie Musselwhite all spent time there, as well. Film work continued with sound design and post for a Nickelodeon pilot called *Rocco's Modern Life*, while advertising projects included Sega video game spots and Hewlett-Packard laser printers.

Leahy later turned his attention to the posh new Crescendo facility, which he helped open in 1997. In 1999, the neighborhood for which Leahy named his second studio became much quieter. That year, he closed the facility and consolidated his operation into Crescendo Studios.

Mobius Music

Though he didn't open Mobius Music until 1977, owner/engineer/musician Oliver DiCicco had been tinkering with audio equipment since the early '70s, when he built his first mixer out of a kit while still in college studying electronic music in New York. At the time, he owned one of the early Moog synthesizers and a couple of 2-track machines; they came with him when he moved to San Francisco to join a friend's band.

Then he stumbled upon a multi-purpose building in Noe Valley, a quiet residential neighborhood, popular because it's one of the sunniest neighborhoods in San Francisco. In that city, that's important. He pegged the large room in the back of his newfound building for a band rehearsal space, but it soon morphed into a recording studio. "I spent time making it into a real studio," he says. "I designed it, did all the wiring, and built it several times through the years. I was pretty much a one-man show."

He also taught himself how to engineer. "In my first studio [in New York] I had an Ampex MR70 4-track; it was huge," he recalls. "And you couldn't just punch in to record, you had to switch from synch to input and then go into record, so it took two hands to do a punch-in. So there wasn't a lot of punching going on." When he opened Mobius Music in San Francisco, it became both a training ground for his own skills and a viable business.

Living in a city founded on the ideas of innovation, experimentation, and a pioneering spirit made it possible for DiCicco and so many others to take this learn-as-you-go approach. "San Francisco was small, it was livable, it was cheap!" he recalls of an era that predates any dotcom presence by a good 15 years. "You could find an apartment for $200 or $300 a month, there were a lot of clubs, and it was the one place where you could get away with putting together a studio on a shoestring and actually make it work. There were a lot of talented people; it was kind of like a garden, it was totally untended, anything could grow and you could be pretty much anything you wanted to be and everybody was cool with it. I think that ethos is still here. It's one of the few places where it's okay to be who you want to be and no one bats an eye."

Because of his live-to-2-track experience, DiCicco recorded a lot of jazz projects; the music suited this style of recording. He had a 16-in 16-out Quantum 168 console, Altec speakers, Crown amps, and a recently purchased 3M 56 16-track. "I got it from American Recording in L.A.," he recalls. "I had scraped up $10,000 to buy this machine. I drove down with a friend in his Rambler station wagon, and his car blew up on the way down. So we hitchhiked to L.A., and got the owner of the studio to vouch for me so I could rent a station wagon to drive back. We were going to tow my friend's car, but we couldn't disconnect the drive shift, so we ended up abandoning the car. It was a nightmare. But those were the kind of things you had to do."

His experiences taught him well, and the more time he spent in his studio, the faster he could get good sounds, which helped him bring in more business. He was three years into his new operation when Dead Kennedys guitarist East Bay Ray came by to check out the studio as a possible site for their first full-length album, *Fresh Fruit for Rotting Vegetables*. He liked the layout and clicked well with DiCicco, who gave the band a reasonable block rate. So, in the spring of 1980 Ray, Jello Biafra, Klaus Flouride, and Ted entered

Mobius Music. Much of what DiCicco learned through his previous jazz recordings promptly went out the window. The band set up in the main room with only a few 4-foot-high gobos between them. (There were no iso booths at Mobius at the time.) "It was kind of like a shoebox," DiCicco recalls of his studio. "There was carpet on the floor, Fiberglas panels on the walls with burlap on them and then bare Sheetrock. It was a small room and isolation was difficult to achieve. It was probably as bare bones of a recording as you could do. It wasn't fancy, but it was going to 2-inch 16-track, so there was plenty of tape real estate to put sound on. Tape hiss wasn't a problem, because the sound never stopped!"

Working nights (bassist Flouride had a day job), the band spent a week on basic tracks, about another week on overdubs, another on background vocals, keyboards, and horn overdubs, and then a week to mix. The band recorded its songs quickly, while the equally efficient DiCicco faced the challenge of cramming "ten pounds of sound into a five-pound bag," he recalls. "With just the drums and bass playing, you could hear things pretty well, but as soon as the guitar kicked in…Ray was like a wall of sound."

The goal, which they had essentially achieved on the "California Über Alles" 7-inch single previously recorded at Jim Keylor's Army Street/BSU Studios, was, as Biafra put it, to "come as close as we could to capture the fire and extremities of a kick-ass live punk rock show. I was hell-bent on burning down the Hotel California!"

Upon the advice of noted punk producer Geza X (who recorded "Holiday in Cambodia" and "Police Truck" with the band at Tewksbury Sound prior to the *Fresh Fruit* sessions), Biafra made sure every word in his lyrics packed a wallop. X also introduced the singer to higher-quality microphones and double-tracking, which added presence and power to Biafra's distinct warble.

"At Mobius, I was using the same Neumann U47 I use now," Biafra says. "I sang a scratch vocal in the [live] room during the basics and then re-did it. By then, I was using the technique I use today, where I usually blast through maybe three or four takes in a row, and then pick and choose which lines I like the best later.

Sometimes I leave a compiled single track, but on *Fresh Fruit,* it's double-tracked."

Under Ray's supervision, DiCicco mixed the album to an Ampex 351 2-track machine—a straightforward process due to a lack of automation and inputs, but challenging nonetheless. Guitars always had to be louder, with voice added on top. Ray usually stayed in the control room with DiCicco, while Biafra listened in the upstairs lounge, where the speakers apparently sounded a lot like the ones he had at home, giving him a good measuring stick for how the tracks would sound outside the studio. "They were mounted on the wall of the room and they had this lamp cord running up to them, so who knows what was going on with the sound of them?" adds DiCicco. "But for some reason, Biafra liked the sound of those speakers, so when we were mixing, he'd be up there listening to the mixes and yelling down to me through this door into the control room, and I'd hear him yelling and I'd think, 'Okay I guess that means turn something up,' and then if I didn't get it right, he'd come in and go, 'No, no, no, no.' He was pretty particular about how things were going to sound. Nothing was ever fast enough or loud enough."

Biafra clarifies, "Ray and [Ted] would argue incessantly that I was being too picky about the mix, but in the long run, I have no regrets about that. As [9 Lives cat food spokescat] Morris the Cat once said, 'It pays to be finicky.' People still like listening to our albums, and part of that is because somebody went the extra mile to make sure they sounded good."

DKs returned for portions of future albums—lead vocal overdubs for *Frankenchrist*, some basic tracks for *In God We Trust*—but Mobius really became more of a spot for jazz, new age, and avant garde than rock and punk. "Ironically, within two years of doing the Dead Kennedys stuff I ended up doing a lot of albums for Windham Hill," says DiCicco. Albums for mandolinist Mike Marshall, Alex DiGrassi, label founder Will Ackerman, Michael Manrig and *Winter's Solstice* and *Winter's Solstice III* all came out of the Mobius facility.

In the mid '80s, DiCicco reconfigured the studio by raising the ceiling, installing hardwood floors, moving the control room back, and relocating the lounge, which made it even more conducive to jazz and acoustic music. Acts such as Bill Frisell, Charlie Hunter, and Henry Kaiser took advantage of the redo.

"This was never a really heavy rock and roll studio, not like Fantasy or The Plant, especially," he says. "But we had our own little niche and a pretty loyal client base. This was never a high profile studio, either. Most of my work came from referrals; I had to do things on my terms and do what I could honestly pull off."

DiCicco closed Mobius Music as a commercial studio business in 2004. He now works as a designer and visual artist, builds musical instrument sculptures, and leads an experimental music project, Mobius Operandi Ensemble. The group rehearses in the former Mobius control room, DiCicco's original intention for the Noe Valley space coming full circle after 28 years.

SECTION FIVE

The Nineties: From Digital Boom to Dotcom Bust

If one looked at every decade in recording history as a roller coaster, the 1990s would have Six Flags' tallest thrill ride beat. The Bay Area continued to produce commercially successful acts through the '90s, and the scene's community spirit remained intact. Crooner Chris Isaak continued to release well-received albums, and locals such as Four Non Blondes, Counting Crows, Faith No More, Metallica, Primus, Mr. Bungle, Tracy Chapman, Third Eye Blind, Train, and American Music Club all reaped commercial success. Tom Waits and the Grateful Dead carried on, and at the end of the decade, Santana made a long-awaited return to the top of the charts with the multi-Platinum *Supernatural.*

Meanwhile, the Bay Area punk scene exploded once again in the mid-1990s, spurred by the remarkable success of Berkeley-based Green Day's major label debut, *Dookie,* which hit in 1994. Their former label, Lookout Records, reaped the benefit from interest in the band's earlier releases, while Lookout acts such as The Riverdales accompanied Green Day on its first arena tour. City dwellers NOFX, another pop-punk favorite, charted well around this time—and the studio that frontman Fat Mike ran with producer/engineer Ryan Greene, Motor Studios, ran no fewer than 16 hours a day for a period in the mid '90s.

The area also produced some hot R&B and hip-hop during this time, most notably from Digital Underground and The Hieroglyphics collective, which counted among its members Del the Funky Homosapien, Casual, Pep Love, Domino, and the group Souls of Mischief. Also making their marks in the Bay Area at this time were Too Short, E-40, M.C. Hammer, Raphael Saadiq (formerly of Tony Toni Toné and Lucy Pearl), and Bobby Brown, among others.

A little farther south down in Silicon Valley, the heart of high-tech, venture capitalists opened their bank accounts to fund an onslaught of forward-thinking computer-savvy entrepreneurs who wanted to take advantage of the new Internet highways and byways via e-commerce companies—the Internet start-up. Progressive San Francisco, an hour's drive from San Jose (Silicon Valley central), became an ideal location for these Gen Xers, who brought their expanding portfolios to the city. They set up offices, mostly in the South of Market neighborhood (SOMA). They wanted apartments there, too.

Competition for rentals became so tough that people would line up around the block just to put in an application for a tiny one-bedroom flat. Landlords and property owners subsequently jacked up the rent on housing and commercial space. The dotcommers didn't much care; they had more than enough money to pay those ridiculous rents. The creative community—the musicians, visual artists, poets, photographers, and writers—found themselves priced out of their own neighborhoods. Buildings formerly used for artist live/work space and rehearsal studios went to dotcom companies for quadruple the rent. To make matters worse, the new arrivals generally didn't much care for live music: too angry, too depressing, you can't dance to it. The DJ culture emerged. Live music clubs transformed into dance clubs; many others shut down. Performing musicians had fewer places to plug in their amps than ever before. So, with no place to play and no place to live, many local artists moved away, heading for Seattle, Portland, Los Angeles—anywhere but San Francisco.

The area's recording studios, historically supported in part by local musicians, felt the effects. Some experienced a slowdown in business and had to close. Others, such as Greg Freeman's Lowdown Studios, Coast Recorders, and Brilliant Studios, were forced out by urban development and/or greedy landlords.

Even with commercial studios closing, the artists who did stick around had more options than ever when it came time to record, thanks to the rise of the home studio. The arrival of inexpensive modular digital multi-track recorders such as the Alesis ADAT and the TASCAM DA-88, followed by the rise of Digidesign's Pro Tools and other computer-driven workstations, made setting up a personal studio a very attractive option for space-confined engineers and musicians. Working at personal studios shaved thousands off an artist's recording costs, but it also took away a large portion of many studios' business at the same time. If these studios wanted to survive into the new millennium, they had to revise their business plan—and soon.

In 2000, the dotcom expansion began to shrivel as quickly as it had grown as capital dried up and investors fled. By 2001, the bubble had burst, leaving a bewildered San Francisco left to pick up the pieces. A music community that had been so vital and full of talent for decades had essentially disintegrated. They're still trying to get it back. Then, on September 11, 2001, terrorists attacked the World Trade Center; the social and economic impact affected every industry nationwide. It was a bad time for everyone, and the places where music happened suffered with everyone else.

Before these turns of events, a few significant new facilities appeared on the scene, while existing heavies such as Hyde Street, Fantasy Studios, Different Fur, Studio D, and The Plant hung on for the ride.

CHAPTER 22

Coast-to-Coast-to…*Toast?*

When we left Coast Recorders on Mission Street (a.k.a. CAM), it was humming along as it had since Bill Putnam assumed the lease on the building in 1970, acting as a home away from home for advertising jingles, jazz, and the miscellaneous electric project. Phil Edwards, who split his time between sessions at Coast and his own facility next door (see Chapter 12), moved out of his studio in 1985 when his landlord tripled the rent. He closed the studio but kept his remote truck, formerly owned by Stu Cook and Doug Clifford of Creedence Clearwater Revival, and moved his business to Hayward, in the East Bay. These days he often parks the truck at Fantasy Studios, where his former boss from the Columbus Recorders days, mastering engineer George Horn, works. Meanwhile, Dan Alexander had a fairly successful operation going at Hyde Street. He based his equipment sales company out of the studio until 1985, when he relocated his offices to Berkeley, and Studio C, now Sandy Pearlman's Alpha and Omega, took care of itself. Then, in 1988, Allen Sides called. He was in San Francisco visiting Coast Recorders, which, he told Alexander, was for sale. Sides suggested he come and take a look. "So I went over there, walked into Studio A and thought, 'Wow, this is like one of the little rooms at United Western. This is great!'"

Not long after that fortuitous phone call, Alexander bought Coast Recorders from Bill Putnam, who owned the master lease.

Putnam was nearing retirement, and the Coast sale was one of Putnam's last studio business deals. Alexander took over Coast in early 1989, but he started fixing up the place almost a year earlier.

Alexander planned to re-equip all three studios, but he had some cleaning up to do first. He didn't have to deal with orange carpet this time; there were just minor cases of neglect. "One day, about three weeks after I started, I was cleaning the main studio and came upon these two piles of telephone books about three feet tall," says Alexander. "I go out to the lobby, a staff of five are sitting around drinking coffee, and I say, 'Do we use these phone books that are in Studio A?' They look at me, they look at each other, and one them says, 'What phone books?'" he laughs. "So that's what it was like at Coast Recorders."

Yellow Pages promptly trashed, Alexander set about upgrading Coast's equipment. Studio A's MCI JH-428B console, an "ancient piece of dreck," as Alexander recalls, and the smaller rooms' Neotek Model 1 and Harrison 3624 console (formerly of The Automatt) all went away within the first couple of years. Alexander installed a 40-input Neve 8026 in Studio A. "The modules came from New Zealand, the frame came from an auction in England," Alexander recalls. "We spent about a year rebuilding it. Another Neve, a 28-input 5305 belonging to a TV station in England, one of two in a series, replaced the Harrison in Studio B, while Studio D (there was no Studio C by this time), a small voiceover room, received an "odd little Neve" 12-input mixer. Alexander also brought in an Otari MTR-90 24-track tape machine, followed shortly by Studer A820 and A827 24-tracks and other equipment.

When Alexander took over CAM, a lot of the longstanding clients continued to work there, unlike what happened during the Heider-to–Hyde Street changeover. Concord Records brought in numerous projects, and acts such as Rosemary Clooney and Tito Puente, who recorded five albums at the new Coast, still frequented the studio. National and local advertising work also kept coming. Clients in the late '80s and early '90s included McDonalds, the San Francisco Chronicle, and Charles Schwab. Even Alistair Cooke broadcast his long-running radio show *Letters From America* from Coast Recorders until 1996.

Coast on Mission's Studio A during the Dan Alexander years.

John Cuniberti

In the early '90s, Coast Recorders officially broke from its "jingles and jazz" recipe, hosting the first of many rock and alternative projects. In 1992 local rap/rock/prog band Faith No More entered Coast with producer Matt Wallace to record *Angel Dust*. Their previous album, *The Real Thing* (covered in Chapter 20), took only a matter of weeks to record and happened relatively smoothly, but *Angel Dust* took its toll on both the band and its producer. "After a couple of weeks my assistant was just kind of never around, which was a drag, so I ended up producing, engineering, assisting, and even answering the phone!" says Wallace.

Personal conflicts upped the anxiety level even further. Faith No More had escalated to the top of the hard rock scene, but they were imploding as a band. Guitarist Jim Martin's father had died just prior to the *Angel Dust* sessions, so he wasn't fully present. Keyboardist Roddy Bottum came out of the closet. Plus, the band didn't like the direction of the record, ironically calling it "gay disco music." "The record was fraught with a lot of tension and turmoil," says Wallace.

The "little" Neve in Coast's Studio B.

At the same time, it was a very creative period for the band, especially for Mike Patton, who had become stronger as a vocalist, and whose vocal experimentations had become more accomplished, if not more unusual. Gregorian chants and other vocal acrobatics, combined with distortion on songs such as "Smaller and Smaller," sound more like another instrument in the band, as opposed to a vehicle for lyrics. After Wallace mixed the album at Scream Studios in L.A., he took a well-deserved three-month break.

Following Faith No More's album, Kim and Kelley Deal's band, The Breeders, came through in 1993, recording their alt-rock smash *Last Splash* at Coast and Brilliant. Other projects that year included local guitarist/solo artist Chuck Prophet, recording *Balinese Dancer*, and other projects from Joe Satriani (with John Cuniberti at the helm), Starship, and Patton's Mr. Bungle.

Wallace came back to Coast with Paul Westerberg (of The Replacements) to finish his first solo album, *14 Songs*, in 1993. They had started the project at RPM Sound Studios in New York and had a few songs down when Westerberg unexpectedly fired his entire band but kept Wallace, who shuttled him out to San Francisco to finish tracking and overdubs. Wallace and Westerberg employed a sort of "guerilla recording" process, which suited Westerberg's intuitive writing and recording style. Westerberg wrote and Wallace recorded "World Class Fad" in about an hour. Westerberg then recorded "Even Here We Are" on his own with Wallace's Fostex X15 4-track in the RPM bathroom. With a talent such as Westerberg, songs surface anywhere, anytime. "I always had to be one step ahead of Paul," says Wallace. "I set up a [Neumann] U47 mic on an Atlas boom stand right behind the console so I could swing it around if I needed to. Once the band got a take on a couple of songs, he came in the room and was so excited at hearing the playback, he wanted to sing right then. So I literally cranked the monitors up, and he grabbed the U47 and sang the song in the control room. Technically, that's fundamentally wrong, but we did it anyway. A lot of the record was about recording the band live and capturing the moment."

Matt Wallace (left) and Paul Westerberg in-session at Coast.

Photo courtesy of *Mix* magazine

Sessions at Coast continued for a couple more years; then Alexander found himself in a familiar predicament. This time, instead of Allen Sides tipping him off to Coast Recorders' availability, it was one of San Francisco's pioneering studios, Golden State Recorders, on the market. Owner/engineer Leo de Gar Kulka decided to retire from the studio business in 1995. Intrigued by what promised to be an exciting opportunity, Alexander paid Kulka a visit. "The studio had a sound that you would just die for," he recalls. Aside from falling for the studio, he had seemingly more practical reasons for purchasing another studio. "At the same time that Golden State became available, Michael Ward [his former Hyde Street partner] bought a 91,000 square foot building on Oak

Street just off of Van Ness for *$1 million*." This elaborate Beaux-Arts structure, originally built in 1914 for the Young Men's Institute, a Catholic fraternal and benevolent organization founded in San Francisco in 1883, now houses the San Francisco Conservatory of Music. "Ward's talked-about plan was to turn the ballroom into this huge recording studio, and when I was at CAM, I was very concerned that this would have a big impact on my business. Of course the studio never happened by a long shot."

Alexander took Kulka's space on Harrison Street, claiming it as the new site for Coast Recorders. He tried to keep studios on both Mission and Harrison Streets running simultaneously, but after a couple of months he knew he would have to let CAM go. The building would keep its original name...almost. We'll revisit that situation a little later in this chapter.

Coast-on-Harrison

After a nine-month or so clean-up time, in 1995, Alexander moved most of his equipment, including the Neve 5305 console that resided in CAM's Studio B, to the considerably larger Golden State Recorders space. Alexander had obtained the Neve's sister board by this time, giving him two identical consoles with sequential serial numbers. He locked them together and made the essential modifications to create a 72-input Neve with GML Automation. He also brought over his Studer and Otari tape machines to Harrison Street. Alexander retained the wonderfully live acoustics of the 40×45–foot tracking room, but he updated the studio by adding four iso booths, a machine room, and a lounge.

Due to its size, historically good acoustics, and the Neve console, the new Coast Recorders proved quite popular. Chris Isaak recorded *Baja Sessions* at the studio, mostly acoustic, mostly live, in single takes. Engineer Mark Needham got it all on tape; Eric Jacobsen produced. Cake and Tower of Power took advantage of the ample space, as well. Kevin Gilbert, fresh off of a hugely successful venture as a sideman on Sheryl Crow's *Tuesday Night Music Club* album, came in to record his solo album, *Thud*, mixed by Cuniberti. Over the next couple of years they would see visits from Red House Painters and Don Johnson, who would drop in to work on music in between shooting *Nash Bridges* episodes. Matt Wallace recorded three tracks with Train just after they signed with Aware/ Columbia Records. He stayed at the studio to mix their hit single, "Meet Virginia" and the song "Free." John Cuniberti visited Coast-on-Harrison as an engineer, doing yet more work with Satriani, among other clients, and he managed the studio from 1996 to 1998.

Double the size, double the fun: The expanded Neve at Coast Recorders on Harrison Street.

John Cuniberti

As the '90s came to a close, Coast, like many other studios, experienced a slowdown in business as some of their regular clients built their own studios. In the '90s, the development of affordable pro (and semi-pro) recording equipment made building a home recording studio about as affordable as buying a nice car, and was more economical in the long run than renting a studio for $1,000 or more a day over a period of several weeks for each album. "You can't bring in enough people from out of town in any given month to support any studio," said Cuniberti. Of the rise of the home studio, he says, "It's a dangerous trend, because it's repeat clients that make or break it."

The rising price of housing and commercial space in late '90s San Francisco, a direct result of the dotcom explosion, led to Coast's demise. The building's landlord was a "billionaire property owner whose new property manager thought she could get brownie points by kicking us out and moving in some dotcom company for 20 [thousand dollars] a month," says Alexander. When they were four days late on their rent one month, the landlord evicted them.

After 35 years and thousands of recordings, the property owners gutted the building completely, right down to the outer walls, intending to sell or lease the building as office space to an Internet startup. That didn't happen. Much to the landlord's chagrin, the building remained vacant for many months, the law of Karma set in motion.

Two Coast staffers try out Coast Recorders' live room.

John Cuniberti

The Coast-on-Harrison era would conclude Alexander's dealings as a studio owner, but he continues to run his equipment sales company, Dan Alexander Audio, out of his Berkeley offices, supplying most of the other studio guys in town with prized vintage equipment.

Hot Toast

When Dan Alexander decided to move his operation over to Harrison Street, he turned over the lease on the Mission Street building to engineer Craig Silvey (John Lee Hooker, Nine Inch Nails, and Pearl Jam) and Philip Steir, who had co-founded and drummed for San Francisco–based electronic/industrial/activist band Consolidated. Signed and sealed, Alexander asked the two musician/engineers what they would call their new studio. In a twisted tribute to 1340 Mission's 25-plus-year legacy, they deemed it...Toast. "I never forgave them," Alexander says dryly.

Alexander also sold them the Neve 8026 he had in Studio A, while Steir and Silvey brought in a Trident TSM 32×24 with Uptown Automation for Studio B, which they intended for overdubs and "budget" sessions. In a 2000 interview with *Pro Sound News,* studio manager Chris Lyon described the ambience of their B studio as being "sort of like a chic California living room."

This living room hang, however, had gear virtually stacked to the rafters. They had Sony 3348 48-track digital, Studer A800 24-track analog and 16-track Tascam D-88s for tracking sessions, as well as a 16-channel Pro Tools III system with Sample Cell and an 8-channel Pro Tools I system with TDM for tracking, editing and/or mixing. Clients could listen as loud as they liked with UREI 813, Yamaha NS 10, Mastering Labs ML 10, Tannoy LGM 12, and Genelec 1031 A monitors. Reverb? No problem. Toast offered an EMT 140 plate, a TC Electronic M-5000, an Eventide DSP-4000, an Eventide H-3000, an Eventide 2016, a Sony D-7, a Sony M-7, an SPX 990, a Roland R880, a Lexicon PCM 80 and a Lexicon PCM 60.

Steir and Silvey also added a thick swipe of outboard gear to Toast. The spread included choice compressors and EQs from UREI, Tube Tech, GML, dbx, and Neve. The Toast team had an equally solid mic selection, including two original AKG C 12s, two Scheops 221 B tube mics, two Neumann M49s, a Telefunken U47, a Neumann Lepzig (U47), and other Neumann, AKG, Shure, and Coles options.

A young, enthusiastic engineering staff, combined with equally young but enterprising owners with strong musical backgrounds and a lot of gear at their disposal helped Toast bring in a hip crowd right away. During their first year of business, Third Eye Blind recorded its multi-Platinum self-titled debut at Toast with producer Eric Valentine. They came back in 1999 to record *Blue* with Jason Carmer.

Carmer joined the Third Eye Blind team thanks to Toast. He had visited the studio a few years earlier to record Geffen act Black Lab at the same time Third Eye Blind was recording their debut with Valentine. "I think [frontman] Stephan [Jenkins] heard what I was doing and thought it sounded good," says Carmer, who had previously recorded Royal Trux and other bands at the Machine Shop, a "crappy" 8-track studio he had on Mason Street down in the Tenderloin. "But they were already doing the record with Eric, so we kept in touch. Then we did a song together for a cartoon and we've been working together ever since."

Toast's next big booking came from alternative rock kingpins R.E.M., who spent about three months at Toast to work on *Up* with producer/engineer Patrick McCarthy. Released in 1998, the album was their first as a trio, after the resignation of drummer Bill Berry.

When frontman Michael Stipe, guitarist Peter Buck, and bassist Mike Mills entered the studio in February of that year, they had only a loose plan of how to compensate for the loss of Berry. They discussed using drum loops even before Berry left the band, but were still largely unprepared for sessions with no drummer.

Buck, Mills, Buck's Tuatara bandmate Barrett Martin, and Beck drummer Joey Waronker all contributed beats at various times. Drum machines, early models culled from Buck's home studio, filled in the gaps. An array of tubular bells, vibraphone, Mellotron, a Moog, and other analog synthesizers added even more color to the standard guitar-bass-drums rock band configuration.

During their three-month stay, frontman Michael Stipe taped lyric sheets for songs-in-progress on the walls leading into Studio A. In the control room, two toy dinosaurs brought in by Peter Buck decorated the mixing desk. Apparently, he had bought the dinos 15 years prior; they presided over every R.E.M. session since their 1983 album *Murmur*. Buck also posted colorful Fillmore and Family Dog posters from the '60s inside the control room, including one from a 1966 Lenny Bruce show. Between sessions for Third Eye Blind, Steir filled in the gaps with his own projects. After Consolidated, he became increasingly in demand as a remixer and producer, and brought projects for Butthole Surfers, Pete Townshend, New Order, Kylie Minogue, Korn, Orgy, Len, Smashmouth, Bush, and Live to Toast. Pretty soon there weren't very many gaps to fill. Carmer became a regular client, recording and/or mixing projects for Korn, Butthole Surfers, Run DMC, and others. Engineer Jaquire King also became a frequent visitor, having worked on projects for Smashmouth and Tom Waits when he wasn't working front-of-house for Bimbo's 365 club over on Columbus Avenue in North Beach. Other producers and engineers to pop in Toast included Rick Rubin, (Johnny Cash, Beastie Boys), Gggarth Richardson (Rage Against the Machine, The Red Hot Chili Peppers), Dave Bianco (Ozzy Osbourne, Tom Petty, Mick Jagger), Joe Chicarelli (Frank Zappa, American Music Club), Mark Needham (Chris Isaak), and Nate Kunkel (Lyle Lovett, James Taylor).

Sheryl Crow, Mary Chapin Carpenter, Lucy Pearl, Imperial Teen, Save Ferris, Neil Young, Me'Shell Ndegé Ocello, Blackalicious, and No Doubt all came into 1340 Mission during Toast's five-year run. In a short time, the studio had become one of San Francisco's most active studios, bolstered by its ability to bring in a solid stream of work from outside of S.F.

Despite all of its selling points, Toast suffered as much as any business after the disastrous new millennium triad of dot-com bust, 9/11, and withering music industry. By 2002, Toast was toast. Steir closed the studio and moved to L.A. to resume his career as a producer/remixer. "The very simple reason why Toast closed," Steir explained in a 2004 interview with *SF Weekly*, "was that bands stopped making albums in San Francisco. Album projects ended." With budgets slashed, the idea of heading out of town for a few weeks or months to record just wasn't feasible for many musicians anymore. The out-of-towners stayed out of town, and a lot of the local musicians had left, pushed out by soaring rents and greedy landlords. San Francisco was drying up just as much as Toast.

CHAPTER 23

The Plant: 25 Years and Counting

In late 1993, Bob Skye sold his interest in The Plant to his partner, Arne Frager. About a year later, Frager put Studio A through an extensive near-$1 million renovation. "We completely demolished the studio to the ground," says Frager, who supervised the rebuild with then-technical director Manny LaCarrubba. "We built up the ceiling to about 32 feet high so we'd have a really big, live rock-and-roll studio." The control room, renovated only six years prior, didn't change much. The SSL 4056 remained in place until 2003, when Frager replaced it with an SSL 9000J, the first in the Bay Area.

But the live room was expanded to 26×31 feet with three iso booths, measuring 3×3, 9×9, and 10×12 feet. Frager also had a dedicated lounge and kitchen built for Studio A. Metallica christened the room in April 1995 by cutting tracks for two albums, *Load* and *Reload*. To announce its presence, the band put a silver skull on the console. Engineers plastered skull-and-crossbones flags and nude pinups to the walls. Contrary to popular belief, Frager did not build the studio *for* Metallica, although they did spend the better part of a year there. He did, however, use the long booking as leverage to obtain funding for the studio. "I built the studio for The Plant, not Metallica," he says. Live, Santana, The Breeders, and Dave Matthews Band followed the metal mayhem.

The revamped Studio A, circa 2000.

Tom Rider

In 1997, the year the studio celebrated its 25th anniversary, Dave Matthews Band and producer Steve Lillywhite settled into The Plant to record *Before These Crowded Streets,* their third album for RCA. As was tradition with Plant guests, Matthews stayed on a houseboat at the nearby waterfront. He could walk to work every day, passing by gardens and taking in the fresh air—warmer air than their previous recording locale in Woodstock, New York. "It just seemed like a really relaxed atmosphere here," Matthews said in a November, 1997 interview with *Marin Independent Journal.* "It's great to be in a new place. All you can do is sort of pray that the spirit here will come out in what we do." The spirit moved them to come back a few years later for *Busted Stuff,* recorded in back-to-basics fashion in two months.

The same year, Frager launched the studio's record label, Pop Mafia, in partnership with Paul Marszalek of San Francisco rock radio station KFOG. They initially released albums from local acts Zero, Eddie Miller, and Blueland, distributed through the

Alternative Distribution Alliance. Pop Mafia ultimately yielded no discernable hits but gave a boost to a handful of local acts.

In the midst of studio and record-label activities, Frager had a Neve 8068 with GML Automation installed in Studio B; this had been acquired from The Record Plant in L.A. Aside from minor renovations that included the addition of iso booths and raising the ceiling height to 18 feet, Studio B still retained most of its original character.

Between 1988, when Frager assumed part ownership of The Plant, and 1997, he estimates $3 million spent in new equipment and rebuilding the studios. And he still wasn't finished!

The Plant's Neve-equipped Studio B.

Tom Rider

In 1998, he negotiated a deal with investor Eckard Wintzen, owner of recording school Ex'pression Center for New Media in Emeryville, which allowed him to not only pump funds into his Pop Mafia label but to also begin work on The Garden, an impressive surround mix room housed in what was formerly Studio 01. In Gary Kellgren tradition, it came with a private garden/lounge with hot tub out back.

Also in the spirit of Kellgren's quirky studio design concepts, Frager and LaCarrubba, who handled the acoustics and designed the custom monitoring system, gave The Garden an elliptical shape. With visual artist/interior designer Rose Greenway, they chose an elaborate lighting system that shines 16.7 million hues out of its LED-based canisters. The overall look of The Garden resembles the inside of a fish tank.

The Garden.

Tom Rider

Creating The Garden's custom surround monitoring system proved to be an equally involving job. "I've been working for some years with the wide dispersion of high frequencies, and I've developed what I call the Acoustic Lens," LaCarrubba told *Mix* magazine in 1999. The mains use the Acoustic Lens for the midrange and tweeter sections. "It's a patented, proprietary device, and it gives a wonderfully flat response curve over a broad horizontal coverage area. Basically, it redistributes a driver's sound power, stealing from the vertical Peter to pay the horizontal Paul. The sweet spot is just stupidly huge, and at the same time, you're getting less splash off the console, floor and ceiling."

When building the studio, they fittingly discovered a huge concrete pit, and it wasn't Sly Stone's Pit. In it, LaCarrubba created two 20 cubic-foot enclosures to house the dual 18-inch subs. Rather than go with the popular SSL 9000J, he opted to save that purchase for later and go with the 8096 G plus with Ultimation, extensively refurbished by Bruce Millett at Desk Doctor in Burbank. They launched the $2 million rebuild anticipating a big demand for surround music mixing, but with record labels' increasingly restricted budgets, surround didn't take off nearly as quickly as expected. The Garden served as a popular mix room nonetheless. Not long after it opened in May, 1999, Primus stopped in to mix *Rhinoplasty*. In the other Plant studios, one might find Kenny Wayne Shepherd, Stabbing Westward, or Guster in one room, Third Eye Blind, Too Short, or The Deftones in another.

The next redo came in 2000 when Frager turned the former Boomtown space, which had been occupied by Talking Head Jerry Harrison and Booker T. Jones, into Plant Mastering, to be run by John Cuniberti, who had joined the facility in 1999 to supervise The Garden's construction. Equipped with a Crookwood UK desk, a SADiE workstation, and 801 Nautilus monitors, among other items, the spacious suite proved a worthy investment. "It paid for itself in the first year and has been a very successful business," he says. More than 1,000 records (and counting) have come out of Cuniberti's studio, including major-label projects for Tracy Chapman, the Neville Brothers, Fela Kuti, Dead Kennedys, and a slew of locals—many for hip-hop label Quannum Records, Rogue Wave, DJ Shadow, Beth Waters, Michael Joy, and many others. Cuniberti still works out of The Plant, and found time in between mastering gigs to engineer albums for Train, Joe Satriani, the Funky Meters, and others.

CHAPTER 24

Two Dotcom Storm Survivors

In 1997, Toast was in its halcyon years, as was Coast Recorders' new Harrison Street location. The Plant, Hyde Street, Fantasy Studios, and Different Fur carried on as usual. Yet, among San Francisco's few "big" studios lay hundreds of demo rooms, mid-size project studios, home studios, and even garage studios hidden away in the densely populated city. The dotcommers hadn't infiltrated yet, which meant more affordable studios for indie bands, with Brilliant Studios being one of the more popular options.

Tiny Telephone

Add Tiny Telephone to the roster. It opened in '97, when current owner/musician John Vanderslice and a team of others decided to form a co-op rehearsal/recording space hidden away in the Outer Mission district, in a gated "industrial shantytown" of metal-paneled buildings housing mechanical art troupes and other creative entities. For years, Vanderslice and friends, one of them a contractor, spent nights and weekends constructing a frame for the studio, nonparallel walls, a control room, double-paned windows—the works. As time went on, everyone in the group dropped out except Vanderslice. Fine for him, as his band at the time, MK Ultra, needed a place to record anyway. Vanderslice gradually began acquiring gear piece by piece: A Quantum Audio Labs QA 2000 here, a fussy Ampex MM1000 16-track there.

The large studio features an 18×25–foot live room, 9 ½×9–foot iso booth, and two smaller booths for guitar amps. He painted the halls and lounge pink, decorated the live room with colored lights, and put cool lamps and a comfortable couch in the control room. Tiny Telephone doesn't have many frills, but it does have Peet's coffee (a draw in itself for many in the Bay Area), tea, a coffeemaker, and a microwave. When he opened the studio, he charged $100 a day.

By word-of-mouth alone, Tiny Telephone began to attract a handful of engineers, drawn by Vanderslice's commitment to analog recording. Local bands, such as Erase Errata, Deerhoof, and the now-defunct Beulah filtered in based on Vanderslice's reputation as a likeable and insanely talented musician, as well as a maker of great-sounding records that he describes as "sloppy hi-fi." The lure of an affordable studio didn't hurt either. When Counting Crows guitarist David Bryson closed his Dancing Dog studio, engineers Damien Rasmussen and Rick Stone and tech Lawrence Mannion brought a lot of their work to Tiny Telephone, along with their Mogami TT cables and mic stands. Mannion did the wiring, snakes, TT bays, cabling, and general maintenance on the console. Vanderslice made room for Greg Freeman's equipment and services after his Lowdown studio was demolished for the San Francisco Giants' stadium (AT&T Park). Bit by bit, he acquired more gear, including a Hammond B3 organ from some kid for $300 (but worth several thousand), a Fender Rhodes, Moog Prodigy and ARP Odyssey synths, a Baldwin upright piano, and other vintage keyboards, as well as Gibson, Fender, and Vox amps, cabinets, and effects pedals.

Within a year, out-of-town bands found out about "Tiny," as it is affectionately known around town, including emo darlings-turned-rock-stars Death Cab for Cutie, Shellac member/producer Bob Weston from Chicago, and Austin's Spoon. Spoon's producer John Croslin even moved to San Francisco in 1999 to work at Tiny Telephone as a partner/house engineer. Meanwhile, the locals kept coming: Creeper Lagoon, Thinking Fellers Union Local 282,

Granfaloon Bus, members of Counting Crows, Dieselhead, Chuck Prophet, and Richard Buckner, to name a few.

As far as studio owners go, Vanderslice keeps a high profile in the clubs and the business end of music, which works to his advantage. As a touring musician, he's consistently surrounded by musicians. If he hears a band he likes, he can court it for an album project for the studio. He has also developed relationships with a number of record labels. As a result, indies such as 4AD, Kill Rock Stars, Merge, Matador, Subpop, and locals Fat Wreck Chords and Lookout Records, not to mention Elektra and Dreamworks, have all brought projects to the studio.

By the time the '90s closed, Vanderslice had upgraded his equipment and upped his rate to $350 a day, with an additional $200 for the engineer. He replaced the Quantum with a Neve 5316 that has 30 33114 EQ/mic pre channels, the circuitry of Neve 8078 series consoles, and Audiomate moving fader automation. He sold the Ampex to local rock band Oranger and brought in a Studer A827 24-track. He augments his "analog haven" with Neve, Millennia Media, and API preamps and EQs, UREI, Tube Tech, dbx, and Empirical Labs compressors, an EMT 140 plate reverb, and ample microphones. He avoids digital recording. For mixdown, he has an Ampex ATR 102 ½-inch and Ampex 440C ¼-inch. He makes a focused effort to keep his old equipment well maintained; upkeep isn't cheap, but the results, in his opinion, are worth it. Only very recently did he purchase a Pro Tools MixPlus system.

Tiny Telephone survived the dotcom boom and bust in part by keeping rates low and maintaining up-front business practices (no sliding scale for major label clients, no hidden fees, no discounts). Even now, the studio rents for half the price of comparable studios, and it is always busy. Still, Vanderslice has admitted that the studio barely breaks even. "People ask me, 'How do you sell out every month?'" said Vanderslice in a June 9, 2004 interview with *SF Weekly*. "And I say the same thing: 'I am totally, completely under market by 50 percent, 60 percent.' The only way that I could ever sustain it is that I have always had outside jobs."

His outside job as a solo artist is doing quite well these days. His latest album, *Pixel Revolt*, out in late 2005 on the Barsuk label, has earned rave reviews and led to a European tour opening for Death Cab for Cutie, as well as a U.S. headlining tour through 2006.

As Tiny Telephone nears its 10th anniversary, it continues to sell out every month.

Studio 880

In a bleak area of Oakland, past warehouses and rundown houses, near the end of a dead-end street, no one really notices the plain building surrounded by a gated chain-link fence. If they hear the high roar of a motor, they probably just assume it's just another motorcycle zooming by on the I-880 freeway, not Tré Cool of Green Day steering a go-cart around the Studio 880 parking lot.

John Lucasey opened Studio 880 in 1998 as phase one of his larger 880 Entertainment plan, which includes a record label, film and music production, and a recording studio. As a longtime musician and producer himself, as well as former stunt double and emerging filmmaker, owning and operating a multi-faceted complex seems to satisfy his creative passions as well as his natural inclination toward risk-taking.

He opened as a one-room studio first, but he quickly expanded to three rooms. A hip roster of clients followed, drawn by the gear and the whimsical-meets-modern atmosphere. A receptionist greets clients from a main floor that resembles the set of an *Indiana Jones* film—palm trees, thick wood stairwells, and beams that look like tree trunks. At the top of the stairs, Tiki Bob, a totem acquired from the first *Scooby Doo* movie, stands guard over the complex. A walk through the tropics leads to the posh studios with maroon velvet wall coverings, stars on the ceiling, and recreational diversions such as a bar.

Studio A, the showplace and main tracking room, originally contained an SSL 4056 G+ console in its 19×24–foot control room, which is fully stocked with new and vintage outboard gear, including

26 channels of vintage Neve preamps. The studio also has 24-track Otari analog machines as well as Pro Tools (upgraded to HD|3). Studios A and B are set up for both stereo and surround sound work. In 2005, they replaced the SSL with a Digidesign ICON system and 32-fader D-Control work surface. As of this writing, plans were afoot to replace the ICON with a to-be-determined analog console.

The 40×35–foot live room has a reputation for producing the "killer" drum sound. The live room also offers two large iso booths and a Yamaha C7 grand piano. When it's break time, clients can retreat to Studio A's private lounge, game room (with ping-pong and pool), or private gym. They can also take advantage of pre-production and rehearsal space and that handy stocked bar.

Studio B, suitable for tracking sessions, overdubs, and mixing, originally offered an Amek board, then received an ICON and HD|3 rig the same time as Studio A (the first two to arrive in the Bay Area). Now, it has an SSL 9000J, which is the first in the East Bay (there's one at The Plant in Sausalito and two at SF Soundworks). At its widest point, the live room measures 20 feet wide by 24 feet deep, plus three iso booths. It was recently treated and redesigned by John Storyk of Walters Storyk Design Group.

In addition to standard bookings, Lucasey has leased the B room on a long-term basis to a few clients through the years, including Chris Dugan's and Willie Samuels' Nu-Tone Studios operation, where they worked with local artists such as Sabrina Stewart and Divit, among others. Green Day, regulars at the studio since their *Warning* album, currently have Studio B locked out for a long, long time.

The last time the band camped out at 880, they wrote, rehearsed, and recorded material for their multiple Grammy-winning "punk rock opera," *American Idiot*. During that time, the band bounced between Studios A and B and worked 12-hour days recording anything that came to mind: Christmas songs, hip-hop tracks, even an entire new wave album. The new wave tunes are assumed to be the tracks on The Network's (presumably Green Day members undercover) *Money Money 2020* album, released on

Warner Bros. in late 2004. In between, they found the creative muse that led to *American Idiot.* "It was really cool to watch that history being made," says Lucasey.

Studio C, now 880's primary mix room, also has a Pro Tools HD system and one of the ICONs from another room (replacing a Control|24 surface), along with a live room containing two iso booths. Quannum Records, home to DJ Chief Xcel and Blackalicious, had this room reserved for about a year in 2004 and 2005. Now Lucasey uses C to mix live-in-studio performances for Wal-Mart's Soundcheck live performance series, featuring acts such as Yellowcard, Switchfoot, Ne-Yo, and Miranda Lambert. Soundcheck's video shoots often take place in Studio A.

Studio 880 has stayed booked almost consistently since 1998 for many reasons. Its laid-back, urban luau setting and great-sounding rooms attract major label acts such as Smashmouth, Iggy Pop, Robert Cray, The Killers, Chris Isaak, Kronos Quartet, and Third Eye Blind, as well as the latest round of "local acts done good," such as Goapele, Lyrics Born, DJ Shadow, Zion I, and Lifesavas. They don't look to the record labels for their only source of income—a wise move, considering the labels fund fewer projects these days. They have pursued film projects with some success. They offer projection in all of the control rooms and live rooms and have several sound-effects libraries available. As a result, they've hosted 5.1 sessions for the *Chris Isaak Show* and handled post-production work for *The Jungle Book 2.* Smashmouth recorded a song for *Austin Powers in Goldmember* at Studio 880. Under the 880 Entertainment umbrella, Lucasey executive produced a Kung-Fu parody called *Kung Phooey,* directed by Darryl Fong. Lucasey also executive produces the Hooman Radio, broadcast every Saturday night on Alice@97.3FM, mixed by Zion I's DJ Amp Live.

880 Records, another business under 880 Entertainment, is officially underway and signing new bands. Their flagship act, May Pole, released its debut, *Mysterium Tremendum,* in March 2006. Lucasey has rented out his second floor to a variety of music- and entertainment-related businesses, which gives the studio the

income stability needed to survive economic slow times. This, combined with bringing in long-term residents and a diversified clientele, serves as a good example of a business model for today's recording facility. The idea of the recording studio as simply a rental service for record labels doesn't work anymore. Studios now have to keep more irons in the fire and find more innovative ways to keep business coming in.

SECTION SIX

The New Millennium: Picking Up the Pieces

San Francisco entered the new, hard-to-pronounce decade (The ohs? The oughts?) in a disheveled state. When the dotcom bubble burst, the metrosexuals and fashionistas of the high-tech world found themselves largely out of work, and their former downtown offices, once home to ridiculously expensive launch parties, were now barren. The DJ culture that they helped build waned, as the once-wealthy skulked their way off the dance floor and pondered graduate school and other opportunities. Still, San Francisco remains one of the top cities in the U.S. for electronic music artists and turntablists. The rock scene, so vibrant for so many years, was pronounced dead during the dotcom whirlwind, but still has a pulse if you look hard to find it. Many performing musicians and songwriters have left to search for affordable housing and rehearsal space elsewhere, and that has hurt the local rock clubs, many of which have closed down or look mostly outside of S.F. for headlining talent.

On a national level, record sales declined and labels signed fewer acts and spent less money on developing new talent, Bay Area talent included. Artists, producers, and engineers who hadn't already left the city by this time migrated to Los Angeles or New York where the labels focused their efforts.

The recording industry felt the effects of these developments and then some. Record labels' shrinking rosters meant less work for studios throughout the U.S. Considering San Francisco's lack of a strong music industry that could support its studios, a lot of the local high-end studios faced dark days. With decreased budgets, labels kept their projects close to home—meaning, not in San Francisco. Adding to their woes, home recording equipment became more affordable and user friendly than ever, thanks to music-production software and digital-recording options. On a grassroots level, this proved a huge asset for the independent musicians, songwriters, and producers. Finally, they had the freedom to spend as much time as they needed to record their music, without worrying about day rates and studio time. Record producers had smaller budgets to work with, and recording most of an artist's record at his or her own studio helped them meet that budget. More independent artists have released albums, EPs, and singles over the last few years than ever before, and with the onslaught of Internet music sites, they had an affordable way to get their music to the masses. Consumers had more music to choose from, too, but they also had to weed through a whole lot of crappy-sounding, self-produced records.

Back at the studios, record labels called less often, and their regular producer and engineer clients brought in only days instead of weeks of work. Few artists travel to record anymore, so San Francisco lost a lot of out-of-town business. Many studios closed between 2000 and 2003. Others wondered if their large, acoustically pristine live rooms, home to many a hit album, had become wasted space. Some struggled to hang on to the "good ol' days" of block bookings and analog recording. Others followed the "if you can't beat 'em, join 'em" philosophy and began looking for new ways to make the monthly nut.

As the remaining studios in town pick up the pieces and do their best to remain vital, the music community also rebuilds. Signs of life appeared in 2003 and 2004, when artists gradually made their way back to S.F. Small pockets of local acts are causing a buzz around the West Coast. At the same time, some home recordists are realizing that their bedroom recordings just don't sound very good and are bringing more of the essential elements of their projects back to commercial studios. More promising still, a few energetic studio owners are hell-bent on a common goal: bringing back the local music scene.

CHAPTER 25

The Old Guard

Remember back in Chapter 11, when Fleetwood Mac spent a year at The Record Plant recording *Rumours*? Today, they would probably spend a week at The Plant, then do the rest at their separate home studios. With a wave of studio closings and not many new openings in the new millennium, we're left with a skeleton crew of survivors. In the Bay Area, some original players survive, while the few new arrivals establish a foothold with innovative and/or diversified business plans.

Coast Resurfaces

Toast, the studio owned by Philip Steir and Craig Silvey, closed in June 2002. Steir, for one, backed out partly due to a slowdown in album recording. The studio's departure left the historic 1340 Mission Street building vacant for the first time in 30 years—but not for long.

Mastering engineer Paul Stubblebine, who had operated his Paul Stubblebine Mastering facilities out of Hyde Street Studios since 1997, wanted to expand his business with two mastering rooms operating side by side, with 5.1-surround capabilities. Hyde Street didn't have the space to accommodate such a facility, and an optimal surround listening environment should really be built from scratch for best results. As an active participant in the Bay Area recording community since the late 1960s, Stubblebine also recognized the importance of preserving the historic Mission Street space and knew what inherently great acoustics, courtesy of Bill Putnam, remained inside.

The same year that Toast moved out, Stubblebine and a silent partner retrieved rights to the Coast Recorders name from Dan Alexander, who had closed the Harrison Street Coast in 2000. They re-christened 1340 Mission as Coast Recorders.

Stubblebine gutted Coast's two smaller rooms down to the bare walls to rebuild the area into two mastering suites, renaming them the Magnolia Room and the Camelia Room. The two suites share a common machine room and can be used for either 5.1 or stereo mastering.

The Camelia Room, used by Stubblebine, features a pair of speakers custom built by Alon Wolff of Magico Loudspeaker Systems for stereo monitoring. Monitoring for the other four channels is provided by Meyer HD-1s, augmented by Bag End ELF subwoofers. The Magnolia Room, where mastering engineer Michael Romanowski resides, also features Meyer HD-1 monitors, augmented by Revel subwoofers.

The studio has a number of workstations available for mastering. Stubblebine works on a Sonic Solutions HD rig, while Romanowski operates a SADiE 5 workstation. They also offer the new Sonic Audio HDSP system, Pro Tools, and Nuendo. For Sony's SACD format, they have Sonoma. Workstations run through a Pacific Microsonics Model 2 D/A converter to analog—usually an ATR one-inch, although they also have ATR 102s with ¼- and ½-inch head configurations.

As for that recording room down the hall, the Putnam-designed Studio A, the room was re-voiced by Bob Hodas (who also supervised the mastering facilities' acoustics) and refurbished with improved AC wiring and audio harnessing. The new Coast contingent brought in new gear, too. They installed a 60-input Neve V3 where Toast's Neve 8026 used to be and rolled in a mix of modern and vintage items, including Pro Tools|HD3 and a Studer A827 with 16- and 24-track heads.

Longtime Toast fan Jason Carmer tried out the revived Coast in 2003 to work on the Star Spangles' Capitol debut *Bazooka!!!*. When it came time to record their follow up in 2005 they went to Carmer's Berkeley home studio, Stupidio, to record in his Chris Pelonis–designed room with Helios console. The new Coast at Mission has hosted a healthy dose of local acts, including rock band Film School, jazz singer Spencer Day, jazz/hip-hop group Shotgun Wedding Quintet, and pop singer-songwriter Kiff Gallagher, all Bay Area–based and regionally successful.

Stubblebine, Romanowski, and engineer Josh Greenham stay busy with a diverse mix of major and independent label projects and DIY acts. Stubblebine's recent credits alone include the Sam Bush/David Grisman album *Hold On We're Strummin* and Riders In the Sky's *Silver Jubilee*, both for Acoustic Disc. He's also worked with Vanessa Carlton, The Mountain Goats (produced by John Vanderslice for 4AD), The Bittersweets, jazz artists Anton Schwartz and Roberta Donnay, the Hot Buttered Rum String Band, pianist Seth Kaufman, and on a 1969 live concert CD by the Flying Burrito Brothers.

The wealth and diversity of local talent coming through this building is encouraging with respect to the health of the music scene as well as Coast Recorders, the city's last remaining Bill Putnam room, bearer of a classic sound that never goes out of style.

Hyde Street Studios

In 1985, Dan Alexander had moved out of Hyde Street to offices in Berkeley and took over Coast Recorders a few years later. Michael Ward, his partner, continued on as Hyde Street's sole proprietor, ultimately responsible for the dealings of the entire building. After Pearlman moved his Alpha and Omega studio out of the C room in 1990, Stephen Jarvis came in, using the live room to store the growing inventory of his equipment-rental company. He sub-leased the C control room to guitarist David Denny to use for various recording endeavors, including some elements of Diesel Harmonics, a five-guitar ensemble that recorded several albums there with Jarvis engineering. The arrangement marks the beginning of Studio C's complicated future as two separate rental spaces.

Shortly after Jarvis' arrival, Ward authorized a complete renovation to Studio A, a year-long process that began in 1991. They installed Neve 8048, which they had extensively refurbished, and added a new master control section and Flying Faders Automation. The 22×38–foot live room got a complete makeover at that time. In 1996, Ward updated the room again by adding two iso booths. At the same time, the mysterious Studio B (there was only an A, C, and D in the early years), formerly occupied by Earwax Productions, was taken over by Bruce Layton. Ward also created a couple more producers' lounges, also with audio and video tie-lines, and updated the whole facility with new paint, carpeting, and cabinetry. After a long line of predecessors, Studio D received an Amek APC1000 with GML Moving Fader Automation.

As the 1990s progressed, Hyde Street became a downtown destination for punk, metal, rap, R&B, hip-hop, and alternative acts; its rough-hewn appearance and urban location provided a good setting for edgy, raw music. Jello Biafra continued to make regular appearances, sometimes with hardcore band The Melvins. Primus, Mr. Bungle, Exodus, Four Non Blondes, American Music Club, Cake, Sun Volt, and a host of others also would pass through.

Matt Kelley's first gig as lead engineer happened in 1990 at Hyde Street. According to Kelley, Digital Underground was frantically searching for a vacant studio after a tape machine at Starlight Studios broke mid-session. At the time, not many local facilities were eager to book a little-known hip-hop group from Oakland who wanted to work the midnight shift. But Hyde Street took them in, and Kelley was assigned the session. "We were ready and waiting at midnight for the group to show up," he recalls. "By 2:30 a.m., they still weren't here, so I decided if they didn't show up by three, we'd call it off. At like 2:59 they walked in. We did the session and we got some really great tracks. Next thing you know, the album [*Sex Packets*] went Platinum and they went on to great success. My phone didn't stop ringing after that." The phone calls led to albums for Spice 1, Tupac Shakur, and George Clinton, who ironically is the source of many Digital Underground samples. Kelley also hooked up with the Hieroglyphics, a collection of hip-hop artists that includes Del the Funky Homosapien, Souls of Mischief, Casual, Pep Love, and Domino.

Photo courtesy of *Mix* magazine

Digital Underground's Shock-G (left) and engineer Matt Kelley in Hyde Street's Studio A in 1998.

After Denny left the Studio C control room area in 1997, Paul Stubblebine, formerly chief engineer at indie mastering house the Rocket Lab, took over the space to open his own facility, Paul Stubblebine Mastering. His Sonic Solutions workstation hummed with projects for David Grisman, with whom he worked during the Rocket Lab days, plus dozens of classical projects for Reference Recordings (seven of which were Grammy-nominated), John Lee Hooker, Roy Rogers, Charlie Musselwhite, Richard Thompson, and a long list of local acts. "We've always been involved with local labels and upcoming bands. They make up a substantial part of our work and we're happy to see them succeed," he says.

In 2002, the Hieroglyphics crew took over the Studio C live room formerly occupied by Jarvis and turned it into their own studio with Matt Kelley as their resident engineer. Solo albums from each of these artists, as well as a Hieroglyphics collective project, were recorded by Kelley at Hyde Street during this time. Their loud playbacks reportedly interfered a bit with the mastering studio next door.

Hyde Street Studios survived the dotcom bust years by diversifying—not necessarily by expanding into new markets, but by making room for more residents. Kelley and Stubblebine had the two halves of Studio C, a company called Datastream

Productions occupied Studio B at one time, and a label/studio called Grooveyard rented another room at Hyde Street. Soon, Ward rented out practically every nook and cranny of Hyde Street. Lounge areas were divided and turned into Pro Tools suites to accommodate more tenants. Local singer/songwriter Chris von Sneidern rented a small studio at Hyde Street, dubbed Studio E, in 1999, which he used to record his own projects as well as other acts. By 2003, a lot of those other acts had either left town or retreated to home studios. Von Sneidern soon sub-leased the control room of his rental space to another engineer and moved his entire operation into a 7×15–foot iso booth. He continues to work on his own music there. At present, Ward has 18 tenants working out of the Hyde Street complex, leaving Studios A and D, the core of Hyde Street, available to rent to outside clients.

Having so many residents in one building has benefits for the tenants as well as the landlord. A rare sense of community exists between the various musicians and engineers working there in an increasingly insular recording industry. If someone needs an extra mic stand or a particular piece of outboard gear, someone down the hall is usually willing to loan it. They might even add a guitar part to a track if they have the time.

In the midst of this activity, the spaces formerly known as Studio C went through some changes. Stubblebine moved out in 2002 to open impressive new facilities at Coast Recorders (see the "Coast Resurfaces" section). Two years later, a group of producer/musicians that had occupied (and promptly trashed) Stubblebine's former spot moved out.

Engineer Justin Phelphs started his career as a house engineer at Coast Recorders on Harrison Street in 1997, and he continued to work as an independent all over the city, including Tiny Telephone, where he was one of Vanderslice's main go-to guys. In the process, he racked up album credits for Spike 1000, Jackpot, Cake, Omar Sosa, MIRV, Chuck Prophet, and a slew of other bands. When he heard about the vacancy at Hyde Street, he seized the opportunity, assuming the lease with partners/engineers Jaime Durr and Mike McGinn with the intention of opening a mix room. But the studio needed a lot of work before that could happen. "When we walked into the C control room, it was a disaster," recalls Phelps. "We had to do quite a bit of cleanup to get it back into shape. Then six months after we got the control room up and running, Matt [Kelley] moved out of the studio."

Kelley went with the Hieroglyphics, who had relocated their label offices and studio into a new building in Oakland. With the C studio space available, Phelps and partners took over that area, as well, and began the process of knocking down walls and rebuilding the place as Studio C, ultimately restoring it to a modern version of its original glory.

They moved in their combined equipment and some outboard gear from Studio B. They purchased a modified Sony MPX 3000 console with Hardy mic pre's and Uptown Automation, Studer A820 2-inch and ¼-inch tape machines, and a Pro Tools|HD rig. They completely remodeled the 21×19–foot live room and treated it with tunable wall panels, which can either liven or deaden the room sound. They created an adjacent 20×12–foot room that can be used as an edit suite or iso booth, as well as another 12×6–foot iso booth. To date, they've opened the doors with much success to such artists as Jolie Holland, Chuck Prophet, Court and Spark, Secret Chiefs 3, The New Up, and The Girlfriend Experience.

Around the 2005 holiday season, a large crowd of local musicians, producers, engineers, and others from the S.F. scene showed up one rainy Saturday night for Studio C's grand opening party. Cocktails, cookies, and random puffs of curious-smelling smoke abounded as the entire Hyde Street facility opened itself to visitors to celebrate Studio C's revival. Chris von Sneidern played a set in Studio A. Chuck Prophet and his wife, keyboardist Stephanie Finch, stopped by to support their engineer friends. Stephen Barncard (who first appeared in Chapter 8) came by to see the new room. He hadn't set foot in Studio C since 1973. Dan Alexander studied the control room arrangement and wiring. As guests toasted the promise of the coming year, rumors swirled about Hyde Street Studios' future. The building's owner had sold the Hyde Street Studios building and four other buildings on the block. "The long-term plans are to tear it down," says studio owner Michael Ward. The building owners have said it would be at least a year or two before that happens; however, given the red tape involved in dealing with the San Francisco Planning Commission and Permit Services department, it could take longer, or not happen at all. But if things go as planned, historic Hyde Street Studios, in operation since 1969 and home to hundreds of hit records, could stand a very real chance of demolition for an eight-story condominium building. If this does happen, Ward says his plans are to relocate rather than dissolve.

The Plant: New Growth

To date, Arne Frager made his last renovation to The Plant in 2003 when he installed the SSL 9000J in Studio A. He's not stopping there, though; he's just taking a break. In an effort to diversify and increase the studio's market share, Frager has reached out to the film world, something that in the late '90s he told the media he didn't want to do. He tended The Garden, originally designed for surround-sound work, to make it more "sound-for-picture friendly," and brought in John Neff as a film mixer and to help expand the studio's post-production capabilities. Neff then mixed Michael Franti's film, *I Know I'm Not Alone* at The Plant, due out in June 2006. "Part of these changes have to do with the fact that the budgets for mixing music in surround really disappeared in the last three to four years because the record labels just didn't find a big market for those products," says Frager. "So we've done what we always do, and that is adapt to change."

Despite rumors to the contrary, The Plant has stayed relatively healthy over the last few years. Studios A and B have hosted acts such as String Cheese Incident, Train, Joe Satriani, The Deftones, the Von Bondies, The Donnas, Sonia Dada, The Noisettes, Roy Hargrove, Carrie Underwood, and Charlie Musselwhite, among others.

In May 2005, Mike Indelicato, owner of vintage guitar store E*Guitars in San Rafael, California, purchased 2200 Bridgeway from Sausalito real estate investment group EMIC Properties for $2.3 million, according to a release issued in the *North Bay Business Journal.* Indelicato plans to work with Frager on his ongoing upgrades.

Different Fur, Different Owners

Through the 1980s, Different Fur hosted a wide variety of artists, from Windham Hill's new age and acoustic music to Oakland rap to Huey Lewis' all-American rock. As technology and the industry evolved through the '90s, founder Pat Gleeson's independent spirit lived on through such diverse clientele as Kronos Quartet, Brian Eno, and Primus. In a new era of recording, though, Different Fur found itself, well, different.

"We were sort of a holdover because we were a full-service studio, which fell by the wayside in the '90s," says co-owner and producer Howard Johnston. "Before, people would start and finish at Fur and then we'd have playback parties. We tried to carry that over into the '90s." But fewer clients had the budget to start and finish at Different Fur, usually taking the home-studio route for the bulk of their project and recording basic tracks at Fur. Whatever the need, Johnston and partner Susan Skaggs met it with their usual efficiency. They celebrated the studio's 25th anniversary in 1997 and closed out the decade with an array of acts, including Lavay Smith and Her Red Hot Skillet Lickers, Robert Cray, Charlie Hunter, Neurosis, and Tuck and Patti.

In early 2004, Johnston and Skaggs sold Different Fur, a decision they had struggled with for some time. Skaggs started thinking about getting out of the studio business in 2002. "I just got tired of working in the studio," she says. "It got to the point where a band could come in and I wouldn't hear a lick of music. The job just didn't seem that creative anymore. Howard and I started talking about selling, and I got my real-estate license, to make some real money for a change. [In 2003] we got serious."

Johnston adds, "When Susan and I bought Fur, we needed to invest to make it state-of-the-art. If we were going to compete into the future, we [would have to invest in more upgrades] and we weren't ready to make that adjustment."

In 2004, the longtime partners sold Different Fur—the building and the studio—to Klepto Records, a San Francisco–based independent record label owned by Jeromy Smith. According to his head engineer, Duane Ramos, Smith was looking for a studio that could also act as a home base for his label. He found it on 19th Street. "I was always concerned that someone would want to buy the building and not the studio," says Skaggs. "But the buyer paid a good price for both, and Howard and I walked away financially happy." Skaggs now lives in San Diego, not far from her family. Johnston works at various San Francisco studios, mainly Different Fur and SF Soundworks (Tony Espinoza's swank multi-room facility in SOMA, covered in Chapter 26).

Most of the equipment—the SSL 4056, the Sonic Solutions, the outboard gear—remain at the studio, though Smith did upgrade to Pro Tools 192 Accel and remodeled the second-floor lounge. The studio's beloved Yamaha grand piano moved to SF Soundworks.

Under Klepto Records' direction, the studio continues to operate as a commercial facility, welcoming such recent guests as vocalist/producer Skyler Jett, gypsy jazz band Hot Club of San Francisco, and a handful of alternative and electronic acts. Different Fur also serves as the in-house studio for Klepto's roster of one, local rock band Ride the Blinds.

Fantasy Studios

Fantasy Studios weathered the '90s as well as any facility. It cruised through the early part of the decade with a lengthy list of pop, rock, jazz, and R&B hits and suffered with everyone else when the economy tanked and the recording industry shacked up at home. On a local level, everything from the 1989 Loma-Prieta earthquake to escalating real estate prices to 9/11 affected just about every local studio, Fantasy included.

Aside from acquiring four now-essential Pro Tools|HD workstations—two for the studios, two for the mastering department—and acquiring additional Grace Audio, Vintech, and Neve mic pre's, they've made only a few changes to the studios themselves over the last two decades. In 1986, they replaced the Neve 8108 in Studio D with an SSL 4000E console. More recently, they installed an SSL 8056 with Ultimation in Studio A. They're considering an upgrade to Studio C.

The long-term recording residents don't come around as often, but they do come. Santana booked many weeks at Fantasy in 1999 to record and overdub a large portion of *Supernatural*, with tracks engineered by Glenn Kolotkin (whom we met in Chapter 10 at Columbia Studios), Jim Gaines (who first arrived in Chapter 14 at Wally Heider Recording), and many others spread among many other studios.

Santana returned to Fantasy in 2001 to record parts of *Shaman*, and again in 2005 for *All That I Am*. All three albums each took at least two years to make, with Fantasy receiving anywhere from two months to a few days' worth of business at various intervals. Gary Burton, Buddy Guy, and Kronos Quartet all visited the studio in 2005.

Fantasy also draws a fair amount of work from independent acts. The studio offers multiple rooms at various price points, which enables studio manager Nina Bombardier to put together a somewhat reasonable package. Artist/songwriter Roberta Donnay used Fantasy Studios to track and mix her 2006 jazz album, *What's Your Story*, but she did all of the overdubs at David Freiberg's FreeMountain Studios. Of course, the decision to work at Fantasy partly came from her producer, the legendary Orrin Keepnews, who oversaw Fantasy's jazz recording department through the '70s and produced hundreds of albums in the building through the years. Chief engineer Stephen Hart, who joined the Fantasy staff in 1999, worked on remixes for a Delaney & Bonnie and Friends album in 2006, and handles most of the studio and live engineering for beloved record store Amoeba Music's new label, Amoeba Records. Inaugural efforts include gypsy jazz recordings from Brandi Shearer, David Grisman, and the Robin Nolan Trio.

Keepnews' and other producers' early work for Fantasy and its various subsidiaries keeps the studio busy with a steady stream of reissues, box sets, and special projects. Much like in the '70s, when Fantasy operated as a private studio, these re-releases give the studio the built-in business needed to offset the diminished amount of outside work.

During the past two years, in addition to remixing and/or mastering old Fantasy albums, the Berkeley studio has seen work from another prominent jazz label, Concord Records, now known as Concord Music Group. In late 2004, Concord Records Inc. acquired Fantasy Inc., and the two labels merged together to form Concord Music Group. Based in Beverly Hills since 1999 when entertainment vets Norman Lear and Hal Gaba purchased the label from founder Carl Jefferson (see Chapter 12), Concord Records was already a leader in the jazz and adult contemporary markets, and Fantasy owned one of the largest catalogs of jazz, R&B, rock, and blues. Coupled with Concord's 2005 purchase of the popular Telarc (jazz, blues, and classical) and Heads Up (contemporary jazz) labels, they've become one of the top independent labels in the country. In recent months, the label has brought in reissue projects for Scott Hamilton, Gary Burton, and John Fahey, among other artists, to Fantasy Studios. Vince Guaraldi's music will soon get a re-do, as Concord prepares to re-release his entire Fantasy catalog.

Though the post-production mix stage known as the Saul Zaentz Film Center closed in January, 2005, Fantasy Studios still brings in steady post-production and ADR/Foley recording. They've hosted post sessions for *Jarhead, Cassanova, Art School Confidential,* and *Grizzlyman* (scored by Hart), as well as voiceover work from Pixar, located only a couple of miles away in Emeryville.

In 2005, after a more than three-decade absence, the Fantasy enterprise welcomed back John Fogerty to the roster. Having gone through years of legal battles with Fantasy Records, when the company became part of Concord Music Group, Fogerty finally saw an opening to reunite with his Creedence Clearwater Revival catalog. The result is *The Long Road Home—The Ultimate John Fogerty–Creedence Collection,* an aptly titled disc that includes early CCR tracks, some of Fogerty's best solo work, and four new tracks recorded live in 2005. A live DVD, taped in September, 2005 at the Wiltern Theatre in Los Angeles, is slated for release in 2006.

In its 35-year history, "The House That Creedence Built" has expanded both its external structure and internal contents. By keeping its original foundation intact, Fantasy has weathered the industry's highs and lows and stands in a position to remain strong in the years to come.

CHAPTER 26

New Blood

SF Soundworks

It takes guts, a strong vision, and a touch of insanity to open a high-end multi-room recording studio during one of the music industry's lowest economic periods in history. In 2003, former dot-com entrepreneur Tony Espinoza took that leap when he opened SF Soundworks, the first significant commercial studio to open in San Francisco in the new millennium.

Located on Natoma Street (the same alley where Commercial Recorders resided) near a seedy block of Sixth Street in SOMA, SF Soundworks grew out of the former home of Focused Audio, a post-production studio that worked on Tim Burton's film *A Nightmare Before Christmas* and the *Gumby* and *Nash Bridges* TV series. When Espinoza first looked at the studio in the late '90s, he saw it as an ideal site for the multi-room facility he envisioned. It had multiple control rooms, all concurrent with one another and running off of a central machine room. It also had a good wiring system and Carl Yanchar's excellent acoustic designs. Espinoza bought the building in early 2000, when record sales were still somewhat high, despite a litany of record-industry complaints against file-sharing and Napster. The build-out took longer than expected—just over three years total—and during that time, the music business tanked. Espinoza built-up three more stories.

In August 2003, Espinoza publicly opened SF Soundworks, his fully realized studio vision in place. The Soundworks complex contains four control rooms, five recording spaces (one of which doubles as an edit bay), a lounge/edit suite, one guest apartment, and the Espinozas' adjoining flat.

He installed an SSL 9072 J Series console and one of five Pro Tools|HD3 workstations in Studio A. Espinoza also brought in vintage gear from Neve, API, Pultec, GML, Tube-Tech, and UREI—much of it from a personal collection that he started when he was 15—as well as additional pieces from Chandler, Pendulum, Thermionic Culture, and Crane Song. Monitoring includes Dynaudio BM15A near-fields, Tannoy Eclipse 8 and 10s, Mackie HRM824s, and the popular Yamaha NS10s, and a pair of soffit-mounted dual 18-inch JBLs. A 19×14–foot live room containing Different Fur's former Yamaha C7 grand piano sits to the engineer's left. Studio B offers another Pro Tools rig, ample outboard gear, and a 20×17–foot, ultra-reverberant concrete drum room designed by Charles Salter and Associates, with access to two additional isolated spaces on the main floor. Studios C and D work for simple overdubs or a private edit station.

One floor above, the Pro Tools Café offers workspace with two more Pro Tools rigs and two Macintosh computers in an open loft area overlooking the gourmet kitchen, with plush red sofas, a fire-place, and a balcony.

One more steep set of stairs leads to a spacious guest flat adorned with modern furnishings, a gourmet kitchen, a heated deck, and a glass front wall with sweeping view of the city. Espinoza and family live in an identical, adjoining flat next door, perfect for the studio owner/producer who tends to work 14-hour days for weeks on end.

The SF Soundworks kitchen area and Pro Tools Café above.

Tony Espinoza. Photo courtesy of *Mix* magazine

Not long after opening, Espinoza checked his voicemail to find a message from L.A.–based engineer/producer Joe Chiccarelli, who apparently heard rumblings about a new San Francisco studio. Chiccarelli became a regular client, helming sessions for acts such as Vanessa Carlton and locals such as Beth Waters and The Animators. Former Different Fur owner Howard Johnston works at Soundworks regularly, bringing in George Winston and Tuck and Patti sessions, among others. In 2004, Espinoza re-aligned with Apple for its iTunes Originals series; he had worked as a product manager for the company in the early '90s. (He helped build the industry's first PDA, the Apple Newton, the first of his many high-tech achievements.) They produced the first recording for the series that year, with Alanis Morrissette, followed by more tracks from The Cardigans, Keane, R.E.M., and New Order. Most of these sessions were tracked and/or mixed by Espinoza. In addition to iTunes recordings, the studio received a regular stream of major-label work from New York (Russ Elevado, John Cale), L.A. (Ice Cube with Lil' Jon), and Europe (David Gray, Robin Guthrie).

The big names are nice, but Espinoza's and Soundworks' true spirit lies in nurturing local talent. "Our core mission has always been to develop a community of talented engineers and producers and empower them with the best tools available to help elevate the quality of independent productions to that of major labels and beyond," says Espinoza. And it's working. Local acts of every type, from nationally known DJ Shadow, Dan the Automator, Lyrics Born, Blackalicious, and Goapele, to those on the brink of national success, such as Rogue Wave, Oranger, Elephone, Jeff Black, MiniPop, Why?, Madelia, and The Sounds, have chosen to record at least parts of their projects at SF Soundworks.

To foster this community, Espinoza realized that he had to make his fancy studio with all of its high-end gear affordable and convenient for the acts he most wanted to support: the ones generally holed up at their separate home studios. Hence, Soundworks' Pro Tools Café, which originally had rates as low as $10 an hour. He also has three small to mid-size rooms that he rents for a reasonable rate. And even though the studio looks swank, there's no receptionist, at the time of this writing no studio manager (except for Espinoza), and no pool table. He does have a team of very capable staff engineers and producers and excellent equipment for them to work on, however. "Our clients come here to work, and when they leave, they take with them some of the most innovative and best-sounding records being made anywhere," says Espinoza. His down-to-business approach has resulted in rooms booked three months in advance at a time when a lot of studios wonder how they'll fill next week.

To accommodate the overflow, in late 2005, Espinoza added another SSL J Series console, purchased from The Record Plant in L.A., which was refurbished and modified to a 9056 to fit into the Studio B control room (now called Studio 2). He remodeled Studio 3 (formerly Studio C) to offer a drum room, large vocal room, and amp room and installed a Digidesign ProControl to pair with the existing Pro Tools HD|3 rig.

He also restructured his rates. When the studio first opened, Espinoza operated on a "sliding scale" basis, charging "card rate" to the major label clients and offering deep discounts to indie bands on a shoestring budget. But now, rates range from $950 a day for Studio 1 (Studio A), $600 for Studio 2, and $450 for Studio 3. "*We* didn't come up with these rates, our customers did," says Espinoza. "The competitive advantage for us is that we're built from the ground up to be affordable. By investing in the last SSL J console made [in Studio 1] and the first [Studio 2], we are optimizing the depreciation curve of analog mix technology." That's CEO Espinoza talking. The one who, after the Newton PDA, designed the first MP3 player, called Rio. The one who co-founded When.com, then sold the company to AOL for a reported $200 million and became VP of AOL Music Services. He's also the one who has played in bands since high school and had a project studio in some form during his entire career in high-tech. SF Soundworks is a long-term goal realized on a grand scale, his passion for music and electronics coming together in a venue where one of the city's greatest assets—the artists—can communicate, collaborate, and create bodies of work that will take them from local luminary status to national success.

FM Recorders

When we left Denzil Foster and Tommy McElroy in Chapter 19, they were camped out in Fantasy's Studio B working on En Vogue's 1992 smash, *Funky Divas*. Their hot streak continued through the '90s with albums from Regina Belle, F Mob (a Foster and McElroy solo project), and continued work with En Vogue. In 1994, they decided to bring their work in-house. They found an old drapery manufacturing building in foreclosure in Emeryville near the Oakland-Berkeley border, but at 16,000 square feet, didn't have the means to fill it. "We just set up shop in one little corner and worked there," says McElroy. They had a small Amek console, McElroy's growing collection of samplers and keyboards, and really not much else.

By 1996, as they began planning En Vogue's next album, *EV3*, they started construction on full-blown recording facilities—which still barely made a dent in the massive warehouse. They named it FM Recorders—possibly for Foster and McElroy or FM radio or FMob...take your pick.

Designed by Chips Davis, the LEDE control room covers 1,200 square feet, arguably one of the largest in the Bay Area. At the front, the dynamic duo installed a Euphonix 2000-M digitally controlled analog mixing desk and a Pro Tools MixPlus system. Stacks of solid-state and tube outboard gear fill a credenza behind the console, with more than enough room left at the rear for a spacious producers' area with leather sofa and desk space for keyboards, laptops, and other gadgets. To the engineer's right, a large machine room houses two Otari MTR-100 24-track analog machines, a Tascam MX-2424 hard-disk recorder, and 24 tracks of Alesis ADATs.

The adjoining live room, now dubbed the "Fish Tank," was also designed by Davis and features panels that can be rotated to alter the room's acoustics. The studio isn't much larger than the control room, but it has enough space for a small classical ensemble, acoustic combo, or a rock band...if they really like each other.

Foster and McElroy maintained the studio as a mainly private operation, but in the early 2000s, they lessened their workload to devote more time to their families (both had young children then). Foster moved to L.A., while McElroy stayed in the Bay Area. In early 2004, they started ramping up their business again and revamped the studio in the process. McElroy brought in producer/musician Sep Valizadeh as an owner/manager and opened FM Recorders to the public a year later, though not in the conventional sense. The studio serves as merely one piece of a larger puzzle; a puzzle that, like SF Soundworks, aims to reinvigorate the Bay Area music scene by turning out high-quality product that with any luck will garner nationwide attention.

The transition began when Valizadeh launched a weekly open mic night at Blake's on Telegraph in Berkeley, where he found a handful of new acts to help develop FM's burgeoning production company. "The idea was, 'Let's do a pseudo open studio policy where we're actively looking for talent and working with them in the studio on a one-on-one basis,'" says Valizadeh. Word got out around town, and soon bands began soliciting *him,* wanting to know how they could get in on this East Bay action. "We couldn't really say no," Valizadeh adds, "because we started to achieve what we initially set out to do, which was create a scene."

In 2005, they modified the studio by making more of the available square footage usable. They created Live Room B, located to the side of the original control room and studio. Live Room B has all of the natural echo one would expect from an old warehouse and serves as a rehearsal space, as a place for really live drum sounds, and for full band tracking sessions. FM also creates and records their own samples and reverbs in this room.

They also added tie-lines everywhere: the hallways, lounge, office area, and even the bathroom can serve as additional recording spaces. They also have Stephen Jarvis' pro audio rental company in the building now, which means endless equipment available just a few steps away.

FM artists can draw from a diverse roster of engineers: Steve Counter, Foster and McElroy's main engineer for many years, is available for hot rap and R&B tracks; engineer Mike Walte is a pro in jazz. Valizadeh takes on rock and alternative music as a producer/engineer, and Mark Wilhelm, Rich Graff, and Ryan Wing are available for a wide range of projects. It's a young staff and as such, the studio has a vibrant atmosphere. Laptops sit on paper-strewn desks in the open office area. Walls are painted purple, mustard, and blue, complemented by a few pieces of contemporary furniture. In 2006, FM plans to launch an Internet-based record label and distribution house catering to a diverse roster of musicians. "We want to take our artists and coach them toward being a powerful independent band with a finished product that they can take to the majors," says Valizadeh. "We all know we need them, so instead of fighting the majors, the best thing we know to do is help bands get to that point."

They're currently working with R&B/hip-hop artist Mike Marshall (frontman for Timex Social Club, from Chapter 20), hip-hop/reggae act Hairdoo, and rock bands The Hills, Breakpoint, and Sodium Channel, among others. "We want to be the Bay Area's buzzmakers," says Valizadeh. "Five years from now, we want the majors to know that if they're looking for the hottest bands in the Bay, they'll find them at FM."

Sonoma Mountain Studio Estate

So this is how the other half lives! These days, few acts have the means to record their albums from start to finish at a high-end commercial studio, expecting four-star treatment every step of the way. During The Record Plant era, the top 10 percent of major label acts fit into this category. Today, this group equates to about one-tenth of a percent, *maybe*. For that upper, upper tier, the Bay Area now has Sonoma Mountain Studio Estate, a new "resort" type studio offering supreme luxury, privacy, and recording services at supreme prices.

Opened in 2003 by former musician and *Fortune* 500 exec Bill Zabit, the reported $12 million studio/estate sits on the ocean side of Sonoma Mountain in Northern California, and it comprises five separate buildings tucked away in a gated compound on nine acres of some of America's most picturesque countryside.

Toward the front of the property, a large building resembling a New England horse barn contains the studio—singular. There are no Studios A, B, or C; just one, which they say allows for a more personal experience for the few elite clients they plan to bring in each year.

With only one studio to equip, Zabit and team made sure to stock it with the best the market has to offer. Built from the ground up by Zabit, who handled much of the interior design, and studio design vet Art Kelm, who did the acoustical and technical design, the main tracking room features 20-foot-high cathedral ceilings with peaks of African mahogany, a cherry wood wall that engineer Scott Church jokingly calls the "money wall," and maple, black walnut, and natural stone accents. A 7 ½–foot Grotrian concert grand sits tuned and ready. Two large iso booths connect to the main room, to a live rehearsal room equipped with a Mackie 24×8 console normalled to the control room, and to a producer's lounge equipped with its own Digidesign 002 system with Pro Tools LE software, a 17-inch Titanium G4 Powerbook, a 22-inch Cinema display, and a host of synths and MIDI modules.

The control room offers a vintage Neve 8048 console, with monitoring provided by a pair of PMC BB5As, tri-amped with Bryston amps and crossovers, with Genelec 1031as, KRK 6000s, and Yamaha NS10s for near-fields. They offer Studer A-827 two-inch 24-track and Ampex ATR 100 ½-inch 2-track for analog tracking and mixing, as well as Pro Tools|HD3 with Apogee converters. Outboard gear sits behind the console and includes an exhaustive list of new and vintage boxes; the same goes for the microphone selection. They have a lot of instruments, too, including a custom Sonar drum set, Gibson and Alembic guitars, and a Hammond B3 with Leslie, among other items.

After a leisurely day of recording, guests can amble back to the three-story main house, built as an exact replica of a 1760s colonial saltbox with pine floors, seven fireplaces, and hardware and fixtures hammered by blacksmiths in New England.

The main house has four suites, each with its own fireplace and Jacuzzi-equipped bathroom, a den with a library, a piano parlor, and a dining room with a long wood table that seats 12 and a fireplace that's at least six feet tall. Building on the exterior's theme, the entire place is decorated to feel like a New England bed-and-breakfast inn, with four-poster beds, antique furniture, chandeliers, and lots of wood.

A two-story carriage house and a garden cottage—next to the vegetable garden and greenhouse—also reside on-site, as well as a tennis court, spa, gym, more gardens, a gazebo, a game room with a home theater system and a pool table, and a secluded two-story tree house. And let's not forget the 'round-the-clock concierge service and complimentary access to the 45-foot Ferretti Italian sport yacht docked in Sausalito.

The studio staff also can arrange for optional services, such as private jet, helicopter, limo, personal trainer, personal chef, personal horseback riding instructor, tennis lessons…just about anything they can arrange for legally.

So who's working here? Producer/lyricist David Kirshenbaum flew in to co-produce Vancouver-based singer/songwriter Melanie Dekker, an act recording under Zabit and Church's production company, Sonoma Mountain Entertainment. Her case is special, as she's part of the in-house artist development company.

No matter what your fancy, Sonoma Mountain Studio Estate will certainly ensure a top-quality recording in a luxurious and very private retreat environment.

Talking House Studios

One of the few ground-up studios to open in San Francisco in the 21st century resides, like SF Soundworks, in the SOMA neighborhood. Talking House, an innovative creative environment spearheaded by Seagate board chairman Stephen Luczo, will include not only a world-class, semi-private recording studio, but also artist gallery space, multimedia editing facilities, graphic design, media presentation rooms, and event space, among other facilities.

Designed by John Storyk of Walters Storyk Design Group, with systems integration provided by David Carroll Associates, the recording studio will comprise about half of the building's square footage, with gallery space, lounges, offices, and a private apartment for Luczo taking up the rest of the building. Talking House will offer three control rooms, all connected electronically and visually to one large live room and four smaller iso rooms. The main control room will contain a 72-channel SSL 9000K console purchased from New York's now-closed Hit Factory, while the other two control rooms will have Digidesign ICON control surfaces at their core. All rooms will be equipped for 5.1 and will include a mix of high-end analog and digital equipment.

Jack Leahy, former owner of Funky Features, Russian Hill, and Crescendo, has acted as a consultant for Luczo and his myriad business endeavors for the last four years, and is essentially serving as project manager for the Talking House studio project. Producer John Paulsen serves as president of Talking House Productions.

A rendering of Talking House's main live room.

Image courtesy of John Storyk, Walters Storyk Design Group

"There are six members of the Talking House production team, and they come from a number of backgrounds," says Leahy. "Together they have capabilities of producing video, audio for video post, artwork, and production. It's a pretty versatile house." Talking House has a tentative completion date of June 2006, with grand-opening festivities planned for October 2006. The city is already talking...

APPENDIX A

Epilogue

If I were to write this book 20 years from now, the stories might read a lot differently.

"I remember one time he cut-and-pasted our vocal part in Pro Tools 50 times!"

Or, *"The guitarist recorded these amazing solos in his bathroom, then he sent them over the Internet as MP3 files to the engineer. Then the singer had to re-do some stuff, so he and the engineer carried the engineer's FireWire external hard drive to Studio X for a couple of days. When it came time to mix, the engineer just FTP'd us all MP3s of the rough mixes so we could listen at home, then we'd just e-mail him back our comments. We never had to see or talk to each other at all! It was magic!"*

Okay, maybe I'm exaggerating a little, or not, but certainly studios face different challenges than they did in the '70s, or even the '90s. And in order to accommodate a leaner, meaner, cyber-leaning music business, studios will have to operate leaner, meaner, and smarter than ever before.

As for the San Francisco "scene," a wealth of new talent is out there covering (as always) a wide range of music. Even though these artists aren't all bumping into each other in the studio that much anymore, a lot of promising stuff is percolating in the city. Bay Area recording studios, ever supportive of homegrown talent, are there to help, and a lot of them plan to stick around for years to come. "The music in the Bay Area is amazing and will continue to evolve," says Studio D's Joel Jaffe. "It's up to us to provide a platform for these acts to get noticed and really do well."

That platform has seen some shaky ground, but as long as studio owners, artists, producers, and engineers continue to operate from the same passion and commitment to quality held during the past 50 years, the commercial music recording studio stands a chance of remaining a vital entity in our ever-changing recording industry.

"Studio guys are tenacious," says Dan Alexander. "If you're not a survivor, if you're not willing to scrabble up the mountain on your hands and knees, you'll disappear from the business real soon. It's a peculiar mental illness."

Hope you enjoyed the tour.

APPENDIX B

Sources and Recommended Reading

Sources

Information for this book was obtained from the following individuals and written sources.

INTERVIEWS

I interviewed the following individuals for this book in the months noted.

August 2004

Russell Bond, Jason Carmer, Howard Johnston, Ken Kessie, Mark Needham, Susan Skaggs, John Vanderslice

August 2005 to March 2006

Dan Alexander, Steve Atkins, Stephen Barncard, Nina Bombardier, Betty Cantor, Fred Catero, Bill Champlin, Roy Chen, Mike Cogan, Jeff Cohen, Steve Counter, John Cuniberti, Oliver DiCicco (August 2005), Maureen Droney, Phil Edwards, Tony Espinoza, Tom Flye, Denzil Foster, Arne Frager, Vance Frost, Jim Gaines, Pat Gleeson, Dan Healy, George Horn, Len Horowitz, Joel Jaffe, Leslie Ann Jones, Matt Kelley, Glen Kolotkin, Jack Leahy, Bob Matthews, Elliot Mazer, Tommy McElroy, Justin Phelps, David Rubinson, Phill Sawyer, Al Schmitt, Tom Scott, Pete Sears, Bob Shumaker,

John Storyk, Chris Strachwitz, Paul Stubblebine, Sep Valizadeh, Narada Michael Walden, Matt Wallace, Michael Ward, Bob Welch, Michelle Zarin

BOOKS

Don't You Want Somebody to Love: Reflections of the San Francisco Sound, by Darby Slick (Snow Lion Graphics/SLG Books)

The Fleetwood Mac Story: Rumours and Lies, by Bob Brunning (Omnibus Press)

San Francisco Rock: The Illustrated History of San Francisco Music, by Jack McDonough (Chronicle Books)

San Francisco: The Musical History Tour, by Joel Selvin (Chronicle Books)

Summer of Love, The Inside Story of LSD, Rock & Roll, Free Love and High Times in the Wild West, by Joel Selvin (Cooper Square Press)

WEB

Phill Sawyer www.precambrianmusic.com Click on the "text" button to read his extensive journal entries about Pacific High Recording, 1750 Arch Street, and Sawyer's other career endeavors.

Joe Strummer www.joestrummer.us This Joe Strummer resource site has commentary from Sandy Pearlman on recording *Give 'Em Enough Rope.*

Studio Electronics www.studioelectronics.biz President David Kulka has posted PDFs of several United and Western Newsletters from 1965 to 1971, with information on Bill Putnam's Coast Recorders, Columbia Studios, and Mercury Studios.

Virtual Museum of the City of San Francisco www.sfmuseum.org Many informative articles about California and San Francisco history are available on this site.

OTHER

Birth of the Dead, Grateful Dead (2003, Rhino Records), liner notes written by Dennis McNally & Lou Tambakos.

Various back issues of *Mix* magazine, *BAM, Billboard, Modern Keyboard, Pro Sound News, Pulse!, San Francisco Chronicle, San Rafael/Terra Linda News Pointer, Marin Independent Journal, North Bay Business Journal,* and *SF Weekly* as referenced in text.

Recommended Reading (and Listening)

If you would like to know more about some of the music and industry leaders mentioned in this book, here are a few good places to start.

BOOKS

Droidmaker: George Lucas and the Digital Revolution, by Michael Rubin (Triad Publishing Company)

The Fabulous Sylvester: The Legend, the Music, the Seventies in San Francisco, by Joshua Gamson (Henry Holt and Co.)

Head Hunters: The Making of Jazz's First Platinum Album, by Steven F. Pond (University of Michigan Press)

Jazz on the Barbary Coast, by Tom Stoddard (Heydey Books)

Rage & Roll: Bill Graham and the Selling of Rock, by John Glatt (Carol Publishing Corporation)

WEB

OTR Studios' Internet Radio www.live365.com/stations/310399 The Internet radio station for Cookie Marenco's OTR Studios in Belmont, California.

Recording Wally Heider wallyheider.com This informative site, managed by Stephen Barncard, is dedicated to Wally Heider and his L.A. and San Francisco studios.

Index

B

C

D

E

F

H

L

M

N

Q

R

S

U

V

Y

Z

THOMSO
COURSE TECHNO
Professional ■ Technical ■ F

SHARPEN YOUR SKILLS, RELEASE YOUR SOUN

with these learning resources from Course Technology PTR

The S.M.A.R.T. Guide to Mixers, Signal Processors, Microphones, and More
ISBN: 1-59200-694-9 ■ **$39.99**

The S.M.A.R.T. Guide to Recording Great Audio Tracks in a Small Studio
ISBN: 1-59200-695-7 ■ **$39.99**

The S.M.A.R.T. Guide to Digital Recording, Software, and Plug-Ins
ISBN: 1-59200-696-5 ■ **$39.99**

The Truth About the Music Business:
A Grassroots Business and Legal Guide
ISBN: 1-59200-763-5 ■ **$29.99**

The Art of Mixing:
A Visual Guide to Recording, Engineering, and Production, Second Edition
ISBN: 1-93114-045-6 ■ **$49.99**

Live Sound Reinforcement, Bestseller Edition:
A Comprehensive Guide to P.A. and Music Reinforcement Systems and Technology
ISBN: 1-59200-691-4 ■ **$49.99**

Networking Strategies for the New Music Business
ISBN: 1-59200-753-8 ■ **$24.99**

Course Technology PTR also publishes a complete offering of books, interactive CD-ROMs, and DVDs on music technology applications.

With various levels of instruction on leading software—

Pro Tools ■ SONAR ■ Home Studio ■ Cubase SX/SL ■ Nuendo ■ ACID
Sound Forge ■ Reason ■ Ableton Live ■ Logic ■ Digital Performer
GarageBand ■ Traktor DJ Studio ■ Soundtrack ■ and many more—

you are sure to find what you're looking for.

THOMSON
COURSE TECHNOLOGY
Professional ■ Technical ■ Reference

Visit our Web site for more information, **FREE** sample chapters, and to or

www.courseptr.con